Linda Frum's Guide to Canadian Universities

CARTOONS BY E. HORE

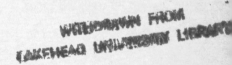

KEY PORTER·BOOKS

This book is dedicated to Eugene Freyssinet — the inventor of
pre-stressed concrete — the man who, more than any other, has made higher
education in Canada what it is today.

I also dedicate this book to my dear brother David. His love and support
(from about grade two on) has been a precious gift and an invaluable
source of strength.

Canadian Cataloguing in Publication Data
Frum, Linda, 1963-
    Linda Frum's guide to Canadian universities

ISBN 1-55013-044-7

1. Universities and colleges — Canada — Handbooks,
manuals, etc. I. Title. II. Title: Guide to Canadian universities.

L905.F78 1987   378.71   C87-094101-1

Key Porter Books Limited
70 The Esplanade
Toronto, Ontario
Canada M5E 1R2

Cover Photo: Paul Ornstein
Design: Marie Bartholomew
Typesetting: Imprint Typesetting

Printed and bound in Canada

88 89 90 6 5 4

CONTENTS

INTRODUCTION

Good news, kids! It's time to go to college! And we know what *that* means — wearing Jell-O on your head! Ice cream for breakfast, potato chips for lunch, and pizza for dinner! Plus beer all day long! And sex! Just ask your older brother about this — the last days of the Roman Empire had nothing on orientation week at your local U. Soon you'll be much, much smarter than you are now, and you'll know heaps of fascinating and impressive facts. And afterwards, you'll sit back and watch the interviewers from IBM, Coca-Cola, Cadillac Fairview, and the Ministry of Industry, Trade and Commerce fight tooth and nail to hire you!

Sound incredible? Well, it's all lies.

Actually, Canadian college students are generally a tranquil lot, and they spend most of their time studying. By the third day of the term, everybody's counting calories and exercising like mad to fight off the "freshman fifteen." Even before AIDS, there was less sex on campus than your older brother wants you to think. Most of the stuff you're going to learn will be tedious beyond belief, and you won't remember any of it the day after you get your degree. As for jobs—can you fry a burger? The part about the Jell-O, however, is quite true.

But wait! This dreariness is not inevitable. You hold salvation in your hands. All it takes is this book and a sense of adventure. This guidebook tells you what you really need to know to make the best decision about where to go to university. You'll find out which schools are hot and which are not. You'll find out where the best parties are, the best teams, the best dorms, the best-looking girls and boys. You'll also get the scoop on the juiciest scandals; an insight into student politics; and a sense of what's going on in the social scene across the country. Most of all, you'll find out where the fun is and how you can get in on it. (I'll give you the address.)

You'll probably notice that I don't spend too much time dwelling on the academic quality of the universities. It's not that I don't care about that stuff, but let's leave that subject to your parents and guidance counsellor. These pages are dedicated to the subjects your family and guidance counsellor are too embarrassed or respectable to talk about.

To find out about the universities discussed in this book, I packed my suitcases and visited every single one. The judgements I came up with are inevitably subjective, but they are based on a year of research and thousands of conversations with students, teachers, administrators, and alumni across the country.

If nothing else, I hope this book will make you aware of the many choices available to you as a prospective Canadian university student. As I discovered on my journey, this country is full of interesting and exciting universities. Use this book, and find the one that is right for you.

NOTE: All figures that appear in this book are the most current available at the time of publication. Readers are advised, however, that statistics, especially those dealing with entrance requirements and fees, change yearly. The numbers in the book are offered only so that readers may get an impression of each university's size, standards and cost.

HOW TO CHOOSE THE RIGHT UNIVERSITY

Most Canadian students choose a university automatically: they pick the closest school, or the one their parents attended. There is no excuse for this. The number of universities in Canada has doubled since your parents' college days, and the differences between schools can be enormous.

To have the college career of your dreams, I recommend that you go far, far away. You've lived at home long enough. Yes, Mom and Dad are swell. Yes, your old room is vastly nicer than anyplace else you're likely to live in. But it's time to grow up.

You grow up a lot faster when Mom isn't doing your laundry any more.

Going away doesn't just build character; it also sharpens your mind by plopping you down among people who talk funny, believe radically different things, hate your province, eat disgusting foods, and yet are still your fellow countrymen. Sadly, the second-biggest country on earth is a narrow and parochial place. Local chauvinism is as fierce as it is ignorant. But there's a simple way to overcome your ignorant stereotypes about Newfoundland, the Maritimes, Quebec, Ontario, the prairies, or BC—live there. You'll be a better and more sophisticated person for it. It's going to impress your friends in Sackville that you know the best disco in Vancouver. And wouldn't it be great to be the only person in Moose Jaw to have tasted genuine Newfoundland cod tongues?

Of course, going to school away from home costs money—money your parents may not want to give you. The solution to this problem is to do something you probably should do in any case: take a year off between high school and college, and work.

Universities in Canada often resemble high schools precisely because they're full of slightly older high-school students. Why not give yourself a year to think about what you hope to get from university? As Robertson Davies says: "Students need some contact with the outside world if they are to recognize the value of the education that a university can give them. Certainly they should not regard it simply as a continuation of high school."

Okay! Now that I've convinced you to leave home, you still have the task of figuring out which far-flung Canadian university will be blessed with your company. Here are some basic questions you must ask yourself before you arrive at a decision.

• *Do I want a big (20,000 or more), medium (5,000 to 20,000), or small (fewer than 5,000 students) school?* The most appealing schools—McGill, Queen's, Simon Fraser, Dalhousie—fall into the intermediate zone. Big schools, with the exception of Western, usually remind one of the sort of places that George Orwell and Franz Kafka so disliked. Small schools are the happiest, but are too often stifling and unintellectual.

• *Do I want a prestigious school?* If so, the University of Toronto is the most; UPEI probably is the least. A university that began as a private school—Bishop's, Dalhousie, McGill, Acadia—will often have more prestige than it deserves. Newer schools — Waterloo, for example — will often have less. Remember: prestige usually reflects what a university was like 20 years ago, and it usually depends upon grossly exaggerated differences in academic performance. Prestige is rarely an accurate guide to present conditions.

• *Do I want to be around people who like to read and talk about what they've read?* Intellectuals congregate at Toronto, above all. They may also be found—though in much smaller numbers—at McGill and UBC. Subscribers to *The Idler* will feel ill-at-ease at St. Mary's and Lakehead.

• *Do I want to live in a city or a small town?* Do you need movie theatres, fashionable clothes, and bookstores? The hopelessly urban will consider only McGill, Concordia, the University of Toronto, or UBC. If you like to wake up to the chirping of birds, try Mt. Allison, Acadia, St. FX, Victoria, Trent, or Bishop's. If the great outdoors is your life, you'll love Lakehead, Laurentian, or UNB.

• *How much do I care about beauty?* Canada has a surprising number of beautiful campuses, most of which are in the Maritimes. Acadia, UNB, St. FX, Dalhousie, King's, and—depending on your taste—Simon Fraser are all magnificent. The University of Saskatchewan, the University of Manitoba, Toronto, Guelph, McMaster, and Western used to be lovely, but have been vandalized by disciples of Mr. Freyssinet. If you can close your eyes when you're near the nasty bits, though, there remains plenty to enjoy.

• *What do I want to study?* I have put this question last deliberately: it's unreasonable to expect a first-year student to know what he wants to do with his life. As a character in a Philip Roth novel unhappily wonders: "What right did that eighteen-year-old have to decide that I would be a dentist?" Delay specialization as long as possible. If you really aspire to becoming a civilized human being, give some thought to the great-books courses at King's and Brock.

The answer to all these questions may depend on the answer to one big question: *How much can I afford to spend on university?* Cost depends not so much on how far away from home you go, but how expensive a city you choose to go to. It can be cheaper to go 3,000 miles to St. John's than 75 miles to Toronto. Many schools that don't look expensive can be ruinous if you want to keep up with the Joneses. Tuition at Western, after all, is only $1,300, and London is a relatively inexpensive city; but the cost of a Mustang convertible (not to mention fraternity dues) can make even the richest father wince. Some cheap-but-fun cities: Winnipeg (really), Montreal, and St. John's. Halifax and Ottawa are surprisingly expensive, but Ottawa is probably the easiest city in Canada in which to get a part-time job.

Warning: Most provincial governments will not lend you money to study outside the province. One exception is Quebec, which will lend money to students going to Glendon College in Toronto.

Above all, instead of trusting hearsay and the memory of your guidance counsellor, be sure to visit any school you're considering. You don't want to end up like the Calgarian who, having in mind the great night-life, applied to U of T and spent the summer looking forward to four years in swinging Etobicoke. Deciding on a school is a deeply intuitive and subjective business. Read this book. Gather all the information you can. Sleep on it, and trust your instincts.

WHAT'S WRONG WITH THE SYSTEM?

It is not the purpose of this book to describe how our system could be better. This book is a buyer's guide, a user's manual; its only purpose is to help individual students make better decisions.

Still, before you make a decision to attend a particular Canadian university, it is not unreasonable to wonder about the state of the system as a whole. We constantly read in the papers that our higher educational system is in big trouble. This is true. We also read that there's nothing wrong with our universities that more money — lots more — cannot fix. This is false. What does money have to do with the following problems?

• Universities that administer literacy tests find that, on average, 40 per cent of their first-year students fail.
• Typically, students have to choose between large schools with good professors but no friends, or small schools with lots of friends but bad professors.
• In the lunch-room at Laurentian University, there is not a book or newspaper to be seen, nor a conversation to be heard, as 300 men and women hive off in little groups to play poker.
• Trent University's Bata Library received a bomb threat at 9 o'clock on a Thursday night, and was evacuated. In the process, it was discovered that, at a university with an undergraduate population of 10,000 students, 40 people were in the library on a week-night.
• Universities claim that they are making their standards tougher by raising the cut-off grades every year. But, since high schools are raising their grades even faster, standards are in fact falling. In 1970, 13.4 per cent of high-school graduates in the province of Ontario received grade 13 averages of 80 per cent or better; in 1984, 25.7 per cent did.

What our universities need is not more money. They may even need less, since we're probably operating more universities than we need. Saskatchewan, with a population of 1,000,000 people, is trying to run two full universities; Manitoba, with a population of 1,069,000 people is trying to run three. What our universities need is a sense of purpose.

What the rest of us need is a willingness to make choices. Do we want a great national research institution to vie with Berkeley and Harvard? If so, we can probably afford only one, and resources will have to be taken from other universities to support it.

Do we want to train students for careers? Then let's not worry about the quality of university life, and let's not try to give the same education to everybody. If we want career training, we should set up scientific and technical universities in major cities, encourage early specialization, and stop wasting money on athletics and orientation parties.

Do we want education to be accessible? Then let's do away with tuition fees, entrance requirements, and exams, and let's equalize spending on universities across the country. Let's also accept that our best students and professors will go abroad.

Do we want knowledge for its own sake? Then perhaps we should do away with degrees. People who just want to learn don't need certificates to show where they've parked their bodies between their eighteenth and twenty-first years.

Do we want humane undergraduate communities? Then let's radically decentralize our big urban universities, accept that we will not be a world leader in scientific research, and put more money into the smaller colleges, especially in the Maritimes.

Of course, among these goals there are contradictions, and they all have some unpleasant implications. We need to choose among imperfect alternatives. It's precisely because we're afraid to choose — because we've been trying, with limited funds, to do half a dozen expensive and incompatible things — that our universities are in such bad shape.

After visiting every anglophone and bilingual university in the country, it is inescapably obvious to me that reform is badly needed. I'm not going to offer a comprehensive plan for radical change. That's not the point of this book. But at no extra charge, I will offer three modest, moderate, and easily implemented suggestions.

1. Raise tuition. Since provincial governments are likely to cut their support by an amount equal to that which universities raise by higher fees, this won't generate much new revenue. What it will do, first, is shift the burden of paying for education onto the person who benefits — the student. Students form one of the wealthiest groups in the country. The 20 per cent of Canadian young people who attend university are almost entirely drawn from the wealthiest 20 per cent of the population. They are also one of the most heavily subsidized groups. Quebec, for example, has not increased tuition in 18 years. The increased cost of tuition will enhance the importance of the choice a student makes when he decides whether and where to go to university. It will promote a community feeling by promoting a sense of commitment. Students now believe, correctly, that their universities belong to them about as much as the Ministry of Industry, Trade and Commerce does. Above all, raising tuition will force universities to worry more about what their students think, and less about what the provincial ministries of education think.

2. Introduce a compulsory first-year curriculum. It's disturbing to discover how anti-intellectual so many of our universities are. Carleton, for example, has almost as many video games and pool-tables as books. Universities should not exist to compete with the CFL, or to save Imperial Oil some of the cost of training its engineers. Universities should exist to create civilized men and women. A student can, of course, create his own liberal-arts degree if he wants to, but many prefer to specialize early in leisure studies or science fiction. Universities should have the courage to say that they can identify what it is that educated men and women need to know. At a minimum, that means a first-year curriculum of history, literature, science, philosophy, and a foreign language. If students then want to devote the next three years to accountancy, at least we know we'll have partially civilized accountants.

3. Raise entrance standards. The University of Toronto claims to be the Harvard of the North. Actually, it has more in common with the University of Indiana (although it's probably harder to be accepted by Indiana). We need to raise our expectations. We should require more from our universities and our students. Entrance standards don't have to be raised everywhere. Desperately overcrowded campuses, like the downtown campus of the University of Toronto, should raise them higher than underused campuses, like Lakehead or the Maritime universities. Universities that purport to be prestigious ought to raise their standards higher than universities that don't.

Higher standards can be sabotaged by grade inflation in the high schools. High university standards are also threatened when universities have to do the work high schools should have done but didn't. In order to improve our universities, we must first improve our high schools, and that will require the reimposition of comprehensive, province-wide examinations. Failing that, universities should make more extensive use of the SAT-style exams used for admissions at American schools.

At the very least we need to be realistic. Between what is euphemistically called "accessibility" — that is, making a university education available to anybody who wants one — and academic excellence, there is an irreconcilable contradiction. If we want our universities to be "universally accessible," we should give up the illusion that they can be any good. Old Friedrich Nietzsche knew this when he wrote, "In large states public education will always be mediocre, for the same reason that in large kitchens the cooking is usually bad."

I should add that there are those who think our universities are even worse than I have suggested. When I asked Irving Layton for the advice he would like to pass on to college freshman, this is how he responded:

"The best advice I can offer to a Canadian college freshman is to delay becoming one for as long as possible. Once he's got his feet on the academic treadmill, he can't prevent his turning into the socialized article approved by the booboisie who run our political, economic, religious, judicial, and educational institutions. His chances of turning out to be a Galileo, Spinoza, Shelley, Thomas Paine, Rosa Luxemburg, Rousseau, or William Blake are less than one in a million. So, my advice to the college freshman is the following: run as quickly as you can to the registrar's office and demand a refund. With that, buy yourself a one-way ticket to India or Tibet or the Bronx and seek out a sage from whom you might learn that the aim of education is ecstasy and insight, not knowledge or the acquisition of marketable skills."

ACADIA

Open your suitcase. Throw in your Ralph Lauren outfits, your penny loafers, your *Animal House* soundtrack, your preppie handbook, your designer stationery, your tennis racket, and your "party till you drop" tee-shirt. Toss your suitcase into your convertible, and then head for Wolfville, Nova Scotia. You're going to Acadia.

Acadia is not for everybody. Situated in a beautiful town, it is a beautiful college for beautiful people. Most people choose Acadia because of its reputation for fun. What many new students don't understand, however, is that the fun times at Acadia are enjoyed mainly by an élite. As one student explains, "Acadia is very cliquey. Get into the right crowd and you've got it made; otherwise, you're out in the cold." The pressure here is intense. And I'm not talking about math class. Acadia is like your worst nightmares about high school all over again. No date for Saturday night? No fancy car? No designer clothes? Can't catch a football? These are meaningful problems for an Acadia student. And don't think being clever will make up for it. In fact, cleverness and an interest in academics can be a definite liability. As one student puts it, "If you want to be in the cool group, studying can't be too important to you. And if you're a girl, being a bit of a bubblehead helps." Other personal attributes of extreme social importance are: what you look like, what you wear, which dining hall — and which table — you eat at, where you live, which team you're on, how athletic you are, and where you come from. In other words, if you hated grade 10, don't waste your time at Acadia.

Acadia has the kind of rowdy, playful atmosphere usually glorified in Hollywood movies about college. There are lots of good-looking girls and guys, lots of parties, lots of nice cars, lots of money, and there never seems to be any homework.

All the amenities of college life are here. Wolfville is the perfect college town. The wealthy residents keep the town looking polished and plush, and there is plenty of excellent student housing available. Classes are a good size, with a 15-to-1 student-teacher ratio. The campus is one of the loveliest anywhere. It is graced by elegant nineteenth-century structures, containing some of the most charming lecture halls in the country. There are also ample modern facilities. The professors are friendly; some even hang out at the student pub. And the legendary Acadia school spirit keeps the campus lively and the alumni money pouring in.

Although there are no fields in which the school especially stands out, it offers a good basic education in almost everything. The business administration program is strong, and there is great pride taken in the biology, computer science, and music departments. The library is adequate, although people with serious research to do visit Dalhousie. One interesting quirk of Acadia's history is its tradition of producing educators. Twenty-six Acadia graduates have become presidents or chancellors of colleges and universities all over the world. They also have an impressive record of creating political wizards. Many members of Ontario's Big Blue Machine went here, as did Premier Richard Hatfield and Sir Charles Tupper (look him up in Trivial Pursuit).

Acadia is a small school that ought to hold 3,000 students but currently has 3,300. Like its students, Acadia is popular. They accept only one-third of their applicant pool each year (1,100 out of 3,100), and they are going to start accepting even fewer in an attempt to bring school size down. But ultimately, to its students, Acadia is not about academics. Above all, Acadia is jock heaven.

The Acadia motto is *In Pulvere Vinces*, which means "in dust you will win." It's a curious concept, yet somehow appropriate for a school that consistently produces football champions. Everyone at Acadia is a rabid sports fan, especially when it comes to football. During home games, about 2,000 noisy people (that's two-thirds of the student body!) will turn up at Acadia's impressive stadium to cheer on the beloved Axemen. Even for away games, Acadia will try to bus in more fans than the host school has, especially when fighting arch-rivals St. FX and Mt. Allison. Basketball and hockey are also popular, but not as dusty.

After football games, everyone heads off to the Swinging Axe lounge in the student union building. This is the favourite Acadia pub, since it is conveniently located on campus and is as good as anything in town. If you are a member of the "in" group, it's especially important to show up — you have to be out and be seen if you are to maintain your status. If you're not a member of the group, you can always show up anyway, to look at the cool people and wish you were one yourself.

Most people agree that serious students go to Dalhousie, Catholics go to St. FX, while Acadia exists for party animals. And Acadia does not betray its reputation. How many other Canadian universities offer free bus service to the local ski hill... daily? How many other rural colleges can entice 1,000 students back to campus for a couple of days each summer (some flying in from the Bahamas and the United States) just to fit in an extra party known as "Summer Extravaganza"? How many other colleges of 3,300 students need 37 intramural softball teams, 33 basketball teams, 28 hockey teams, 15 soccer teams, 12 flag-football teams, and 22 volleyball teams just to keep up with demand? Fun is serious at Acadia.

This celebrated love of fun is probably why Acadia is able to attract so many foreign and out-of-province students. At almost nine per cent, Acadia has a higher percentage of enrolled foreign students than Dalhousie does. Most of these students come from the Bahamas and Hong Kong. Students here joke that the popularity of their school abroad only reflects the fact that Acadia is listed first, alphabetically, in directories of Canadian schools, and it's therefore the first and only school foreign students bother to read about. The large number of students from foreign countries, as well as New England and Upper Canada, gives Acadia a jet-set quality that most people are proud of. But being considered foreign isn't always an advantage. Newfoundlanders and Cape Bretoners complain about the stereotypes they have to contend with when dealing with other students. Says one Newfoundlander, "People assume that, if you're a Newfie or a Capper, you eat fish and drink beer all the time. And if you don't, they want to know what's wrong with you."

Acadia encourages its students to live on campus, and has excellent housing for more than half the student body. Most people live in residence in first year (about 600 out of 800 people) and they find that their social lives revolve around their dorms. Residents develop ferocious and irrational emotional commitments to their dorms. The way people talk about them, you'd never believe that residence rooms were assigned to students at random. It is impossible to know which ones are best: anyone you ask insists that the one he lives in is the greatest anywhere. This intense loyalty seems to develop early, but in candid moments students agree that it doesn't matter where you live because you'll love it soon enough. There are 12 residences, which hold a total of 1,800 students. Only three of them are co-educational.

Fun is not limited to the residences. Many students live in nearby, magnificent old houses which they rent. Like everything else at Acadia, decisions about where to live off campus are guided by considerations of coolness. The best houses and apartment buildings have names that are familiar to everybody. "The Coop," "the Swamp," "the Igloo," and "the Stack" are highly desirable places to live, although any house on Prospect Street or Summer Street will do. Inhabitants of these houses play host to many of the exclusive parties on campus. For students living in a confining residence room, the problem of how to throw an exclusive party is solved by renting the "50/50" lounge in the student union building. Campus security will co-operate with you by ensuring that only those people whose names appear on a guest list posted at the door are admitted. This way you can keep any riff-raff from crashing the party.

If you aren't invited to parties, don't panic. Although Wolfville is small, there are still places one can go for a good time. The open parties in the student union building, "SuperSubs," are always packed, and there's one almost every weekend. Be sure to buy tickets early, as they are often sold out by Wednesday afternoon. The campus disco, Exit 10's, is another favourite spot. If you want to go into town, which people do only occasionally, there is the Anvil for drinking, the Colonial Inn for eating, and, if you want to impress a date, there's Casablanca Restaurant, which is dark and expensive.

The decision to come to Acadia is a life-style choice. There are the magnificent setting, the beautiful campus, the winning teams, the elegant parties, the rowdy school spirit, and that exclusive feeling. For some, Acadia is paradise. For others, it's like going through the dark days of adolescence all over again.

THE FACTS

Founded:	1838
Address:	Wolfville, Nova Scotia
	B0P 1X0
Tuition:	$1,540

Cut-off grade for general admission (per cent):	60
Enrolment:	3,252
Undergraduate full-time enrolment:	3,096
Percentage of foreign students:	8.7
Percentage of students from outside the province:	36.8
Residence fees:	$3,145–3,590
Percentage of students in residence:	55
Male-female ratio:	55:45
Athletic facilities:	About to be great: super-duper gym to be built in honour of 150th anniversary (1988). Good stadium, ice rink, and lots of playing fields.
Team name:	(M) Axemen, (F) Axettes
Colours:	Garnet and blue
Most popular major:	Business admin.
Fraternities/sororities:	None. But people treat their residences and homes as though they were clubhouses.
Typical garb:	Polo outfits, loafers for men. Designer clothing, pearls for women.
Campus political attitude:	Deeply conservative.
Best-known fact:	Acadia has great teams that usually win everything in Atlantic region conferences.
Least-known fact:	Artist Alex Colville is chancellor, and is often seen riding around campus on his bicycle.
If you had to put it in one sentence:	"Most people here are rich dough-heads." — *Inebriated Acadia alumnus, class of '81, visiting summer extravaganza*
Alumni:	Norman Atkins, Dalton Camp, Sir Charles Tupper, Richard Hatfield,

Loring C. Christie (first Canadian
ambassador to the United States),
Edgar Rhodes (premier of Nova
Scotia, 1925–30), Elmer MacKay,
H. Harrison McCain.

DO'S AND DON'TS

DO bring formal wear with you to school. The Homecoming and Winter Carnival proms are the biggest events on campus all year.

DON'T expect to have a private sex life. At Acadia, everyone knows everyone else's business.

DO be careful where you smoke your drugs. Last year, the RCMP and campus security forces raided several residence rooms in an attempt to arrest student dealers.

DON'T miss the chance to roll on the muddy floor of the Bay of Fundy when it's at low tide. It's a favourite campus pastime.

DO take a friend and a picnic and visit: Blomidon Mountain and Lookoff, Dykelands, Cape Split, Scott's Bay, Ridge Park or Three Pools. The area surrounding Wolfville is beautiful, private, and romantic.

UNIVERSITY OF ALBERTA

Albertans love business and they love malls. Naturally enough, when the University of Alberta wanted to create a focus for student extracurricular life, it didn't bother with such effete central-Canadian refinements as reading rooms, debating halls, games rooms, art galleries, or imposing dining halls. Instead, it built its own Eaton Centre. Alberta students love the tubes, projecting inner balconies, and the great, arched glass ceilings of the lavish Hub Mall, even though — in utter defiance of the Albertan profit ethic — it loses money.

On the first floor there are restaurants, bars, clothing stores, record stores, jewellery stores, sporting-goods stores, coffee stands, and even a choice between Treats and Mmmuffins for breakfast. Above them are three floors of residences. When an Albertan student in residence wakes up in the morning, he can stroll to his window, throw open his shutters, look down and behold the lovely sight of dollars changing hands, or look up and see his tuition money going through the ceiling, as millions of dollars of heat escape through the glass roof into the subzero outdoors.

Nobody at U of A seems to think it's weird that the university owns an on-campus shopping mall. "I honestly never thought about it," says one typical student. "I just assumed every campus had its own mall."

The University of Alberta is simply not your typical place. Consider the following motion before the U of A Students' Council.

"Be it resolved that: The Students' Council endorses and supports those student organizations which work towards the peaceful abolition of apartheid."

Now, the abolition of apartheid in South Africa — the *peaceful* abolition, no less — is the number-one student-motherhood issue of the 1980s. There is not a student government in North America — or Europe, Asia, or Africa, for that matter — that does not feel that reforming South Africa is its number-one priority, way ahead of planning the Homecoming, or even banning nuclear arms. So, can you believe that any student council, anywhere in Canada, could defeat this resolution by a two-to-one margin? Well, the answer is yes: the Student's Council of the University of Alberta.

"We just felt," explains the council's vice-president, "that it was unfair to single out South Africa in a resolution when there are so many other countries which even Amnesty International recognizes as having a much worse human-rights record."

People unfamiliar with the political atmosphere on Canadian campuses may not appreciate that this is a highly eccentric point of view. "I guess you could say we're conservative," admits the vice-president. "Well, goodness, everyone knows Alberta is a Tory place. But it's not that we don't care about the rest of the world; we just want to proceed in a reasonable way."

The editor of the student newspaper, *The Gateway,* on the other hand, is doubtful about the social awareness of U of A students. "I say you have to hit people here over the head before you can get them to notice any issue. You wanna know something that's big on this campus? The Edmonton Oilers, now they're big!"

Actually, what's really big at U of A is U of A itself. The University of

Alberta at 35,000 is now the second-largest university in Canada. (UBC has fallen to third place.) Not many greetings are exchanged in the hallways. It's hard to make friends with 35,000 people. A former U of A professor, now working at the University of Lethbridge, remembers that "on my last day at U of A I walked around for half an hour until I saw a familiar face to say goodbye to."

U of A may not be cozy, but its degrees pack clout in Alberta. And by local standards it is the acme of sophistication. A transfer student from Mohawk College in Red Deer says hopefully, "I used to have my hair in a mohawk at Mohawk. It didn't go down too well. I think I'll try again though. It should be okay here." Does he have a surprise coming!

Why are Albertans so impressed with U of A? The dean of students thinks that "it seems to be a case of 'bigger is better.' We've got more staff, more equipment, more facilities, more money. We tend to be favoured when it comes to funding. Our government is very generous with us. So there are more choices and opportunities for students at this university than at the others." When Alberta struck it rich in the 1970s, a far-sighted Premier Lougheed determined that a lot of the petro-money would be spent to fund Alberta's universities, and to create a first-rate medical research complex at U of A. The good times are gone now, but earmarked accounts in the Heritage Fund have saved U of A from the 1980s destitution of the other prairie schools. This is one of the few universities in Canada where resource-intensive subjects (science, engineering, and an expensively computerized department of business administration) are taught as successfully as the inexpensive humanities. U of A can afford to do everything well.

The new U of A research hospital fills several city blocks. Thanks to its faculty and modern equipment, U of A undergraduates enjoy some of the finest scientific facilities in the country.

It isn't just money that draws Albertan students to U of A rather than to Calgary or Lethbridge. An indulgent provincial government bestowed upon the univerity the only schools of dentistry, pharmacy, forestry, home economics, and agriculture in the province. Many students come to U of A for its special facilities for handicapped students. U of A and St. Mary's University in Halifax have been chosen by the federal government as special resource universities for Canada's handicapped. Machines to enable deaf students to "hear," scooters so the immobile can move, and seeing-eye people to lead the blind from class to class are only the most visible elements of an astonishing program, which is directed by a sensitive and knowledgeable staff. They are assisted by 150 student volunteers who, in turn, make up one of the largest student activity groups on campus.

Fraternities and sororities matter more at U of A than at most

Canadian universities. Several have clubhouses just off campus. Luckily for the public, but unluckily for the boys of *Delta Upsilon*, the most attractive clubhouse of all — theirs — has recently been turned into a museum. *Delta Upsilon* house was once the house of Lord Rutherford, the premier of Alberta from 1905 to 1911. Rutherford was also the first chancellor of U of A and gave his home, then the most magnificent in Edmonton, to the university after his death. Somehow the lucky boys of DU got it... at least for a while. On tours of the house, the guides point out Peter Lougheed's old room.

Joining a club, a fraternity, a team, or *something*, is essential at U of A. This is a difficult place to make friends, as any one of the hundreds of students eating lunch alone in the student cafeterias would tell you. Living in residence is one solution. Hub Mall apartments are, understandably, hard to get, but the other residences on campus almost always have vacancies. Students blame an expensive meal plan for the unpopularity of residence living; but mostly, it just seems to be not in fashion.

The many happy students at U of A say that the campus is friendly, and not at all the intimidating, miniature city that frightens newcomers. The most popular of the three campus pubs, the Room at the Top ("RATT" to one and all) bustles so furiously that there's not only a line-up to get in, there's also a "line-up to get into the elevator that takes you to the line-up to get in." Humanities students like the Hub Mall's pub, Dewey's. Concerts and large dances are staged in Dinwoodie's, in the student union building.

As a prospective student at either of Alberta's urban universities, you must choose between big (U of C) and immense (U of A). At U of A, you can go all day without seeing anybody you know; your classes will be huge; you'll probably never talk to a professor; and the line-up for the 5 o'clock buses may bring to mind the last train from Paris in 1940. On the other hand, the choice of specialties and courses is vast; the equipment in the professional schools and in the scientific departments is gleaming and new; and the library is the second-best in Canada. It's easy to see why U of A is thought by many to be the best school west of Toronto. And then there's the choice between two brands of muffins.

THE FACTS

Founded:	1908
Address:	Edmonton, Alberta T6G 2E5

Tuition:	$878
Cut-off grade for general admission (per cent):	60
Enrolment:	29,107
Undergraduate full-time enrolment:	21,527
Percentage of foreign students:	7.2
Percentage of students from outside the province:	9.2
Residence fees:	$2,490–3,330
Percentage of students in residence:	15
Male-female ratio:	53:47
Athletic facilities:	Excellent: facilities left over from Commonwealth Games in 1982. "ButterDome" provides indoor track and field facility.
Team name:	(M) Golden Bears, (F) Pandas
Colours:	Green and gold
Fraternities/sororities:	Yes. 13 of them and counting.
Typical garb:	Jeans, ski jackets, canvas knapsacks slung over one shoulder.
Campus political attitude:	Small-"c" conservative in a big way.
Best-known fact:	Joe Clark practised being prime minister here.
Least-known fact:	The University of Alberta is the second-biggest school in Canada.
If you had to put it in one sentence:	People who choose to come to Alberta subscribe to the "bigger is better" theory of life.
Alumni:	Joe Clark, W.O. Mitchell, Susan Natress (champion trapshooter), Peter Lougheed, Roland Michener, Ronald Martland (retired Supreme Court justice), Sam Belzberg, Doris Anderson, Jim Coutts, Harvie Andre, Thomas Siddon.

DO'S AND DON'TS

DO be sure to take advantage of the "Exam Registry" run by the student union. You can buy your professor's old exams for a couple of bucks, and get some clue as to what your own exam will be like.

DON'T run for the position of vice-president for finance of the student council unless you are prepared to manage an annual budget of five and a half million dollars . . . the largest budget of any student council in Canada.

DON'T assume, if you are from out of town, that Edmonton is a total cultural wasteland. There are in fact some good theatres and museums that students should take advantage of.

I REMEMBER...

I hope that I made some contribution to the University of Alberta in the period between my matriculation in September 1917, and May 1920 (take away October, November and December 1918 playing truant in the RAF) but I am sure that the University gave me much more in knowledge, confidence and above all — friends. — *Roland Michener*

BISHOP'S

"I'm going to say something very controversial now," said the new principal of Bishop's during an interview. "We, at Bishop's, have decided," and here he paused solemnly, "to be specialists in undergraduate education."

That's it? That's the controversial part?

"Don't be fooled," said Principal Scott, "that's more controversial than you think."

At a time when Canada's youth are having anxiety attacks about jobs, "education for education's sake" can be an unpopular concept. The problem with the idea comes when you examine just who it is that can *afford* to go to university simply for the thrill of it. (Here comes the controversy.) It is, you see, a very unpopular group of people: Toronto's private-school kids, graduates of the Westmount high schools, the off-spring of eastern Canada's old Anglo-Saxon families, and assorted other members of the privileged classes.

It's not that it costs so much more to go to Bishop's; it doesn't. But once a school gets labelled as rural, residential, non-professional, non-technical, and sports-oriented (in short, "a specialist in undergraduate education"), it begins to draw a self-selecting crowd of young folk who "just wanna have fun." You've heard of the University of Western Ontario? Well, welcome to the University of Eastern Quebec!

Certainly not all of Bishop's 2,100 undergraduates are rich kids, but only the kids at Bishop's know that perception is *not*, in fact, reality. To the outside world, Bishop's has long been known as a resting place for Quebec's Anglo élite. "But today," says one student, "we're a very middle-class bunch, a real mix of things. We've got French and English people, small-town folk, and city slickers from Toronto. There are a few people who are really well-to-do, but it's generally frowned upon to show off."

Everyone agrees that Bishop's has changed a lot in the past few years. Although its reputation as "a country club" remains intact, now, instead of a country club for dumbos, Bishop's is aiming for a new status as a country club for smarties.

"It's not for nothing that this place is called a country club," explains the student council president. "Take my case for an example. If I walk out my front door, I immediately hit the dining hall. Through my back door are the tennis courts. The golf course isn't far, and the new gym is just amazing. We're surrounded by beautiful old buildings and rolling countryside. For a Bishop's student, this is just part of going to school."

But there's a new part to going to school at Bishop's — work. "Bishop's decided it was time to get serious about academics. The administration has really cracked down," says one senior. "There are more assignments now. It's harder to get good marks, and there are stiffer penalties for late assignments. I am retaking a course I failed last year, and it's gotten a lot harder this time around."

The most noticeable change has been in the admissions office. The cut-off grade for automatic acceptance has risen from 65 per cent to 70 per cent. The hike is partly caused by the growing popularity of Bishop's and partly by a deliberate effort on the part of the administration to improve Bishop's academic reputation.

"The reputation of this school used to be in the basement. It's crawled up a few floors, but still has a way to go before it hits the top storey," says one sixth-year Bishop's student. "It used to be Party, Party, Party; now we only party with a small 'p,' and we do a lot more work."

If Bishop's used to be known as a party school, and would like to be known as a party and academics school, it is in fact becoming known as a party and sports school. The Gaiters are an awe-inspiring football team. "Bruce Colter is the God of Canadian football coaching," explains one student. "Lots of kids come here just for him. And the Gaiters have never had a losing season."

Bishop's takes its football very seriously. During a recent game against the mighty UBC team, Bishop's alumni came from as far as Florida just to see the match. "Nobody can figure out how a little college can always come up with such a great team. The Gaiters have made Bishop's famous; they got us on *The Journal*."

"We're proud as hell about our football team," says Principal Scott, "but I'm afraid people think all we do here is talk about football. What we want to do is make our whole school just like our football team. We want excellence everywhere."

Most Bishop's people are willing to admit that the university has a long way to go before it can take a place among the leading universities of the country. "I'd say we're catching up to Brock," says one student, sincerely. "Bishop's would be a great university if it just won the Lotto 6/49," says another. "As it is, we're much too short on resources." While the provincial government is not generous towards it, Bishop's can rely on its fiercely loyal alumni. "We get a lot of support from them, so underfunding isn't quite as bad as it could be." Still, the campus looks dilapidated compared to Western or Queen's.

With so many alumni staying in touch with their alma mater, Bishop's is obviously doing something right. In a promotional brochure, graduate Norman Webster (class of '62), now editor-in-chief of *The Globe and Mail*, relates: "My main memory of Bishop's is of a feeling that everything was wide open to anyone who wanted to have a shot at it — sports, theatre, debating, student government, journalism."

There is currently a movement at Bishop's to initiate a fraternity system, and another movement to start a varsity crew. As far as most students are concerned, Bishop's just can't do enough to be more like Western.

Most Bishop's students live in residence for at least part of their careers, and then move to apartments off campus. The Oxford Apartments are most popular, but it really doesn't matter where you live. As one student explains, "Lennoxville is our student ghetto." A favourite residence is Divinity House, a beautiful 95-year-old sprawling mansion in the middle of campus that is reserved for quiet upperclassmen.

When it's time for drinking, everyone heads off to the Red Lion, a great Lennoxville institution. It doesn't matter who you are, student, professor, or townie, this place is always the first choice. It's partly owned by a very popular Bishop's economics professor. There are only three other entertainment choices. The G (actually Le Georgian) is a rowdy tavern that's open until three. One night a year, the G sponsors a special event in which patrons are invited to smash their empty beer bottles against the wall or each other. The Len is for Bishop's artsy students, and the Elmwood is for the older crowd and offers billiards and card tables. On campus there is a pub which is open only three nights a week, and a quiet bar, open Monday through Saturdays.

Above all, students socialize at the mailboxes in the student union building, where every student comes every day to see whether his or her L.L. Bean catalogue has arrived yet.

Bishop's is one of Canada's smallest universities. Some think it is one of Canada's best-kept secrets. For students who cannot go three years without an intellectual conversation, Bishop's may not be the best choice. But if you want a university experience guaranteed to make you sigh nostalgically 30 years later and think "those, those were the days," choosing Bishop's could be the happiest decision you ever make.

THE FACTS

Founded:	1843
Address:	Lennoxville, Quebec J1M 1Z7
Tuition:	$730
Recommended grade for admission (per cent):	70
Enrolment:	1,799
Undergraduate full-time enrolment:	1,148

Percentage of foreign students:	3.8
Percentage of students from outside the province:	20
Residence fees:	$3,010–3,390
Percentage of students in residence:	29
Male-female ratio:	53:47
Athletic facilities:	Excellent. Stadium (seats 2,000), arena (1,200) and brand-new sports centre.
Team name:	Gaiters
Colours:	Purple, white, and silver
Fraternities/sororities:	Working on it.
Typical garb:	Preppy or stylish.
Campus political attitude:	Leave that stuff to the French students at neighbouring Champlain College.
Best-known fact:	The Bishop's Gaiters are one of Canada's best football teams.
Least-known (but useful) fact:	The director of admissions at McGill medical school is a Bishop's alumnus.
If you had to put it in one sentence:	"This place is a beer company's heaven. After all, there's not much else to do."—*Senior student*
Alumni:	Norman Webster, John Bassett Sr.

DO'S AND DON'TS

DO expect to see a lot of vehicles on campus "ranging from Mercedes Benzes to bikes." A scooter is ideal.

DON'T bother bringing a car with you to school. "Where would you go?" wonders one student.

DO have confidence that not everyone at Bishop's is a snob. Although the school has a snooty image, it's not true that everyone there is a spoiled brat.

I REMEMBER...

What I remember best about my time at Bishop's was meeting my first wife, who was a fellow student. — *John Bassett Sr.*

UNIVERSITY OF BRANDON

One thing you learn at Brandon is the art of changing the subject gracefully. When asked about the 1984 firing of the university's Tory-appointed president by the NDP government, the $500,000 settlement of his wrongful-dismissal lawsuit, and the continuing bitterness between the faculty who supported him and the faculty who didn't, Brandonites say, "Yeah, yeah, but that's all behind us now." When asked about the suspension of the Brandon Bobcats from amateur athletics for offering star high-school athletes money to choose Brandon, they hastily bring up the nationally acclaimed music department. The visitor learns quickly not to expect answers to embarrassing questions.

Certainly it would be wrong to conclude from the Bobcats episode that students must be bribed to attend Brandon. It's much too well loved for that. It would even be wrong to conclude that the Bobcats could not have won honestly. Trent Frayne, *The Globe and Mail*'s spirited sports columnist and a Brandon alumnus himself, says about the Bobcats: "Great team, great team." When asked about the scandal he, too, replies soothingly, "Well, that's all behind them now."

Nobody at Brandon deludes himself that this is one of the country's leading academic institutions. As one student admitted, "You don't need to be too swift to go here." But Brandon has a job to do, "serving the population of southern Manitoba," as an administrator puts it, and it does that job well. "We have the only small campus in the province. People from small communities feel comfortable here."

The students agree. "Brandon is a good place to do your pre-professional studies. A lot of people here need to work to put themselves through school. It's helpful to be able to live at home. Maybe later we'll move on to U of M."

Brandon is one of the few rural universities that was not slapped together during the 1960s' good-times education boom. Brandon, founded as Prairie College in 1879 is, in fact, the second-oldest university in the west. Somebody took care to harmonize the new buildings with the old, and the pretty campus is neatly organized in four downtown blocks. Still, students dread it when they have to change buildings: "It may not be a very far walk, but you're sure as heck going to freeze your buns off anyway." Brandon is located in the coldest university town in Canada.

One building looms over all others: the huge new music building that Queen Elizabeth opened in 1982. It, and the adjacent auditorium, form the centre of the university and are the pride of the town. In the middle of the lonely prairie, Brandon university pours out weekly concerts, music competitions, CBC broadcasts, and jazz festivals. Unhappily, even Brandon's favoured music faculty cannot escape the economic plight of the west. The Manitoba government's decision to concentrate its scanty resources on the Winnipeg universities means that two of the music building's three floors are closed and empty. On a recent visit, Prime Minister Mulroney promised to raise one million dollars to finish the building, but so far the promise has not been kept.

Although none of Brandon's other departments is quite as notable as the music department, one Brandon education professor, Gerry Neufeld, recently put the school on the map with his North American best-seller, *Inside Commodore DOS*. The book is a computer manual with information about Commodores that even Commodore didn't know. The university is also proud of its native-studies program and Bachelor of General Studies degree, but music is just about the only field that attracts students from far-away places.

Not that everyone at Brandon is from Brandon. The university attracts a good number of students from Saskatchewan, and some from Winnipeg as well. These students are clearly attracted by Brandon's small size and rural focus. As the housing director points out, "If you're from Winnipeg and you want to get away from home, Brandon's a good choice. After all, you're only two hours away. And for kids from small communities in Saskatchewan ... Brandon is going to feel the most comfortable."

Still, there are not enough "foreigners" to fill Brandon's residences. Only 470 of the 550 spaces in residence are occupied, and while the university blames cheaper rents in town (where a house with rooms for four or five people is only $500 a month), the students blame the excessive strictness of university rules. "We were treated like children.

You had to sign guests in after eleven o'clock, and you couldn't bring alcohol into your room after midnight. I hated living in residence."

Students who don't live with their parents are always able to find accommodation close to the university. "Nothing in Brandon is farther away than a fifteen-minute drive, anyway. We've only got one bus route. No transfers."

Although the university's budget is tight, a brand-new student union building — complete with pub — has just been built. This will give Brandon students the campus hangout they've been waiting more than 80 years for. It may also help foster a greater sense of attachment to the university than students currently feel.

The new student union pub will bring the number of bars in Brandon to four. The three others are: Spats, "a trendy dance club that's the nicest place," the Unwinder, "a big barroom filled mostly with Brandon University students," and Encounters, a disco dedicated to what its name suggests. It seems, however, that not many Brandon students expose themselves to the opportunities that await them at Encounters. There aren't many couples at Brandon, and students say it's not a terribly romantic place. "The problem is," explains a native of Brandon, "that we all know each other already. We've known each other forever."

If you like the hustle of the city, Brandon might seem claustrophobic, but few of Brandon's students feel trapped. "People like Brandon, and would stay here all their lives if they could. Trouble is, if you want to be a corporate executive someday, there's not a lot of hope you'll find that kind of job in Brandon." Brandon students are satisfied, in an undemonstrative way, with their school. "You don't get a lot of jumping up and down for Brandon U, but you do meet a lot of people here who feel that, for this stage of their lives at least, Brandon University is good enough."

THE FACTS

Founded:	1879, originally as Prairie College.
Address:	Brandon, Manitoba R7A 6A9
Tuition:	$947
Cut-off grade for general admission (per cent):	60
Enrolment:	2,853
Undergraduate full-time enrolment:	1,419

Percentage of foreign students:	6
Percentage of students from outside the province:	7
Residence fees:	$3,030–3,462
Percentage of students in residence:	16
Male-female ratio:	41:59
Athletic facilities:	Fair.
Team name:	Bobcats
Colours:	Blue and gold
Most impressive major:	Music
Fraternities/sororities:	None.
Typical garb:	Jeans, jean jackets, sweat-shirts. "Not University of Western Ontario style, for sure!"
Campus political attitude:	"This campus is becoming bluer and bluer every day."
Best-known fact:	The Bobcats are a great team when they're not suspended.
Least-known fact:	This is the second-oldest university in the west.
If you had to put it in one sentence:	"Brandon is probably more apathetic than your average apathetic university." — Student
Alumni:	Tommy Douglas, Stanley Knowles, Olive Diefenbaker, David Kilgour.

DO'S AND DON'TS

DO attend the well-organized Brandon film series and spring film festival in the Evans Theatre. A good way to impress a date.

DON'T try to make friends with a jock unless you're one yourself. After the Bobcats episode there's been a real rift between athletes and non-athletes, and people like it that way.

DO be careful what you choose to study if you are planning to transfer to U of M to complete your degree. U of M will not accept some Brandon credits, so check ahead of time.

DON'T despair too much about the state of the scantily-stocked library. Help is coming. A new government grant is going to pay for an extension that should be ready soon.

UNIVERSITY OF BRITISH COLUMBIA

Before OPEC, no matter what UBC did it just couldn't help being the best school west of the Ontario border. Now, UBC is a great Canadian university on its way down. The University of Alberta has overtaken it in size and wealth. The best professors and graduate students are deserting to accept higher salaries over the Rockies. And civil war — always an ominous possibility in polarized and quarrelsome British Columbia — may break out any minute between conservative students and leftist faculty.

In British Columbia, UBC is still enviously viewed as the school of the wealthy and the established. "UBC is more traditional, more old-fashioned," says a student, who refers to the students at Simon Fraser as "the Marxists on the hill." An administrator concurs. "Of the three universities in BC, I think most people's preference is to go to UBC. It is seen as the place where the great repository of scholarly opinion lies. Whenever a radio show needs an expert, they'll call UBC."

Perhaps that's why the administration can get away with maintaining that the university's problems are negligible when seen in perspective. All administrations do that, of course — that's what they're paid for — but UBC's denies reality with unusual flair. "The perception of our situation is more damaging than the reality," the academic services vice-president insists. As for the faculty exodus, "The administration tries to put a good face on the loss by saying 'we'd be in trouble if other universities *didn't* want to steal our professors,'" according to the president of the UBC student council. "They actually think it's good: they're always saying 'look at all the people who get recruited from UBC.'"

So why does everybody still think that UBC is a top university? Perhaps because of the stunning impact of two words on the Canadian mind: No Snow.

The human organism is really a primitive thing. When the sky is grey and the wind is cutting, people get grumpy and mean. When the sky is blue and the sun is shining, they have a friendly word for everybody. UBC is one of three universities in the country where students can converse outside comfortably any day of the year, instead of nodding briefly and rushing to class before hypothermia sets in. "We have a lot of high-quality individuals who accept lower salaries just to be in Vancouver," says the vice-president of academic services, himself a recent defector from Waterloo. And, says a young student from Quebec City, "I came out here for Expo and never left. I love this city."

You can't have everything. While it's climatically possible to chat on the sidewalk at UBC, first you have to bump into somebody you know. And that just isn't going to happen. "In the two years that my brother and I have been here," explains one UBC student, "we have not bumped into each other once. And we both spend a lot of time here." Says another student, "If you don't like crowds, then don't come here. Sometimes you feel like you are walking around with a big computer number on your chest. Like a convict." Says still another student, "There's so much to do here, so much intellectual and physical stimulation that you never have to feel lost. But paradoxically this is also one of the most alienating environments around, particularly if you don't know anybody when you get here."

Alienation? In lotus-land? Everyone has heard about the legendary beauty of UBC, the snowy mountain peaks, crystal-blue lakes, overgrown emerald foliage. But turn your back to the mountains and face the part of the campus that man made, and you see a concrete-mixer's vision of paradise. At UBC, the orthodox faith of Canada's university planners — that a student in a concrete box is a happy student — prevails.

However, most students are not at UBC to be happy. They're at UBC to get a job. "That place is a real grunt school," says one ex-librarian disapprovingly. "Students there have very narrow ideas about education." The students themselves substantiate this opinion. "It's very competitive here," says the student president. "Take commerce, one of the most popular programs. Every year there are 1,700 applications for 425 spots. Then, even if you are one of the 425, you still have to be at the top of your class to get your third-year specialty option. You're simply forced to be at the books. There's no second chance. No choice of jobs."

A journalist on the student newspaper agrees. "There's no incentive to take anything other than pre-professional courses because no one has the desire to build up an enormous debt fooling around with the humanities. The financial climate discourages people from learning. They just want to get their degrees and get out." Programs currently popular are commerce (especially Pacific Rim studies), forestry, engineering, computer systems, and biotechnology.

Not everybody at UBC is a pre-professional zombie. While the faculty wait for the NDP to return to power and solve all UBC's problems by writing an enormous cheque, and while the administration denies that anything much is wrong at all, the leaders of the UBC student body have quietly assumed the responsibility that their elders shirk. UBC students annually contribute $15 each to a student building fund, now worth five million dollars. Over the past 30 years, student money has put up some of the university's best-used buildings: the Thunderbird Winter Sports Centre (1963), the Student Union Building (1969), and the Aquatic Centre (1978). The fund plans a daycare centre and recreational facilities. No other student body in Canada can boast such an active, responsible role in the physical development of their university. Bravo UBC!

Mercifully, there are some at UBC who believe youth can be fun. The engineers (called "geers" locally) rely on noisy, drunken bravado and feminist-baiting. "We basically rule the world," the geers say in the UBC student handbook. But that was before they found out that, in fact, feminists do (at least in that part of the world under the jurisdiction of UBC).

The geers' legendary midwinter parade, the Lady Godiva Ride, had traditionally been led by a semi-nude, long-haired woman on horseback. In 1987, campus feminists forced the university to ban the Ride. To protest, the engineers staged a mock funeral, parading a coffin with four horse's legs sticking out to lament the death of "Mr. Ed." Later, safely inside a UBC auditorium, "Lady Godiva" put on a strip show. Naturally, campus feminists disliked this event even more than the Ride.

Fraternities and sororities are second to the engineers in the fight against apathy and alienation at UBC. After paying the highest tuition in any Canadian province, many students willingly pay frat dues of as much as $500 annually. "Frat kids are the ones with money to throw around," says the student president. Many of them pursue expensive sports like skiing, sailing, and California-girl-chasing. (Los Angeles is about one day's drive away.)

Not everybody admires the contribution the frats and geers make to

UBC life. "In Vancouver," says the manager of UBC's radio station, CITR, "there's a big difference between youth culture and college culture. They are two totally different phenomena. Our alternative music is more popular off campus than on. UBC kids find the music we play weird. They just want to hear the Rolling Stones, the Beatles, and *Animal House* over and over again. The whole concept of *Animal House* is bigger now than ever before. Beer gardens, toga parties, drinking out of jugs instead of glasses, that's UBC today."

Those who don't like frats and geers can take comfort: they don't make much of a dent on the grey blahs of UBC life. When UBC defeated Western in the 1986 Vanier Cup match, Western went wild with disappointment. At UBC, however, "People thought it was nice that they won but no one really cared." Don't come to UBC if you like to play sports before a cheering throng. National championships, continental championships, world championships, galactic championships — none of it matters. There's accounting homework to do!

One graduate recalls the sobriety of the campus with amazement. "Nothing ever happened. I don't believe I went to a party the whole time I was there. I don't have a scrapbook full of pictures showing my friends squeezing toothpaste all over each other's heads. That stuff just doesn't happen at UBC."

UBC has one plausible excuse for its dullness. Like Simon Fraser, UBC is located far, far from downtown. It's also located far, far from the suburbs. "It's not so bad," says a tolerant student, "it only takes me forty-five minutes to get to school." Opinions differ whether the bumper-to-bumper rush hour — 7:45 to 9:15 a.m. and 3:30 to 5:30 p.m. — is more nightmarish inside your own car or inside a city bus packed with other commuters. All agree that, either way, it stinks.

Once you're on campus, you need hiking shoes and a compass. UBC occupies more than 1,000 acres. (By comparison, the more than ample Alberta campus sprawls over 154 acres.) With all that land, you'd think they'd have plentiful, cheap parking, but the UBC creed apparently holds that traumatic parking ordeals build character. Bring a bike. Or a horse. Or a helicopter.

Fortunately, thanks to Expo 86, spaces in residence are easily had. Unfortunately, they've been stuck on the fringes of the campus, making them almost as inconvenient as off-campus living. UBC has the largest number, though not proportion, of students living on campus. Commuters envy residential students their tight-knit friendship, although even residence students have a hard time developing a sense of belonging at amorphous UBC.

UBC's wide selection of clubs do a little to foster a sense of belonging. At least they'll keep you on campus long enough to miss the rush hour.

Club options range the whole gamut of extremist British Columbian viewpoints, from an Anarchist club ("Last year we held a Latin American film festival, showed anti-authoritarian Canadian films, discussed anarcho-feminism in Japan, the struggle of the Greenham Common women, and the Big Mountain matriarchy, and crocheted to Emma Goldman tunes. Join us and overthrow.") to an Accounting club ("One of the main objectives of the Accounting Club is to provide a link between students and professionals within the accounting field. We provide opportunities where everyone is welcome to meet and share drinks with CGAS, CAS and RIAS, visit CA firms and listen to career planning sessions. For people considering life after UBC, the club holds résumé and interview clinics.").

If you're going to UBC, you will need to plan ahead if you don't want to spend your life gloomily doing your homework. Persuade ten friends to come with you. Join a club or a frat. Live on campus if you can. And whatever bad things happen to you while at UBC, remember this— you've come as close to experiencing the University of Hawaii as you can in the Great White North.

"Club options range the whole gamut...from an Anarchist Club
to an Accounting Club..."

THE FACTS

Founded:	1915
Address:	2075 Westbrook Mall Vancouver, British Columbia V6T 1W5
Tuition:	$1,584
Cut-off grade for general admission (per cent):	60
Enrolment:	27,303
Undergraduate full-time enrolment:	18,210
Percentage of foreign students:	4
Percentage of students from outside the province:	19
Residence fees:	$2,744–3,204
Percentage of students in residence:	15
Male-female ratio:	53:47
Athletic facilities:	Excellent. Stadium (seats 3,200), Winter Sports Centre, Aquatic Centre.
Team name:	Thunderbirds
Colours:	Blue and gold
Fraternities/sororities:	Yes. An expensive pastime.
Typical garb:	Faded jeans, Hawaiian shirts, sun-glasses.
Campus political attitude:	Strong support for everything from anarcho-feminism to free trade.
Best-known fact:	David Suzuki teaches here.
Least-known fact:	Students get nowhere near David Suzuki.
If you had to put it in one sentence:	"Student life at UBC means eating a cinnamon bun in Buchanan Lounge."—*Graduate*
Alumni:	Pierre Berton, Allan Fotheringham,

Mrs. Norah Michener, Pat Carney,
John Turner, Roy MacLaren, Earle
Birney, Jack Austin (Senator), Peter
Worthington, Michael Harcourt.

DO'S AND DON'TS

DO try to do your jogging in Stanley Park as often as possible. There probably isn't a lovelier place to jog in any Canadian city.

DON'T let UBC's system of registration turn you off UBC forever. It's true that UBC is one of the only places left where registration is aggressively non-computerized, but what's one day out of your life? Some even say that running around campus looking for the right signature can be fun.

DO listen to CITR, labelled the "hottest" radio station in Canada by *Flair* magazine.

DON'T go to the UBC bookstore unless you're loaded with money. It's not that things are so expensive, but you'll be tempted to buy something from the best collection of college-labelled sportswear anywhere in Canada. Not only does the store sell great clothing, it also sells TV sets, Sony Walkmans, luggage, jewellery, and extensive art supplies. There are a lot of books, too.

I REMEMBER...

"The only regret I have in my life (I mean, the only one I will admit to) is that I was at university for only three years. I greatly envy those who were at university for five, seven, nine years. The only education I ever got (if any) was in wandering around Europe for three years later, but I really wish I had been able to spend a more leisurely time on campus — reading, chasing girls, and beating up on engineers."
— *Allan Fotheringham*

"My years at UBC were among the happiest of my life. The west coast was buoyant and our optimism was limitless. University life exploded with the return of our men and women from the armed forces. We worked hard, we played hard, we were confident of our future." — *John Turner*

"I went to UBC and Carleton. I got interested in sports, especially boxing, and began devoting all my time to that, and skipped school. I did well in Golden Gloves tournaments, but lousy in classrooms, and distinguished myself by writing a Philosophy 200 exam by accident instead of Philosophy 100 — and passing, which was used by the

professor to underline the flaws in the education system. I took
French 100 with John Turner, but he was more diligent than I. Also
worked for student newspaper, *Ubyssey*, doing sports, which got me
into journalism. Colleagues were Fotheringham, Joe Schlesinger,
Peter Sypnowich, Pat Carney. I went to university more or less
because I had no goals, and found UBC wonderful." —*Peter
Worthington*

BROCK

What do Brock students like about their university? Well, the student
president says, "It's great — it's so small." The editor of the student
newspaper says, "People like the place because it's small." A second-year
transfer student from York says, "I like it here; it's small." A third-year
student from Europe says, "The best thing about this school is that it is
very small." Brock's liaison officer says, "The best-selling feature of our
school is that it is small." A student in residence says, "What do I like
about Brock? It's small."

Brock University, as you may have gathered by now, is small (only
4,300 undergraduates). But there are other appealing features. For
example, the food is very good. So good, in fact, that Brock's chef, Dave
Gibson, is the subject of much favourable local press. "The food here is
delicious," says one student, tucking into a big helping of Beef Tostada.
"Yeah, for cafeteria food, this stuff is great," says another student, who is
enjoying the day's other special, Veal Scallopini.

Good size, good food, what else? Good location! To quote a Brock
promotional pamphlet: "Brock University in St. Catharines, Ontario,
sits in the heart of the scenic Niagara peninsula. Surrounded by vine-
yards and bordered by Lake Gibson, our campus is a part of the
beautiful Bruce Trail, one of Canada's best known nature and hiking
areas. Niagara Falls and historic Queenston Heights are a few miles
away; Hamilton and Toronto are within easy driving distance." The
campus itself, though modern, is pretty. It's woodsy and somewhat
futuristic-looking, like something from the set of the movie *Rollerball*.

And then there are the academics. There is nothing really wrong with Brock in this regard. It's just that there's nothing right either. Brock is still a new university, and universities of only 21 years rarely have terrific academic reputations. It is possible that, with time, given Brock's desirable location and vigorous administration, a favourable reputation will develop. "We still have to prove ourselves," says the student president. "Everybody here realizes that reputations don't come overnight. You have to earn them."

If anybody has earned a glowing reputation at Brock, it is the PR department. Is any high-school student in Ontario unfamiliar with the charming "Isaac Brock Wants You!" campaign? This famous slogan and the Uncle Sam-style poster are so colourful and winning that a Brock survey shows over half the 1986 entering class was influenced by it. (The campaign's creator has since been snatched by Western.) In fact, so many people have been impressed with the campaign that, since 1980, applications to Brock have risen 375 per cent.

A large proportion of that 375 per cent are drawn from outside traditional Brock territory, that is to say, the Niagara region. Sixty per cent of Brock students come from beyond the Golden Horseshoe. Brock is gaining popularity in places like the Ottawa Valley, Kitchener/Waterloo, Belleville, and appropriately, Brockville. It also appeals to students in Toronto's outlying boroughs: Scarborough, Etobicoke, Peel-Halton, North York. However, according to the liaison officer, "A certain snob factor prevents students in downtown Toronto from applying." For others, Brock offers a pleasant, residential college environment that's not too far from home.

Very few students choose Brock because of the programs offered, but the administration is working on developing some specialties. Brock is proud of the concurrent B.A./B.Ed. program in child studies; the school of administrative studies (the co-op accounting stream is the most popular — you'll need low eighties to be accepted); and perhaps the best-known of Brock's departments, physical education and leisure studies. Brock also considers its science department to be first-rate. "On a per faculty basis, the number of funding grants we've received for science is the highest in the country," says a member of Brock's liaison office. "For science, biology, chemistry, physics, math, you can't do any better than Brock."

Brock also offers a special degree in liberal studies. Although this program is not especially popular, it is probably one of the best. Students spend four years studying great books, "the major developments in mathematics and the great experiments and breakthroughs in science."

This program is similar to that at King's College in Halifax, except that this one is extended over four years. Year one starts with Aristophanes and year four ends with Kafka. A lot of good stuff gets read in between. In all departments, Brock uses the seminar system, in which students are divided into small groups, and are required to talk and make presentations, even if they don't want to.

Like everything else at Brock, the sense of community is improving. "Brock students have a good sense of balance," says the student president. "They are serious about their work but they also want to have fun." Although there are no frosh weeks or initiations, the student council does run orientation parties in September and "disorientation" parties in January. The German pub theme, complete with polka music, is a favourite. There are several clubs on campus which, in the words of one student, "are organizations created to obtain money for holding parties." The student council also tries to bring in bands during the school year. In 1984, they brought in Billy Idol, just months before he became a mega-star.

For a really rocking time, students generally favour Niagara Falls, New York, where bars stay open till 3:00 a.m. and the atmosphere is "hopping." The on-campus pub is pleasant and well liked, especially on Thursday nights when there are specials. But on weekends the place is dead: the kids who have come to Brock because it is close to home, go home.

Residences at Brock have not been able to keep up with demand. The DeCew Residence on campus is the most popular, but has room for only 418. There are other residences, but they are located in downtown St. Catharines. Queenston is an old nurses' residence and Leonard is an old motel. These dorms (with 315 rooms) offer the benefits of residence combined with independence. First-year students with an 80 per cent high-school average are guaranteed a space in residence. For the rest, it's the luck of the draw. If you don't get a room, expect waiting lists 400 people long.

Off-campus housing in St. Catharines is no problem, however. St. Paul's Street, downtown, is the best. It's not even expensive. There are some apartments here that have been passed down from student to student for 15 years. Be warned: bus service in St. Catharines closes at 11:00 p.m. Few people off campus spend much time on the campus at night-time. (The escarpment on which Brock is located is beautiful, but distant from the main drag.)

The number-one off-campus Brock bar is Gord's. "Gord's is very new wave," explains one regular patron. "It isn't a pick-up bar. It appeals to everybody, although sometimes the skinheads like to beat up the Brock students." Brock sponsors regular "Brock nights" at Gord's and these are the safest nights to come.

Brock's students believe in themselves. They know what the outside world thinks of their school and they don't care. "Look," says the editor of the newspaper, "what I like about this school is its small size. The fewer people who want to come here, the better." Says another student, "I didn't think I'd like it here at first. People just teased me and put down the school too much. But the people who put this place down haven't been here. It's a great place to go to school. And I am proud of it."

THE FACTS

Founded:	1964
Address:	Merrittville Highway St. Catharines, Ontario L2S 3A1
Tuition:	$1,330
Cut-off grade for general admission (per cent):	65
Average grade-13 mark of entering class (per cent):	69.3
Enrolment:	8,054
Undergraduate full-time enrolment:	4,375
Percentage of foreign students:	4.2
Percentage of students from outside the province:	4.2
Residence fees:	$2,892–3,193
Percentage of students in (on-campus) residence:	10
Male-female ratio:	48:52
Athletic facilities:	Excellent, housed in the Physical Education Centre.

Team name:	Badgers
Colours:	Red, white, and blue
Fraternities/sororities:	None.
Typical garb:	Low-fashion, casual.
Campus political attitude:	Deeply interested in Canadian politics circa 1812.
Best-known fact:	Brock has the best promotional posters in Canada ("Isaac Brock wants you!").
Least-known fact:	Brock's cafeteria food is delectable.
If you had to put it in one sentence:	"I like this school. It's small."—*Everyone*
Alumni:	Father Sean O'Sullivan.

DO'S AND DON'TS

DON'T be surprised if you always fall asleep in the library. The fans produce so much "white noise" that concentrating is almost impossible.

DO go to Alphie's Trough (the campus pub named for General Brock's horse, Alfred) for morning coffee and Tim Horton Donuts. A good way to start your Brock day.

DON'T be surprised if someone here calls you a "Brock-oli." It's a favourite derisive term.

UNIVERSITY OF CALGARY

The 1988 Winter Olympics: nothing this big has happened in Calgary since the price of oil fell below $25 a barrel — except this time, everyone's in a good mood. The xv Winter Olympiad hosted by the University of Calgary has invigorated Alberta's usually inert number-two school.

There's always been some bitterness in Calgary about being number two. When Alberta became a province in 1905, it was agreed that Edmonton would get the capital, and Calgary the university. But to Calgary's chagrin, piggy old Edmonton took them both. In 1966, the University of Calgary became at last an autonomous university, instead of the second and neglected campus of the University of Alberta. It has struggled ever since to catch up. "Yes, we're definitely getting better," says one student leader. "I just don't know if we're getting better fast enough."

That student's anxiety matches the observations of outsiders: the vice-president of the University of Manitoba, while conceding that the University of Calgary is one of the best of Canada's new universities, notes, "With the money they've got, they should be much better than they are."

Students may be bothered by Calgary's academic defects, but they are even more dejected by its listlessness. There's no spirit, pride, or camaraderie at U of C. According to the student council vice-president, no matter to which faculty U of C students belong, "They treat coming here like a job. This is a commuter school, and it's empty, I mean *empty*, by five o'clock. You can't get students here interested in anything besides their work. I don't care if you hit them with a two-by-four, they still won't react."

The editor of the student newspaper, *The Gauntlet*, agrees: "It's very hard for us to get a response to anything we write. Students here just don't care. Part of the problem is that the school is just too young to have developed any traditions. After all, we only had our first homecoming in 1986, celebrating the first 20 years." The vice-president concludes "There's no spirit here, you know? No leather jackets like you see at U of T and Waterloo."

The University of Calgary is a little smaller than the University of Alberta: 14,000 full-time undergraduates versus 22,000. Like most big Canadian schools, Calgary inspires little loyalty or love. You'd think the consecutive 1984 and 1985 Vanier Cup victories (the national undergraduate football trophy) of Calgary's Dinosaurs would rally Calgary students. But one of their fans complains that "the Dinosaurs get pathetic turn-outs for their games, even the Vanier Cup games."

The management department, installed in Scurfield Hall (a delightful new building — it looks like a greenhouse for people), is responsible for most of the good in U of C's reputation. For the eight years from 1978 to

1985, U of C has placed either first or second in "biz" schooldom's top event, the annual Queen's Intercollegiate Business Competition. In 1985, after winning at Queen's, the U of C team went on to take first place at the world competition in Atlanta.

Calgary also offers an unusual physical education program, in which students can major in distinctive specialties like adolescent studies, pre-adolescent studies, and dance education. There's even a degree in outdoor pursuits — which is exactly what it sounds like — under the direction of Rusty Baillie, one of the mountaineers in Canada's Mount Everest expedition.

Most students, however, begin their studies at U of C in the general studies department. General studies is composed of interdisciplinary courses. Some, like Greek and Roman civilization, you could find anywhere. Others, like communications studies; ethnicity and folklore; leisure, tourism, and society; and peace and war studies, are a little more flaky. Serious students stay in the department only long enough to meet the requirements to enter the grown-up faculties of education, management, social welfare, humanities, or natural and social sciences.

Perhaps one reason why students are so eager to flee the campus the moment classes are over is that the University of Calgary is so strikingly ugly. It ranks with the worst in the country: Laurentian, Regina, York. Nasty, white, concrete high-rises with slatted windows stick out at irregular but large distances in a huge expanse of suburban land. Trees are rare.

Crossing the campus in winter tests the mettle of even the toughest Canadian hide. "Premier Lougheed said it was cheaper to let students freeze a little than to build a tunnel system. That's easy for him to say. He doesn't have to walk around this place in the middle of winter," complains a frost-bitten member of the student council.

Because of the Olympics, an extension has been stuck onto the already large student centre. A new fine-arts facility has been tacked onto the top of a new multi-storey parking lot. The gym has been expanded, and there's a new skating rink, as well as an undergraduate residence. Calgary has also put up a pair of new buildings without any Olympic uses — the new management faculty and a new research lab for the medical school.

Because the university was built on the outskirts of town, anything a student might want to do, other than attend lectures, necessitates a bus ride. Students may rent apartments or small houses in the local Hillhurst-Sunnyside area, but the cafés and good bookstores are all downtown. Calgary students seem to avoid living in residence, because "the university is not the only show in town. People would rather live around a little more action." There are usually vacancies.

Calgarians love their city. "You think it's boring here," they say defensively to visitors, "but we have a lot of great bars." And, if a great bar is your idea of a good time, it is true that you won't be bored in Calgary. Banditos, Singapore Sam's, the Yonge Street Café ("Talk about an insecure city," one patron wryly observes), Manhattan's (and that goes double here), and the Blackfoot Inn are all favourite student joints. Any night-spot on 11th Avenue (known as Electric Avenue) is cool.

When the 1988 Olympics are over, will the slight jolt of life it's brought to the University of Calgary also expire? With any luck, the new resources of this comparatively wealthy school will be used efficiently so that its students can "proudly roar for the Dinosaurs" instead of being processed like cheese.

THE FACTS

Founded:	1966 as the University of Calgary. Was previously second campus of U of A, and before that was known as "Normal School."
Address:	2500 University Dr. NW Calgary, Alberta T2N 1N4
Tuition:	$857
Cut-off grade for general admission (per cent):	60
Enrolment:	20,557
Undergraduate full-time enrolment:	14,102
Percentage of foreign students:	4.5
Percentage of students from outside the province:	7.5
Residence fees:	$2,005–3,562
Percentage of students in residence:	8.5
Male-female ratio:	52:48
Athletic facilities:	Sumptuous.

Team name:	Dinosaurs
Colours:	Scarlet and gold
Fraternities/sororities:	Yes. Five male, three female. "You always know a sorority girl because she's so much better dressed."
Typical garb:	Scaled-down urban chic. One pierced ear for men. "It's like a fashion show on the first day of school, but people get casual after that."—*Student*
Campus political attitude:	"Even the NDP group on campus represents the conservative branch of the party."
Best-known fact:	University of Calgary biz students are a dazzling group who tend to win every competition they enter.
Least-known fact:	The city of Calgary has more college-educated citizens per capita than any other Canadian city.
If you had to put it in one sentence:	"Even during the height of the hippy era there were no demonstrations here. This has always been a very conservative, quiet place."—*Student*

DO'S AND DON'TS

DO go to Dinosaur football games. They are just about the best team in the country.

DON'T assume that because this is Alberta everyone is a hick. "Because of the oil industry, students here usually have lived and travelled all over the world. Calgary students are very sophisticated."

DO take the course offered by the former lieutenant-governor of Alberta: "Special Topics in Prairie History." You'll learn interesting stuff like how many pigs there were in Red River in 1810.

DON'T bother buying a cowboy hat. It really isn't the fashion here.

DO bring your skates. Calgary now has the only enclosed Olympic-sized speed-skating oval in Canada.

UNIVERSITY COLLEGE OF CAPE BRETON

There are 1,900 students at the University College of Cape Breton, and they're all here for the same reason: money. "I can live with my parents, save money, and postpone the expense of moving away by studying here," says a level-headed student. "And anyways, this place isn't so bad."

UCCB is Canada's newest university in one of Canada's oldest, most depressed regions. It was formed in 1982 when the College of Cape Breton was upgraded and granted university status by the Nova Scotia government—bringing the total number of universities in the province to seven. Previously, students would study at Cape Breton college for two years, and then make the expensive move to a degree-granting institution on the mainland, usually to St. FX or Dalhousie.

Today UCCB awards its own Bachelor of Arts degree, Bachelor of Business Administration, and a diploma in engineering. However, students wishing to earn an engineering or science *degree* must still transfer elsewhere after their first or second year. Holders of engineering diplomas can transfer automatically to TUNS—Technical University of Nova Scotia—for their final three years of study. Science students seem to prefer Dalhousie. UCCB will probably be granting its own science degrees within a few years.

The administration of UCCB has imposed strenuous requirements on its students. Courses in spoken and written English, math, the humanities, and the social and natural sciences are all compulsory. All students must pass a literacy test. At the moment, students choose among only seven majors: English, history, philosophy, theology, political science, sociology, and psychology, but there is hope that foreign languages and economics will be added in the near future.

While the curriculum is structured, entrance requirements, in keeping with UCCB's mission of higher education for all, are minimal. Grade 12 is all it takes.

There are no residences at UCCB. Students take the bus, or their parents drop them off. By the end of the day, no one wants to hang around campus for social events. The student council throws parties occasionally. They're well attended at the beginning of the year, but "after a while, people realize that partying on campus is not all that convenient," according to a student who lives 10 miles off campus.

Students would rather date, or go to the local taverns. Favourite drinking spots: the Old City Pub, Daniel's, or Smooth Norman's. "But," says a student, "you really couldn't say that this is a party school." UCCB may remind many first-year students of the high school they have just left. The university is housed in one 360,000-square-foot structure with lots of glass corridors and brightly painted rooms. Despite the cheerful motifs, students say that depression sometimes hangs over UCCB. "You should see winter here," says a student, shaking his head sadly.

Although most students look forward to the day they leave Cape Breton, they show real gratitude towards UCCB. Without it, many would be unable to afford a university degree. Because of it, they can look towards the future with some optimism. Perhaps that is why this school, which has almost no extracurricular life, cheers so hard for its athletic team, the Capers, and their mascot, Chiever the Caper Beaver. "This is going to be a good school someday," says a student munching on a sandwich brought from home. "All it needs is time."

THE FACTS

Founded:	1982
Address:	P.O. Box 5300, Sydney, Nova Scotia B1P 6L2
Tuition:	$1,524
Cut-off grade for admission to B.A. program (per cent):	50
Enrolment:	1,900
Undergraduate full-time enrolment:	1,900
Male-female ratio:	48:52
Athletic facilities:	Good. Sydney was the site of the 1987 Canadian Winter Games.
Team name:	Capers
Colours:	Green, orange, and white
Most popular major:	Psychology
Fraternities/sororities:	None.
Typical garb:	Jeans, Capers team shirts.
Campus political attitude:	Here they say Saint Alan with a straight face.

| Best-known fact: | UCCB is located in one of the most stunning but depressed regions of Canada. |
| If you had to put it in one sentence: | "None of us would be here if we could afford to be somewhere else." —*Second-year science student* |

Best-known fact: UCCB is located in one of the most stunning but depressed regions of Canada.

Least-known fact: UCCB has its own university press and has recently published *Songs and Stories from Deep Cove, Still Standing,* and *Gigglesnatch.*

If you had to put it in one sentence: "None of us would be here if we could afford to be somewhere else." —*Second-year science student*

DO'S AND DON'TS

DO mutter the school motto, "Perseverance Will Triumph," to yourself as you try to get through the bleak winter months.

DON'T neglect the university's art gallery. Local artists, craftsmen, and students display their talents here.

DO keep in touch with your friends who are going to university off the island. You'll probably want to visit them...a lot.

CARLETON

The polite describe Carleton University as Canada's great experiment in universally accessible education. The rude call it "Last Chance U." According to its vice-president, Carleton perceives its mission as enabling "the fellow who scraped his way through high school to develop his potential. We believe that any student who graduates from grade 13 or its equivalent should have access to a university education."

There's a catch, of course — in fact, more than one. The students at Carleton grumble that "the classes get really big, and you don't ever get much attention." Worse, at least for the student who wants to cap his career of scraping through high school with four years of scraping through university, at Carleton students genuinely worry about flunking out.

"Sure, it affects your morale, knowing they are trying to cut out twenty per cent of the entering class," confesses a survivor. "You feel they're lying in wait for you, hoping you'll trip up." In popular departments, the students who are still registered congratulate themselves like veterans of the Somme. In engineering, for example, "by third year, a quarter to a third of the class will be gone. Courses are designed solely to weed us out." A disheartened political scientist rather sadly believes that "the words 'fun' and 'university' don't go together."

Don't assume, though, from its admissions policy and the startling failure rate, that Carleton is some kind of refuge for the stupid. The average grade for entering students in arts and science is 72 per cent. The engineering and architecture faculties won't accept applicants unless they score at least 80 per cent in grade 13, and journalism cuts off in the high 70s.

Carleton was the first university in Canada to offer a degree in journalism, and it remains the best-known school of journalism in Canada. "Whenever I meet a student from Vancouver I always say 'You must be in journalism,' and I'm usually right," says Carleton's vice-president. "Our program has a very high national profile."

"There's no typical Carleton student," says a representative on the student council. "We have lots of international students, students from all across Canada, diplomats' kids. Some kids got accepted by the skin of their teeth and others are brilliant." A recent graduate agrees. "There's a real freedom from peer pressure at Carleton. There's no dress code, no distinct social groups — it's a real mix."

One common denominator, however, is that students speak the same language. Says one refugee from the University of Ottawa and its bilingualism, "The best thing I can say about Carleton is that everyone speaks English here."

Feeling that unilingualism is the best thing about Carleton does not prove that you're a bigot, but perhaps only that you've recently come from one of Carleton's densely packed classes. Ontario's other universities have grown by 15 per cent over the past five years — Carleton, by 30 per cent. Consequently, classes are huge, and there can be as many as 75 undergraduates for every teaching assistant. The student-professor ratio is even worse.

To make room, additional floors are being laid atop the computer science, architecture, and physics buildings. The library is doubling in size — at present it's so small that it can hardly hold the university's modest collection of books, and has no room at all for students to study. New fine arts, theatre, and social science buildings are planned. If this new construction resembles what's already built, the additional space will make life a little more comfortable at Carleton but will add another nasty blot to the already disfigured south Ottawa landscape. A visitor to the horrific Carleton campus will be amused to discover that the university purports to have an "architectural policy." No, it isn't to be the world's largest consumer of Formica. "Our policy," explains the vice-president, "is to have buildings styled according to the most up-to-date architectural trends. We want whatever is newest, that's always been our policy, and that's why no two buildings on campus look alike."

You'll have plenty of time to admire the results of that policy as you make the long hike from the parking lots to class. Over 90 per cent of Carleton's students live off campus, and since Carleton is plopped on the empty plain near the airport, students must drive or take the bus.

As consequences of commuting go, frozen toes from the death march across the parking lots are painless compared to loneliness. Last year, the student council created a new "off-campus students' centre" in a brave effort to welcome commuters. The individual, however, must still present herself to the office staffers and ask for help, saying something like, "Hi, I'm Wanda. I'm looking for friends." An alumna does caution that social life at Carleton could be worse — "it's not Queen's, but let's keep this in perspective; it's not the University of Toronto, either."

As for romance... well, two attractive young women reacted to the topic with, "Would we be sitting here if this were a romantic campus?!"

Once a year, however, Carleton goes nuts — on the day of the Panda Trophy football game against the University of Ottawa. The Carleton student handbook gives the following instructions to Panda partiers:

1. Buy wineskins early. Ottawa stores run out weeks before the game.
2. Get coveralls and paint anti-Ottawa slogans on them.
3. Start Panda week at Oliver's [the campus pub] on Wednesday. Continue with pubs and concerts Thursday and Friday nights.
4. Pace yourself Friday night.
5. Pre-Panda breakfast party 8 a.m. Saturday. Loud music and drinking begins.
6. Paint face black, red, and white like Panda Bear.
7. 12 noon join Panda Parade.
8. Arrive Lansdowne Stadium.
9. Beware of waterbombs from Ottawa U side.
10. Victory parties back on campus.

By 10:00 a.m. on Panda morning, Carleton's residences are utterly blotto on a panda punch served from garbage cans. Yum! Oh, if you go to the game, be prepared to sidestep a lot of vomit.

On the other 364 days of the year, however, Carleton mimics the capital: dull and prosaic. On the other hand, the university's location in Ottawa has allowed it to develop specialties in the disciplines related to government: politics, public administration, Canadian studies, and journalism. "One thing about Carleton," says an otherwise loyal alumna, "it doesn't have a great abundance of creative people. Wildly artsy types should go someplace else."

THE FACTS

Founded:	1942
Address:	Ottawa, Ontario K1S 5B6
Tuition:	$1,263
Cut-off grade for general admission (per cent):	60
Average grade 13 mark of entering class (per cent):	68.8
Enrolment:	15,780
Undergraduate full-time enrolment:	9,455
Percentage of foreign students:	7
Percentage of students from outside the province:	11
Residence fees:	$2,780–3,165
Percentage of students in residence:	14
Male-female ratio:	56:44
Athletic facilities:	So-so. 50-metre pool, gymnasium (seats 1,100).
Team name:	(M) Ravens, (F) Robins
Colours:	Scarlet, white, and black
Coolest major:	Architecture

Fraternities/sororities:	None.
Typical garb:	Video arcade fashions.
Campus political attitude:	"Given that we're located in Ottawa you'd think there'd be one, but there isn't. This is a very apolitical place." — *Student*
Best-known fact:	Carleton has a great school of journalism.
Least-known fact:	Lester Pearson was chancellor. David Lewis was a founder.
If you had to put it in one sentence:	"At Carleton, it's not difficult adapting to the norm: there is no norm. This is a low-pressure environment."—*Student*
Alumni:	Conrad Black, Linda MacLennan.

DO'S AND DON'TS

DO participate in "Meet Your Ten" — a program created by two Carleton students to match up lonely hearts. After filling out a questionnaire, students receive a list of 10 Carleton students who are deemed compatible. "It gives people a chance to talk to each other," says the organizer.

DON'T believe everything you read.* Twenty-five Carleton students missed an exam last year when a practical joker put up a notice informing them that their sociology exam was cancelled. As a general rule, exams are *never* cancelled. (*Except in this book.)

DO recover from the Panda game in time to attend the "Baldachin" game against Queen's. It's a little less rowdy, but not by much.

DON'T wait two months before you say hello to the person sitting next to you in class. The best way to study at Carleton is in study groups that you have to organize yourself. Ask the people who sit near you if they want to join.

I REMEMBER...

"I enjoyed my days at university just as thoroughly as I disliked my years of school, which may explain why I went on from Carleton to Laval and from Laval to McGill, and retained a university connection long after the launching of what has since proved to be my career.

Naomi Griffiths and John Strong are the professors whom I remember most fondly from Carleton, although the most agreeable memories of all from those times are probably of my prolonged dalliances in the taverns of Hull, Wakefield, and, when I was in Quebec City, the Rue Saint-Jean." — *Conrad Black*

CONCORDIA

Students considering Concordia University will be relieved to learn that the student council has voted to make Concordia a military-free zone. Army fatigues and water pistols should be left at home.

Concordia made its big splash in February 1969 when a group of radical students, boasting that they would "bring the university to its knees," occupied the university's computer centre, set fire to it, and threw computing materials out the window. Four million dollars' worth of damage was done. The group charged the administration with racism when a black student received a bad grade on an essay.

Although they have refrained from arson and defenestration lately, Concordia students continue to distinguish themselves by their activism and awareness. In a typical fall week, a Concordia student can choose to attend an array of political events ranging from the sober to the goofy. Some examples: guest lectures on the USSR under Gorbachev and the Ukraine after Chernobyl, demonstrations by campus clubs concerned about Soviet Jewry and human rights in El Salvador, an audio-visual presentation by an "anti-sexist" men's group, and a travelling Third World crafts show. Concordia is one of the very few Canadian universities where a passionate advocate of animal rights would feel at home.

There's a lot to do at Concordia, but students are despondently conscious of the university's one big problem. Concordia has little, if any, prestige. Many students freely admit that "I came here because I didn't get into McGill." One student claimed that "my best friend was offered a $1,000 scholarship at Concordia, but chose to go to McGill without a scholarship instead." Another student laments, "You just never stop feeling like a second-class citizen. You never stop feeling like you'd rather be at McGill."

This feeling of inferiority was not helped much when some snooty McGill students circulated buttons reading, "If you can't go to university, you might as well go to Concordia."

The lack of prestige is not undeserved. Says one disgruntled student who transferred to McGill after two years at Concordia, "The library is a joke, most teachers are terrible — they don't give two hoots about their students. Anybody can get accepted, and hardly anyone actually speaks English — it sometimes seems like Bulgarian is the university's official language." (Concordia is an essentially English-speaking university, although a unilingual francophone would get along fine.)

"Ever heard of a university where you have to line up to study? Well, our library is so small, the moment one free chair becomes available, it's like musical chairs when the music stops." However, while the library may be short on books and staff, it does feature a full-scale model of Michelangelo's *David*.

Concordia is not, however, a total academic disaster. Its fine-arts and communications departments are among the very best in the country. And the Concordia commerce department is considered to be better than McGill's. Says one commerce student, "I chose Concordia even though I got into McGill's program. My friends who are doing commerce at McGill are only there for the name. They admit that I'm probably getting the better education."

One of the most annoying things about Concordia is that it is spread over two campuses that aren't remotely close to each other. When Sir George Williams University merged with Loyola College to form Concordia University in 1974, the new school kept both campuses. The Sir George Williams campus is downtown, scattered around the Guy metro station. The Loyola campus, a former Jesuit school allegedly designed to look like an Oxford college, is located in Notre Dame de Grâce, a Montreal suburb 15 minutes away from downtown by car.

To transport students between the two campuses, Concordia runs a shuttle-bus service. For some reason, it's nearly impossible to have all your classes at either one campus or the other. Almost all students must take the shuttle bus at least once a day. "It's ridiculous," says one student, "a bunch of adults being stuffed into orange school buses. It's just embarrassing." Still, on the shuttle bus you will see what is inspiring about Concordia: students of every age, wearing all varieties of dress, speaking dozens of languages. Many students at Concordia are mature students, many attend on a part-time basis, and many are new immigrants unfamiliar with either of Canada's official languages.

Concordia has never tried to be McGill. It was founded for a different purpose: to serve members of the Montreal community who don't fit into, or could not get into, other institutions.

Most Concordia students live at home with their parents. "There are a lot of ethnic kids here," explains one student, "and they're expected to live at home until they're married, especially the girls." For students who do live on their own, there is no distinct Concordia ghetto, although Lincoln, Matthew, and St. Mark streets are popular. Otherwise, there's nothing wrong with a place in the McGill ghetto.

To hang out, the Peel Pub on St. Catherine street is the first choice of Concordia students. The bars on Crescent Street are popular, too —each Concordia student will have his own favourite among Montreal's plethora of wonderful joints. On campus, there's Reggie's Pub (named in honour of a former Concordia janitor), and the fourth-floor cafeteria dubbed "the zoo," because "you have so many different people from every possible ethnic group yapping away in a million different languages." Occasionally the Concordia student union sponsors parties, but, says one student, "they're rougher than most college parties. At McGill parties you may get some beer on the floor. At Concordia, you get beer all over your face and clothes. People get really knocked out."

While Concordia may not be the place to rub shoulders with Montreal's young élite, it is a place that attracts many off-beat, unconventional characters. Because of the fine arts department, there are a lot of weird-looking artsies (some of whom may even have some talent). And the wild-eyed, anti-militaristic politicos are also worth hearing out. Concordia may not be posh, but it isn't boring either.

THE FACTS

Founded:	1974, when Sir George Williams (1873) and Loyola (1898) were merged.
Address:	Sir George Williams Campus 1455 Maisoneuve Boulevard West Montreal, Quebec H3G 1M8
Tuition:	$450
Cut-off grade for general admission (per cent):	60
Enrolment:	26,136

Undergraduate full-time
enrolment: 11,599

Percentage of foreign
students: 3

Percentage of students from
outside the province: 3

Residence fees: $1,264–1,470

Percentage of students in
residence: 2

Male-female ratio: 51:49

Athletic facilities: Located at Loyola Campus,
                                  excellent. Stadium (seats 5,000),
                                  arena (1,500).

Team name: Stingers

Colours: Maroon, gold, and white

Most popular major: Accounting (15 per cent of students
                                  are enrolled in this program).

Fraternities/sororities: Yes.

Typical garb: *Très* urban.

Campus political attitude: Off-the-map left.

Best-known fact: Sir George Williams was home to
                                  Canada's most turbulent student
                                  demonstrations in the 1960s.

Least-known fact: Concordia's Simone de Beauvoir
                                  Institute helps keep Concordia at the
                                  forefront of feminist and lesbian
                                  thought.

If you had to put it in one   "This is a good university. Sure, it's
sentence: got its faults, but hell, nothing's
                                  perfect." — *Third-year business
                                  student*

Alumni of Concordia,   Brian Gallery (mayor of Westmount),
Loyola, Sir George: Don Ferguson (*Royal Canadian Air
                                  Farce*), Michael Warren (former
                                  Canada Post boss), Victor
                                  Pappalardo (founder and president of
                                  City Express Airlines), Hana Gartner
                                  (CBC television), Mordecai Richler.

DO'S AND DON'TS

DO make sure you get a copy of Concordia's student handbook; it is one of the best student-produced handbooks in the country.

DON'T believe a word anyone says about a new Concordia library in the making. A "new" library has been in the planning for 20 years now and little progress has been made.

DO check out some of the more off-beat clubs: the Atheists and Agnostics Club, the Computer User's Group, the Fantasy and Gaming Simulations Association, the Helsinki Monitors, and the Sparklers Club (for people over 55 years of age).

DON'T be afraid to flaunt your sexual orientation, whatever it may be. At Concordia, anything goes.

DALHOUSIE

At Dalhousie you are on your own. This is a school for grown-ups. You will never be forced to play moronic ice-breaking games. Intrusive "get-to-know-each-other" orientation sessions are strictly optional, and are confined to the summers when everybody's gone. *Never*, even if you want them to, will your classmates paint you purple and throw you into a pool of green Jell-O. There is no football at Dalhousie. There are pep rallies, but nobody goes.

The student council and the orientation committee keep trying and failing to turn Dal into Queen's or Western. They have even created an "off-campus frosh squad," which sends out militantly cheerful frat-types in "frosh squad" tee-shirts to spot the youngest faces in the milling mob, and ask them whether they're happy. Such efforts provoke contempt from Dal's sophisticated loners, who enjoy cracking cynical *aperçus* like, "This isn't a community, it's a big, grey mass." That's only true if you're comparing Dal to clubby Acadia or St. FX: compared to the Ministries of Concrete known as UBC or the University of Alberta, it's one big happy family.

It is also the finest academic institution in the Maritimes, and the best place to study outside central Canada. It lacks the money of Alberta, the facilities of UBC, and the Dionysian exuberance of Acadia. But it has charm, perfectly adequate facilities, interesting people, a great town, a good library, and a sense of history. Dal's law school was the first in the country to teach common law, and Dal has the oldest dental school in the country.

The average age of students at Dal is 26. That's because 40 per cent of Dalhousie's 10,000 students are graduate students. Their tedious work dampens the gaiety of life on campus; on the other hand, Dal women don't have to settle for men who like pulling jock-straps over their heads and belching.

Dalhousie's campus is unnervingly attractive. Introductory courses are taught in the stately neo-Georgian arts and administration building (the A&A, as it is called by students). Next door is Dal's grandest edifice: the ivy-covered Faculty Club. Handing the best building on campus over to the professors for a lunch-room quietly indicates who counts most at this university. Students, however, can always try to scrounge an invitation, or failing that, a part-time job as a busboy.

The student union building, though not so nice-looking as the vice-presidents' and professors' buildings, provides undergraduate clubs and the student government with ample office space, as well as a theatre, a pub, student lounges, a huge selection of junk-food machines, and even a decent cafeteria. Dal's impressive bookstore is here, too.

Politics do not flourish at Dalhousie, but the athletic and social clubs and the student media do. "Although they are not as vigorous as some clubs at other schools," says a Dal graduate, "they are more casual and approachable. People recognize that clubs are one of the few ways students can meet each other." *The Gazette*, whose popularity rises and falls depending on its radicalism (the less the better), is Canada's oldest university paper, and Dal's radio station is the centre for Dal's sophisticates.

However delightful the exteriors of the classrooms, the interiors don't always satisfy students. "I found that with all that boasting about the academics at Dalhousie, the reality was somewhat lacking. Their liberal arts program leaves a lot to be desired." Of course, the problem is money. Nova Scotia has more universities in proportion to population than any other Canadian province; consequently, every school is squeezed for funds. Even though Dalhousie was the recipient of the largest single bequest in Canadian history (30 million dollars from the widow of stockbroker, Izaak Walton Killam, in 1965), it still doesn't have the money to keep up with Toronto, Western, and the University of Alberta.

Dalhousie has therefore chosen to specialize. The liberal arts may be disappointing, but the pre-med sciences are better than average, and marine biology, meteorology, and oceanography appeal to the budding scientist with out-of-the-way tastes. A new life-sciences centre treats biologists to the latest equipment — though even fourth-year students have vanished in its mazelike interior after taking one wrong step.

Dalhousie considers its political-science department, defined in the Dalhousie calendar as the study of "Who gets What, When, How," one of its best; it's also proud of its theatre department, where students may study stagecraft, acting, and costume design. Shelley Peterson, wife of the premier of Ontario, studied here. Artsy students should be warned, however, that there is no art history department, and only one film and one architecture course. Dal tries to make it up to its artsies with its ambitious Russian studies program, which sends 42 students to Moscow or Leningrad for four months each year.

All students must satisfy a writing requirement, and B.Sc. students must take one mathematics class. In 1985, only four first-year arts and science courses had more than 100 students.

Dal has set the hearts of every other Maritime school aflutter with envy with its new "Dalplex," an extraordinary athletic facility. The football team was economized out of existence some years ago, so hockey, by tradition and default, is the number-one sport here.

For small-town kids, the chance to live in Halifax makes up for any of Dal's faults. "Dalhousie is a lot more exciting than Glace Bay," says one satisfied Cape Bretoner. For natives of Halifax whose high-school friends will follow them to university, Dal may also be a good choice. "But," says a Torontonian, "trying to parachute in is not always easy. You get sick of hearing Upper Canada this and Upper Canada that."

Dalhousie has only two undergraduate residences on campus: Shirreff Hall for women and Howe Hall for men. They have room for only 969 students. (There are 1,000 other university-owned rooms available, but they are located some distance off campus.) Rooms in residence are coveted, partly because of amenities like the charming old dining rooms, antique common-rooms, and spacious bedrooms of Shirreff Hall, and partly because finding a place to live in Halifax is the closest thing Dal has to an entrance exam.

Every student in Halifax can instantly cite the city's current vacancy rate: 1 per cent. Horror stories abound about how nine or ten students share a two-bedroom apartment, or of students forced to drop out of school because they couldn't find a place to live. Dalhousie has a helpful housing office, but can only do so much. To the regret of many students, Dal is only in the placement, not the construction, business.

The housing crisis is the most obvious explanation of Dal's mopey school spirit. Another may be that students prefer to spend their time in town —Halifax allegedly has more bars per capita than any other city in Canada. No one bar ever stays popular for very long. Currently among the favourites are Cabbagetown, the Misty Moon, Lawrence of Oreganos, the Palace, Rosa's, and the Jury Room.

Before you decide to come to Dal, you should figure out how you feel about Halifax. Some find Halifax too provincial. Some believe that Dalhousie is more hospitable to Haligonians than to outsiders. Others will love Halifax's antique charm and its small-city warmth. The ideal Dalhousie student values his independence, doesn't mind sharing a bedroom, plans to study science, hates wearing name tags, and can stand to wait a month or two for the latest movies to come to the local theatre.

"They have pep rallies but nobody goes."

THE FACTS

Founded:	1818
Address:	Halifax, Nova Scotia B3H 3J5
Tuition:	$1,525
Cut-off grade for general admission (per cent):	60
Enrolment:	10,530

Undergraduate full-time enrolment:	6,133
Percentage of foreign students:	6
Percentage of students from outside the province:	33
Residence fees:	$3,240–3,535
Percentage of students in residence:	9
Male-female ratio:	52:48
Athletic facilities:	Excellent. Arena (seats 1,600), outdoor/indoor track.
Team name:	Tigers
Colours:	Black and gold
Fraternities/sororities:	Yes. Low profile.
Typical garb:	Lopi sweaters, pin-striped shirts, jeans, team jacket, Grebs.
Campus political attitude:	Very little acceptance of deviation (i.e., homosexuality or weird clothing). Conservative.
Best-known fact:	Dal has great grad schools.
Least-known fact:	Dal has its own nuclear reactor.
If you had to put it in one sentence:	"What you've got a Dalhousie is a very passive crowd."
Alumni:	Joe Ghiz (premier of PEI), Robert MacNeil, Lily Munro (Minister of Culture, Ontario), Gerald Regan, Robert Stanfield.

KING'S COLLEGE

King's College is to Dalhousie University what Quebec is to Canada: theoretically a part of the whole, but in fact separate, aloof, and happily convinced of its own superiority. Demurely sipping sherry in a leather wing chair in the succulent opulence of the wood-panelled, Persian-carpeted faculty lounge, the registrar of King's College happily concedes that, "Yes, this place has always had its Oxford and Cambridge pretensions."

We come here to a stark question of taste. Some are going to find those pretensions wonderful, exactly what they came to college for. For others — well, "precious" is the word that may spring to mind. On Wednesday nights, students and faculty wear their black robes to dinner in King's very plausible imitation of an Oxbridge hall, where the faculty sits at a high table and sclerotic old men glower from behind thick coats of varnish. The mostly native Canadian faculty all seem to speak with plummy English — and I don't mean Liverpool or Lancashire — accents. (Granted, over half of them have graduate degrees from either Oxford or Cambridge.) Students are not taught by professors but by "dons," "tutors," or "fellows." Residence rules are strict, and night-watchmen carefully scrutinize the comings and goings of King's female population. (Men are spared such "security.") And there are regular High Anglican chapel services.

Commendably, King's does not content itself with imitating Oxonian frills; it has also adopted a new and intensely serious attitude towards undergraduate education. The new seriousness was at first a product of desperation. Founded in 1789, King's is the second-oldest college in Canada, but somehow it never quite got off the ground. In 1923, it affiliated itself with upstart Dalhousie, but continued to flounder. In 1973, it finally hit on a justification for its existence — a freshman "great books" program. Not an original idea, perhaps (it was originated by the University of Chicago in the 1930s, and was subsequently adopted by, among others, Columbia), but a good one that has worked.

Every student in the program (the program itself is optional) must read 73 assigned texts during his first year, and *The Catcher in the Rye* isn't on the list. The Bible, Homer, Dante, Aquinas, Erasmus, Machiavelli, Thomas More, Hobbes, Hume, Adam Smith, Tocqueville, George Eliot, Marx, Nietzsche, Freud, Joyce, and Sartre are.

Classes meet in small seminars, and students are expected to discuss the texts thoughtfully. "There's no faking it if you haven't read the text," claims one tutor. Students must write exams often, and no fewer than six papers are expected each term.

In my opinion, King's offers the most exciting, most demanding, and most valuable first-year program in Canada. There is, however, a price to be paid — and it's not just listening to your tutor pretending to be Sebastian Flyte.

King's is strictly a one-year school. After you complete your great-books course, you then spend the next three years at Dalhousie, taking Dalhousie courses and earning a Dalhousie degree. From second year on, King's is just a dormitory for most of its students. (And for students who opt not to take the foundation-year great-books course, it's really never anything more than a dormitory.)

King's itself offers only one degree, in journalism. This may be taken either as a one-year graduate course, or as a four-year honours under-graduate course. The four-year course begins with the foundation year; then "J" students take a year of arts at Dalhousie before taking two years of practical journalistic training. "There's no emphasis on the theoreti-cal, no communications theory," says the director of the journalism faculty. "We teach how to write better, how to produce TV and radio shows." Admission to the journalism program is fiercely competitive.

Admission to King's for non-journalists remains easy. Some students are accepted with "C" averages from high school.

King's is a small college of only 540, and it can assure almost all its first-year students a room in residence. Even after the first year, the sense of belonging to King's is powerful. Freshmen, upperclassmen, dons, and tutors mingle in the dining hall. A surprised student says "It's not unusual to take your meals with members of the faculty." The King's pub is similarly one of the most bustling meeting places on the otherwise bleak Dalhousie campus.

One other attraction at King's, besides the intimacy and the founda-tion year, is its strong Anglican religiosity. According to a don, "You find more than your average measure of piety here."

Within the bland confines of Dalhousie, King's has created an élite club for overachievers, jocks, Anglicans, and Anglophiles. "There's a real rugger-hearty atmosphere here," brags a professor, with the charac-teristic King's penchant for English private-, sorry, public-school slang. A student sums King's up neatly: "King's people never join frats. It's just not necessary."

THE FACTS

Founded:	1789
Address:	Halifax, Nova Scotia B3H 2A1
Tuition:	$1,530–1,572

Cut-off grade for general admission (per cent):	60
Enrolment:	543
Undergraduate full-time enrolment:	531
Percentage of foreign students:	2
Percentage of students from outside the province:	22
Residence fees:	$3,240–3,535
Percentage of students in residence:	50
Male-female ratio:	47:53
Athletic facilities:	King's has its own small gym, but serious athletes use Dalplex.
Fraternities/sororities:	Students may join Dal frats, but few do.
Typical garb:	*Brideshead Revisited*-style clothing is preferred.
Campus political attitude:	Queen Anne Tories.
Best-known fact:	In 1989, King's will be the second Canadian university to celebrate a bicentennial.
Least-known fact:	King's has the largest collection of *incunabula* (really old books) in Canada.
If you had to put it in one sentence:	At King's, Anglophilia reigns supreme.
Alumni:	Charles G.D. Roberts, Rowland C. Frazee, Roland Ritchie.

DALHOUSIE AND KING'S DO'S AND DON'TS

DO make frequent visits to the Dalhousie Arts Centre, which regularly has outstanding exhibits, plays, and concerts. "A real godsend" is how one student describes the place.

DON'T miss the campus's favourite party, the Domus (Law Frat) pub nights.

DO sit around in the nearby, gorgeous, Halifax Public Garden when school life is getting you down. It can't help but cheer you up.

DON'T let your daddies scare you out of coming to Halifax because it's a port town, girls. Unless you go out of your way to find them, sailors are not going to be a big feature of your life.

DO try to do as much of your studying as possible on the top floor of King's library. It's an utterly charming place to work.

DON'T expect to get a room in residence if you are from the Halifax area. Sorry.

I REMEMBER...

"I dropped out of Dalhousie after two years, thinking I was God's gift to the stage. I wasn't. I resumed at Carleton and, working full time at radio stations and the CBC, it took me three more years part-time to get a degree. I never felt comfortable in college; always impatient for life to begin. The best thing I got from both institutions was about 10 English courses — a treasure for the rest of my life. I guess the most exciting moment in college was after a performance of *Romeo and Juliet* at Dalhousie (I played Mercutio and the Apothecary) — a CBC previewer came backstage and asked me to do some acting on the radio. I did a lot and it led to a lot of other broadcasting jobs. I do not look back on school or college as golden years or my happiest days. I couldn't wait to get it all over with." — *Robert MacNeil (The Mac-Neil/Lehrer Report)*

"In my days you were supposed to have Latin to qualify for Dalhousie Law School. It was not one of my strengths, but somehow I got admitted on the undertaking that I would pass it by the end of first year. When I didn't, Dean Vincent MacDonald, who had a way with words, called me in and said, "Mr. Regan, you are an albatross around my neck." I finally got the Latin, primarily by memorizing Cicero's oration against Cataline which I can recite to this day." — *Gerald Regan*

"King's College provided the ideal transitional environment, in moving as I did from over four years of military, back to civilian life. At King's, we veterans, although certainly an oddity, were given every opportunity to learn, to play, and to prepare ourselves for a useful life in our great country." — *Rowland C. Frazee*

UNIVERSITY OF GUELPH

If you still think of Guelph as Cow College, you're out of touch with current trends. At the campus radio station, a male staffer with a doubly pierced ear, a short blond pony-tail, three days of stubble, a mass of silver bracelets, and a black beret pulled over his ears, says he feels perfectly at home at Guelph. "I don't get it," he says in a puzzled tone as Spanish folk-songs play in the background. "Why would you think I'd feel out of place here?"

Until 1964, "Guelph" was a federation of three colleges, the Ontario Veterinary College (1862), the Ontario Agricultural College (1874), and the Macdonald Institute (1962). When the Wellington College of Arts and Sciences joined in 1964, Guelph became a full-fledged university, ready to assume its place beside Princeton and Padua among the great liberal-arts institutions of the world. But the aroma of pig dissipates slowly.

Five years ago, a desperate Guelph attempted to transform its public image. An aggressive advertising campaign was launched. The most notorious of the campaign's posters depicted an attractive couple lying in the cool shade of a mature tree, staring at each other knowingly. The text read, "Get into yourself. Come to Guelph." The picture implied, "Come to Guelph and get laid."

"It was an attempt to find a way to get Guelph into the public mind," says Guelph's provost defensively. In that sense, the campaign was a success. As an effort to demonstrate Guelph's class, sophistication, and scholarship, it flopped. What self-respecting university steals its theme from condom ads? The campaign was not, however, a total loss. "The whole point of the exercise was to get more people here," says one student who was around at the time. "It seemed to work. Enrolment was down, and after the campaign, it went up. Besides, in those days people were using sex to sell everything, even yogurt."

Let's forgive Guelph the occasional bout of tackiness — the university is understandably frustrated by the unwillingness of the public to notice how it's changed. Here's some of the news Guelph's trying to get out:

- One-third of Guelph's students are in the faculty of arts, making it the biggest faculty on campus.
- Four thousand students, almost half the student body, live in residence, the largest on-campus population in Canada after UBC.
- Over 95 per cent of students come from out of town. Most off-campus

students live within half a mile of the school. Guelph is one of the most cohesive academic communities in the country.
• Guelph has a beautiful and (partly) historic campus.
• While Guelph only requires 65 per cent to enter, the average grade 13 mark of Guelph's science students is 77.
• There are Guelph students who wear spiked hair, miniskirts, and psychedelic lipstick.

Guelph is neither as square nor as bovine as you might suppose. Guelph is more like a poor man's Queen's than Truro Agricultural College. All the same, Guelph students feel inferior. "People here are insecure, they often get defensive about the place," says one student. "In sports, the season is not complete unless we beat Western. You know, all those people from your high school who are really stuck up—it feels really good to get their team."

There's enough school spirit here to get three or four thousand people out to the games. Townies come, too. And, says one student, "the only reason you don't hear people shouting 'Guelph! Guelph! Guelph!' all the time is because it's too hard to say."

Many students choose Guelph because it has cleverly put together a schedule of unique and unusual degrees, like family and consumer studies, environmental studies, family and child studies, international development, settlement studies, ecology, fisheries biology, marine biology ("They actually have seals here!" exults one gleeful marine biologist), meteorology, toxicology, zoology, agricultural economics, human kinetics, and hotel and food administration. More conventional degrees are offered too, among them fine arts, classics, and music. Guelph is the third-biggest research centre in Ontario, after U of T and McMaster.

When students aren't working hard on their weed-out courses, they drink. There are more bars at Guelph than at any other university in Christendom. The whole campus is a licensed establishment. Alcohol is sold in all cafeterias, as well as at special lectures, club meetings, and sporting events. At Guelph it is possible to drink just about anywhere. In the University Centre alone there are at least seven places to get a drink. No wonder the Guelph smoke shop sells hats emblazoned with "I'm only here for the beer."

Guelph also operates its own disco, open six nights a week. Called the Bull Ring, the disco occupies all of a ring-shaped, one-storey building. "It's one hundred years old and it really used to be a judging arena for livestock." The more things change....

For people who are too shy to find love in a livestock pit, Guelph offers a more contemporary method for romance. "The latest trend here is to put personal notices in the newspaper," says the newspaper's advertising director. A typical entry:

To the figure skater wearing the red sweater and black miniskirt in the A.C. Sunday Feb. 1. I was wearing a white top and white shorts and playing volleyball against the team you were cheering for. We talked briefly, and I thought you were gorgeous! I'd like to take you to dinner. If interested, please reply P.O. Box 350 or next week's *Ontarion*.

Does it work? "From the number of ads we get, it must!" says the *Ontarion*'s advertising manager. But does this mean students don't meet each other in the usual way? "If you're not a super-outgoing person, it can be hard here," she replies.

The quietest times at Guelph are the weekends, when many students pack up and go home. "This is a suitcase school," students say. When they do stick around and if they tire of the on-campus hangouts, students go to the Albion Hotel, "a laid-back bohemian place," or O'Toole's, "a roadhouse where you should wear your tight jeans and lots of make-up."

The most popular club on campus is the Royal Order of Buffalos — remember *The Flintstones*? The three hundred or so lodge members party together in rented bowling alleys, and can be recognized by their purple felt hats with horns. Members greet each other with an "Ak-ak-a-dak" mating call that will bring back happy childhood Saturday mornings. Other, more sophisticated but less popular groups on campus include the Marxist-Leninists, the Political Historical Military Studies and Simulations Group, and the Guelph Committee against Imperial War Preparations. Politics veer left. Advocate free-market agricultural policies at your peril.

Finding a place to live in Guelph can be very difficult. Residence rooms are guaranteed for first-year students, but older students may eventually have to live in town. Vacancy rates in Guelph rival Toronto's. Students take what they can get. "It's very expensive here," complains one student from BC. "I'm paying $200 for a small room in a house with eleven people in it." Rent of $300 is in fact more normal. All the same, living off campus is cheaper than living in residence, and most students are able to find housing near the campus.

The mood at Guelph is peaceful, warm, and, to use a favourite local expression, "down-to-earth." For scientists, Guelph is an eminently respectable choice. For artsies, while Guelph may not impress your friends, life here can be awfully sweet. And, for country lovers, while this may be Cow College no more, there still remain plenty of cows — not to mention horses, sheep, pigs, and *seals*.

THE FACTS

Founded:	Ontario Veterinary College, 1862. Ontario Agricultural College, 1874. Guelph University, 1964.
Address:	Guelph, Ontario N1G 2W1
Tuition:	$1,228
Cut-off grade for general admission (per cent):	65
Average grade 13 mark of entering class (per cent):	70.1
Enrolment:	12,349
Undergraduate full-time enrolment:	9,700
Percentage of foreign students:	3
Percentage of students from outside the province:	5
Residence fees:	$3,170–3,400
Percentage of students in residence:	41
Male-female ratio:	47:53
Athletic facilities:	Okay. Stadium (seats 5,100).
Team name:	Gryphons
Colours:	Red, gold, and black
Coolest major:	Veterinary sciences
Uncoolest major:	"The Dips" — Two-year diploma program in agriculture technology.
Fraternities/sororities:	Only off campus. Unrecognized by university. Agriculture frat major organization on campus.
Typical garb:	"Perfect hair-dos. Tawdry clothing." Jeans, work boots, school jackets.
Campus political attitude:	Middle-of-the-road.
Best-known fact:	Agriculture is a big deal here.

Least-known fact:	Most Guelph students are artsies.
If you had to put it in one sentence:	"This is a cosmopolitan, heterogeneous community. You don't have to be a scientist to be comfortable here."—*Provost*
Alumni:	John Kenneth Galbraith, George S. Henry and Harry Nixon (premiers of Ontario), John Bracken (premier of Manitoba), J. Walter Jones (premier of PEI).

DO'S AND DON'TS

DO try to get invited to the Aggie Ball—the most important social event on the Guelph calendar.

DON'T be amazed when you see women dancing with each other on Tuesday nights at the Bull Ring—that's gay night.

DO try to open an account with the CIBC before you come to school, since their instant-bank machines are right in University Centre.

DON'T ever try to catch a bus in Guelph on Sunday. They don't run on Sunday.

LAKEHEAD

Back-bacon, tuques, beer, doughnuts, Grebs, blizzards, trees, more trees, and a university president known to all as Uncle Bob. Welcome to Canada! The real Canada—the home of Bob and Doug McKenzie, Pierre Berton, and mukluks.

What, for example, could be more Canadian than a university that specializes in northern studies and brags about its accomplishments in forestry? What could be more Canadian than a university founded in 1965? What could be more Canadian than a university located in a place that is *really* cold? Nothing. Sorry, Royal Canadian Yacht Club: Lakehead is Canada, Canada is Lakehead, and we're having moose-steaks for dinner.

It isn't just uncivilized northerners who appreciate the McKenzie Brothers' approach to education — 40 per cent of the students at Lakehead come from southern Ontario, and another 12 per cent come from southern points in other provinces.

This is especially puzzling when one recalls that the reason for the creation of Lakehead was to spare the young people of northern Ontario the expense and culture shock of going south — in Thunder Bay, everything south of the city limits is "the south" — for their degrees. But pushy southerners, as is their wont, have taken over.

Okay, so why? The Toronto-raised president of the student council explains that he chose Lakehead because "it's more laid-back here. Even the girls wear construction boots. It's a very comfortable, very close-knit campus."

But the student president is also prepared to admit that Lakehead is one of the few universities in Ontario that can make York students feel superior. "There is a joke here that if you can't get into York you go to Lakehead," he says. But although Lakehead is certainly one of the less choosy schools, that's not enough to explain why students pick it over, say, Brock or Laurentian.

"Lakehead people are tree-huggers," says one professor. "They love the wilderness and they love this part of the country." "I really enjoy the outdoor stuff," says one student from London, Ontario. "I love the way I can just open my back door and start cross-country skiing. And downhill skiing is only fifteen minutes away. This is a great place if you're into outdoor recreation. It's not so good if you're into fresh vegetables."

Lakehead's campus is certainly smack in the middle of the great outdoors. It was built in the no-man's-land between the former cities of Port Arthur and Fort William, which now together make up the city of Thunder Bay. "We get a lot of compliments on the beauty of our campus," says the student president. "It's nice the way all the buildings are so bunched together. It makes it easy to meet people."

The campus is built in a pinkish brick with a lovely rosy hue. A man-made lake, full of salmon in the spring and a skating rink in the winter, laps up against the campus's principal building. "Our own Rideau Canal," says the only university president known as Uncle Bob proudly. As modern Canadian campuses go, this is one of the best.

But, warns one student, "Don't get fooled by the literature that says that the campus is convenient and that there's great shopping nearby. You can't walk to the downtown. It's at least five miles away and that's where all the shopping is."

Lakehead is definitely isolated, not only from Thunder Bay but from the entire country. The closest neighbouring "city" is Sault Ste. Marie, and even it is a seven-hour drive away. Winnipeg is 12 hours away and Toronto is at least 15. These distances constrain Lakehead from playing in intercollegiate sports events. They also explain why the university feels it has more in common with northern Swedish and Norwegian universities than the universities of southern Ontario.

Dr. Rosehart (Uncle Bob's real name) believes that "Lakehead serves a major role for the future of this area. Over three-quarters of our students are in professional programs. We have one of the highest percentages in Ontario of students enrolled in career-related programs."

Professional faculties at Lakehead include nursing, engineering, business, education, and social work. The bedrock programs — forestry and outdoor recreation — are overwhelmingly filled by southerners. A diploma of library technology is available. And students majoring in chemistry, geology, and physics can minor in something called energy and fuel sciences.

Lakehead also offers a unique opportunity to technical school graduates, who may upgrade diplomas in engineering and business to degrees in only two years. Dr. Rosehart is very proud of this program, as he is about anything at Lakehead that smacks of innovation. "What attracted me to Lakehead from southern Ontario was — though I hate the term — a pioneering spirit. Seeing as our programs are still maturing, there is great opportunity for anyone who comes here to shape programs. That's what attracts a lot of our faculty here."

A graduate student was drawn to Lakehead by "the interdepartmental co-operation. Everyone knows each other, and people have a familiarity with the work of others, which is the best thing for grad research." Lakehead does, however, have severe problems. A transfer student from the University of Toronto notes a petty one. "The profs are always so defensive. They insist on being called 'Doctor.' It's important to them that we know that they have their Ph.D.s. They need to prove that this is a good school, so they build pedestals for themselves."

Worse, the library — as a student puts it with great gentleness — "isn't too good." "If you have any serious work to do, you have to use the interlibrary loan system."

Perhaps worst of all: other than outdoor recreation, there's not much to do at Lakehead. A happy consequence of the lack of temptation is Thunder Bay's disproportionate contribution to Canada's Olympic teams. An unhappy consequence is terrible student boredom. The bookstores in Thunder Bay are terrible, there are no art galleries, and no repertory cinemas. (There are, thank God, three ambitious theatre companies.) Even the shopping is boring. "What I miss most," a student from the south says dreamily, "is some kind of sophisticated jazz club. Or any club of any kind."

The one and only student club in Thunder Bay is the Expressway Lounge in the Landmark Hotel. It's the only place in town that brings in known bands. Other, but less exciting, drinking spots include Button's II, Spinner's, Casey's, and O'Toole's.

The housing situation at Lakehead is good. There are some apartments very near the campus, though they are so popular you might have to wait for one. If you can't wait, the student president advises that "You can save a lot of money living in town, renting a room. In exchange for some chores, you can pay as little as $150 a month for room and board. It's great having someone to do your washing and cooking. I think it's the best way to go." The battle to get one of the 650 university residence beds can be tough; there are always waiting lists in September. It's best to apply as early as possible. If you do get stuck off campus, a car is advisable.

Although students insist that Lakehead is a warm community, they say it's not an especially romantic place. "You certainly don't see a lot of smut in the hallways," reflects the student president.

But Lakehead's biggest problem is not its lack of romance, but its lack of respect (even the locals mock it). "People who live here love to denigrate this university," says one student. Says another, "The kids from Thunder Bay who go south to school are insufferable when they come back. They think they're too good for you. They don't want to speak to you."

A degree from Lakehead is nothing to be ashamed of. Some local employers even prefer it to degrees from other, less Canadian universities. Any student who chooses it should expect that he will be called on to shape Lakehead as much as it shapes him.

THE FACTS

Founded:	Lakehead University, 1965. Lakehead College of Arts and Science, 1957. Lakehead Technical Institute, 1946.
Address:	Oliver Road Thunder Bay, Ontario P7B 5E1

Tuition:	$1,262
Cut-off grade for general admission (per cent):	60
Average grade 13 mark of entering class (per cent):	70.1
Enrolment:	5,206
Undergraduate full-time enrolment:	3,581
Percentage of foreign students:	6
Percentage of students from outside the province:	6
Residence fees:	$3,027–3,185
Percentage of students in residence:	17
Male-female ratio:	58:42
Athletic facilities:	Excellent.
Team name:	Nor'Westers, Lady Nor'Westers
Colours:	Blue and white
Fraternities/sororities:	None.
Typical garb:	Kodiaks and ski jackets.
Campus political attitude:	Anti–southern Ontario. Pro-trees.
Best-known fact:	This is the most physically isolated university in Canada.
Least-known fact:	The place is overrun with southerners.
If you had to put it in one sentence:	"This is a very close-knit campus because there's no place else to turn to."—*Student*

DO'S AND DON'TS

DO visit the Aesthetics Lounge upstairs in the student union building. Try to figure out why a room of white concrete blocks, orange carpets, brown plastic chairs, and green Arborite tables is named thusly.

DON'T forget to pack all your winter wonderland sporting gear. For lovers of the great outdoors, few campuses could be more pleasing.

DO everything you can to take advantage of special student rates and seat sales for your airline tickets to and from Thunder Bay. The regular fare is shockingly expensive.

DON'T behave badly while in the student pub, the Study. The pub's house rules warn patrons that "vomiting in or around the Study area will be reason for immediate removal from bar and/or ban." "Throwing beer or other items, unauthorized movement of pub furniture, boat races, mooning, dancing/standing on tables or chairs, using illegal drugs on the premises" will also get you the boot.

LAURENTIAN

The PR department of Laurentian University in Sudbury, Ontario, distributes to every high school in the province glossy pamphlets in vivid colour, advertising "The Laurentian Experience." Clean-cut, handsome, well-dressed students laugh with their professors under the bright summer sun, and toss autumn leaves into the air with joyous abandon. (The Laurentian experience seems not to occur in winter.)

"My first bit of advice for a potential Laurentian student would be to disregard everything the university's promotional materials suggest to you," says the editor of Laurentian's student newspaper. "That stuff gives people the wrong message. That stuff isn't Laurentian," insists the editor. "The Laurentian Experience has nothing to do with the Western Experience, and thank God. A good picture of the Laurentian experience would show a student and professor staggering out of the pub, arm in arm, drunk out of their skulls. Now that's the Laurentian experience!"

"Tell all those preppy bastards not to get fooled by our literature. That crap misrepresents our school. Tell them we don't want them here," says the editor.

There really is little danger that Laurentian will ever be overrun by preppies. This place is not preppy style. Laurentian is not old — it was founded in 1960. It's not pretty (although the orange plastic trim on the concrete buildings is a nice touch). And it's not prestigious.

"What I like least about Laurentian," says one student, "are the low admission standards. Some people in my classes are really slow and it's very annoying." Other students are less annoyed and more amused by Laurentian's standards. The editor of the student paper says, "People will admit they're here because they didn't get in anywhere else. But we just laugh about it. Once you're here, you end up feeling glad to be at Laurentian."

"It's just like our attitude when we lose at sports, which we do a lot. You just head off to the pub, have a beer and a cigarette, and keep laughing."

Laurentian exists for political reasons. In the 1960s, provincial governments seemed to be handing out universities to everybody else, so northern Ontario wanted one, too. And it exists to serve political ends, especially the preservation of the bicultural character of a region that is 30 per cent francophone. For Laurentian University, or L'Université Laurentienne if you prefer, is bilingual. But like the university boom, Laurentian's language policy didn't quite work out as it was meant to. In fact, in the words of Laurentian's first president, bilingualism at Laurentian is "a total failure."

Students do not come to Laurentian to learn the other national language. "The way it works," complains one student, "is that the French students speak French to each other, and English to the English. The English students speak English to everybody." That doesn't mean, though, that the English and French speak to each other very much. Mixing between the two groups is limited. There is a separate student newspaper and a separate student government for each language group.

The emotions felt between the two groups are reminiscent of the emotions felt between the French and English in Quebec 20 years ago. There is tension and buried hostility.

An English student complains, "Things are so much easier for the French. Standards are lower for them. I'm supposed to be on an English floor, but there are two French people here already, and more are coming." A French student counters, "There is much better course selection for the English. There are so many more of them here. It's important for us to keep some things separate." Like, for example, the student government.

A recent proposal by the English student government, the General Students Association, to merge was rejected by the offended French student government, the Alliance des Étudiants Français. "They kept talking about all that stuff about cultural identity and so on," the disappointed Anglo author of the proposal laments, "but I think a merger would have been good for Laurentian, bilingualism, and, moreover, biculturalism. It would bring French and English together." (A more cynical explanation for the proposal: the English students believe that their student fees are used to subsidize the French students, who attend the English dances and social events but do not sponsor their own.) French students feared a power grab by the bigger and richer English student government.

Most courses at Laurentian are taught in both languages, but education is taught in French only, while philosophy and the sciences are taught in English only. The most popular program, sports administration (known as SPAD), is English only. All nursing students must study at least one year in English, but need not study in French at all. The tilt of Laurentian's bilingualism towards English is justified by the university's francophone vice-president for academics: "Most francophones in Ontario are bilingual. They have no trouble with English. In fact, one of the problems we have in developing our French programs is that francophones are more confident in English."

The structure of Laurentian was modelled on the college system of the University of Toronto: Sudbury College is Catholic; Huntington is United Church; Thorneloe is Anglican; and University College is non-sectarian. Sudbury is reputedly the strictest, with "no overnight guests and no playing Caps [a drinking game involving beer-bottle tops] in the halls." University College is the wildest. Each residence provides a kitchen for student use, but there is only one dining hall located on the main campus — which means that breakfast is a very long, cold walk away.

Living off campus may bring your Frosted Flakes within easier reach, but it will cramp your social life. Social life, outside of the colleges, occurs on Thursday nights in the Down Under student union pub, known universally as "the hole." "People come, get drunk, and always leave with somebody. Here's to the Laurentian experience! If you don't have the Laurentian experience within the first week of school, you're a real loser."

If you do live off campus, be prepared to have your preconceptions about Sudbury shattered. "People don't realize," says the English student president, "what a beautiful town Sudbury is. There's a lake in the middle of the city, and our campus is entirely surrounded by water. We even have our own campus beach."

Laurentian officials seem to believe that public relations contains the answer to the school's difficulties. "A couple of years ago," the student council president insists, "we were in a real slump, but slowly people are beginning to take pride in their school. All we have to do now is to teach the students to get over their inferiority complex. Yes, many of them are here because they didn't get into Queen's or Western, but so what? Laurentian people would never feel comfortable in those places anyway."

The student newspaper editor puts it more bluntly. "Sure, you may not have a lot of brilliant people here. You may not have a lot of exciting people, with a lot of flair. But what you do have is good-hearted people, decent, down-to-earth people. And that's the key."

THE FACTS

Founded:	1960
Address:	Ramsey Lake Road Sudbury, Ontario P3E 2C6
Tuition:	$1,264
Cut-off grade for admission (per cent):	60
Average grade 13 mark of entering class (per cent):	69.5
Enrolment:	5,580
Undergraduate full-time enrolment:	3,390
Percentage of foreign students:	3.5
Percentage of students from outside the province:	1.4
Residence fees:	$2,320–2,600
Percentage of students in residence:	35
Male-female ratio:	48:52
Athletic facilities:	Good. 50-metre pool. Tartan Track, 400 m (seats 1,700).
Team name:	Voyageurs
Colours:	Royal blue and gold
Coolest Major:	SPAD

Fraternities/sororities:	None.
Typical garb:	Conservative. "Not a spiky-hair kind of place." Favourite shirt is a parody of ROOTS shirts. They say "ROCKS" instead, and feature a pile of rocks instead of a beaver.
Campus political attitude:	Deeply interested in linguistic issues.
Best-known fact:	Swimmer Alex Baumann trained for the Olympics here.
Least-known fact:	Sudbury is a very beautiful city.
If you had to put it in one sentence:	The atmosphere at Laurentian is like that of Quebec 20 years ago: tense.

DO'S AND DON'TS

DO bring a pack of cards with you to school. At lunch-time in the cafeterias there are more students playing poker than eating.

DON'T get kicked out. Laurentian is the kind of place students come to after they have been expelled from other universities. After Laurentian, "you'll have to try community college. It's all that's left."

DO bring cross-country skis, skates, and other winter wonderland gear. A car would be nice, but it's not essential.

DON'T be afraid to apply to the married people's dorm, even if you aren't married. They sometimes accept singles, and they are a good place to live.

UNIVERSITY OF LETHBRIDGE

Hunkered behind the rough Coulee hills, straddling the winding Old-man River, dominating the windy prairie, and smack on top of the city sewage plant stretches the University of Lethbridge. Acclaimed by architecture-lovers the world over for its dramatic sweep across the Alberta landscape, Arthur Erickson's famous one-building university inspires only weary resignation in University of Lethbridge students. "Yeah, so it's beautiful to you," says one, "but trust me: you try to spend eight months a year surrounded by poured concrete, and see if you don't get depressed." (Even more depressing: the university is slowly tipping over, and is in danger of sliding into the Oldman River. Structural changes are in the works.)

Most students come to this university because they live nearby. "I chose Lethbridge because it's close, and Harvard was too expensive," says one self-assured student. Actually, it isn't that close. Most of the people of Lethbridge suspect that Erickson deliberately put his monument on the wrong (empty) side of town in order to enhance its impact. The university is 15 minutes by car from downtown, but, even though it's stuck in the middle of the prairie, there's no place to park.

It's a shame more Albertans don't consider the University of Lethbridge. A contented student says, "Lethbridge is the perfect size. There's a very warm atmosphere and a greater chance for personal happiness and growth. You get real opportunities for one-on-ones with your professors. They probably know you by name, and are not afraid to kick you in the ass when you need it."

Despite its crazy physical grandeur, Lethbridge is only one-tenth the size of the University of Alberta. The virtues of smallness, however, do not appear to appeal to Albertans. The huge and equally upstart University of Calgary commands far more respect in Alberta than Lethbridge. In Alberta there's nothing wrong with being young, but being puny is regarded as a defect. Think of the West Edmonton Mall.

Even Lethbridge students feel ashamed of their un-Albertan smallness. "What's the best way to impress your U of L friends?" one student jokes. "Transfer to the University of Alberta." Transferring can be hard. Students gloomily complain that the University of Alberta "downgrades our marks on transfer applications. Just shows what they think of our university."

Lethbridge's biggest liability is its location. Few Canadians have even heard of this town, let alone its university. And that's too bad, because some departments are excellent. The fine-arts facilities are outstanding. The popular drama department runs a performing-arts series, which has hosted Karen Kain and the Winnipeg Symphony Orchestra, among others. With the excellent Banff School for the Fine Arts nearby, southern Alberta can claim plausibly, as it does, to be a Canadian cultural centre.

The university is also distinguished by an excellent native studies program, which attracts some non-native students, but mostly serves the neighbouring Blood band reserve, the largest reserve in Canada. The program develops self-government skills, but also offers courses in language and culture.

The university specializes in the liberal arts. Students must satisfy a two-year "breadth" requirement before declaring a major, and must do at least one credit's worth of independent study. The curriculum is divided into five categories and students must take at least two courses from each. Scientific illiterates need not panic — "modern astronomy" and "human nutrition" look manageable.

Students at Lethbridge hang out in packs, and, within packs, according to my unscientific research, there are more public displays of affection than at almost any other university in Canada. Students kiss, hold hands, and sit in each other's laps. Kissing couples seem to be as immobile an element of the hallways as the big, orange-carpeted block benches that line them.

The explanation for all this lovey-dovey stuff? "Twenty per cent of our students are Mormons. They believe in early marriage and are paired up by the time they're eleven," says one student. Another student has a different explanation. "There are a lot more girls than guys at this school. Once a girl's got her man she wants everybody else to know it. The message is: stay away from him."

The large Mormon population in the area has, to the irritation of the non-Mormons, set the social tone at Lethbridge. Pressure from the Mormon community in the town has prevented the establishment of a regular student pub on campus. Instead, on Friday afternoons the student council sets up a makeshift pub in the school's daycare centre. "Welcome to Canada's Bible Belt," says a student cheerlessly.

By necessity, most conviviality takes place off campus, which is where the vast majority of students live anyway. Favourite haunts are Smart Alec's Bar and Deli (the absolute fave-rave), O'Rileys with its "Old Fashioned Novelty Decor," and the Cadillac Bar and Diner, which bills itself as "the most amazing new nightclub in all of Lethbridge."

Few students live in residence, known either as the "Cement Dungeon" or the "Shoebox." (Again, more complaints of "it may be beautiful to you but....") Experienced students advise that apartment living is more congenial. They especially recommend the Hillhurst complex.

Lethbridge students may be a little insecure, but they are essentially content. Their university is friendly, modern, unintimidating, and really cool-looking. For a small, unknown school in a small, unknown town, this university has a surprising amount of potential.

THE FACTS

Founded:	1967
Address:	4401 University Drive Lethbridge, Alberta T1K 3M4
Tuition:	$930
Cut-off grade for general admission (per cent):	60
Enrolment:	3,091
Undergraduate full-time enrolment:	2,633
Percentage of foreign students:	.01
Percentage of students from outside the province:	9
Residence fees:	$2,234–2,834
Percentage of students in residence:	11
Male-female ratio:	46:54
Athletic facilities:	Very good.
Team name:	Pronghorns
Colours:	Royal blue, and gold
Fraternities/sororities:	None.
Typical garb:	"The Mormons dress up, wear lots of pastels and pretty clothes. The rest of us dress like slobs." — *Student*
Campus political attitude:	"Conservative by trend, apathetic by nature."—*Student journalist*
Best-known fact:	Arthur Erickson designed the university.
Least-known fact:	Lethbridge University is located in a town that claims to be the irrigation capital of the world.
If you had to put it in one sentence:	Lethbridge is the only small-sized option in a province that doesn't like small-sized options.

DO'S AND DON'TS

DO join the university ski club. It's the rowdiest, most popular club on campus, and most members don't even ski.

DON'T fail to get acquainted with the interlibrary loan system. You'll need it.

DO encourage your grandparents to come back to school. Tuition is free for anyone over 65.

DON'T count on convenient parking for your car. Parking lots are far away and expensive.

DO attend the "Loose Ladies" party held by the ski club each year. If you can handle the concept — women are supposed to dress like prostitutes and men like customers — it is said to be the best, most popular party all year.

McGILL

Life's returning to Montreal. The PQ is gone. The Sun Life Company is back. And McGill University is once again the *hottest* school in Canada. If you want to be cool, McGill's the school for you. It's true that 10 years ago things were looking pretty grim for the university that once dominated higher education in Canada. No one knew what country it was going to be in, the imposing campus was rotting, a hostile government was starving it of funds, and a group of radical — and, interestingly, Anglo — faculty and students was noisily agitating for a revolutionized "McGill *français*," in which neither the English language nor English people would be welcome. Not surprisingly, McGill's popularity among conflict-averse Anglos dwindled. It's now reviving.

It's a good thing, too, since much of McGill's traditional charm is based on its ability to attract diverse and eccentric students who benefit from one another's presence, even if they do hate each other. Over half the graduates of Upper Canada College applied to McGill this year. (Ten years ago, virtually none did.) Once they arrive on campus, they will share classes with punk rockers and conservatives, bitter-end separatists and Westmount survivors, militant lesbians and sorority girls, geniuses and dumbos, and, most interesting of all, a whole lot of French preppies. In an ironic twist of history, McGill is now home not just to the children of the English establishment, but to those of the French élite as well. Today almost one-quarter of the student body is French (as opposed to four per cent 10 years ago) and they come to McGill for the chance to speak English. Which brings us to the most-often-asked question about McGill: Do you have to be able to speak French? Emphatically not — you could easily live in Montreal for three years and never speak a word of French. Of course, the question remains, why would you want to?

The people who choose McGill choose it because it is in the heart of French Canada. When they say McGill is a great institution, they really mean that Montreal is a great city. Put McGill in Tuktoyaktuk and they wouldn't be quite so enthusiastic. The best moments at McGill are spent munching on croissants and sipping *cafés au lait,* touring Montreal's *beaux-arts* palaces, getting drunk in the bistros of St. Denis Street, shopping for fresh groceries on St. Laurent, skiing on Mount Royal, and going to hockey games at the Forum. The worst are spent at the reserve desk in Redpath Library, lining up for one of the three copies of a text you and 500 other people are being tested on the next day. Or looking for the indoor track at the gym (there isn't one). Or trying to have a civil conversation with the registrar's office (impossible).

Another of the great blessings of Montreal, and therefore McGill (one begins to use the names interchangeably), is the abundance of student apartments. Traditionally, the McGill student ghetto is bordered by Pine Street to the north, Sherbrooke Street to the south, Stanley Street to the west, and Park Avenue to the east. Rent in Montreal is much cheaper than in Toronto, Ottawa, Vancouver, or even Antigonish — another reason, besides the cheap tuition (unchanged after 18 years), for McGill's return to favour. Most McGill students will live off campus for at least two of their three years.

There are only 1,050 places in the five McGill residences, and your chances of getting one are about one in 12. Preference in allotting the scarce residence rooms goes to younger-than-normal applicants and to applicants from far away. A foreign country is best, but British Columbia will suffice. McGill residences vary greatly in charm and comfort, but with 12 applicants for every bed, don't expect to be offered any choice.

Douglas Hall, with suites rather than rooms, is best. All-female Royal Victoria College, known as "the Nunnery," is the least desirable.

If you don't get into residence, don't panic. Only a small part of McGill's social life happens in the residences; the rest happens in the clubs. No other university in the country has more active clubs, especially political clubs, than McGill. If you hate El Salvador, you'll never be lonely. At McGill, people don't meet in the cafeteria line, they meet in the picket line. Every trendy political cause is embraced with enthusiasm — even hysteria — at debates, symposiums, special lectures, meetings, boycotts, and riots. Political rallies displace the more customary student shindigs: proms, spring flings, pub nights, orientation highjinx, and so on. If you don't hate El Salvador, theatre can fill a lot of extracurricular hours. Culture-starved English Montreal gobbles up McGill plays, which are often reviewed in the *Gazette*.

While McGill's extracurricular life is exciting, curricular life lacks a certain something: excellence. Too many professors seem to hate their students. Academic requirements can be laughable. Introductory courses are depressingly overcrowded. Finding books printed after 1930 in the library can be difficult and frustrating. To make matters worse, Montreal does not have a single good English-language bookstore. Let's just say that if you want to do serious research, you'd better go to the University of Toronto.

After sitting on cold concrete steps in a lecture hall, taking notes on your knee, listening to a professor shout into a microphone, you're going to want a beer. McGill students care where they drink their beer — the campus pub, Gertrude's, is strictly for engineers, frat boys, and the unfashionable. (Going to Gert's when you're supposed to be in class, however, is decidedly cool.) Don't make a habit of it after freshman year, but do visit the Old Munich beer hall: it's rowdy and fun. The chic-est area in town these days is the north end of St. Laurent and St. Denis boulevards: the chichi-est spot is L'Express. For a romantic, cheap evening (bring your own booze), any restaurant on Prince Arthur Street. To impress a date or hear excellent jazz, go to L'Air du Temps in Old Montreal. For sheer high-sodium, high-calorie pigging out, you want the pastrami with extra fat at Schwartz's. Listing hangouts in Montreal is ultimately futile: there are a million wonderful places to go, with new ones opening every day — the joy is taking a good friend and discovering your own.

Sadly, finding a good friend can be more difficult than finding a good restaurant. This is not a school where you will see many couples wandering around hand in hand. But students at McGill do worry about herpes, not to mention AIDS. Few romances begin at the big parties in the student union.

Romance breaks out all the same, and McGill is a contented place, especially now that its new popularity has forced its admissions standards up (better have an average of at least 70 per cent in your last three years of high school to be sure of getting in). McGill students are confident about themselves and their school. It will be a while, however, before they are confident that they won't have to move to Toronto after graduation.

"Let's just say that if you want to do serious research
you'd better go to the University of Toronto."

THE FACTS

Founded:	1829
Address:	845 Sherbrooke St. W. Montreal, Quebec H3A 2T5
Tuition:	$570
Cut-off grade for general admission (per cent):	70
Enrolment:	20,601
Undergraduate full-time enrolment:	12,818
Percentage of foreign students:	10
Percentage of students from outside the province:	18
Residence fees:	$3,424–4,425
Percentage of students in residence:	8
Male-female ratio:	50:50
Athletic facilities:	Medium to poor. Stadium (seats 20,000), hockey arena (1,650).
Team name:	(M) Redmen, (F) Martlets
Colours:	Red and white
Most popular major:	Political science
Fraternities/sororities:	Once were a big deal; now all that's left are some splendid clubhouses and a few die-hards who wish it were still 1955.
Typical garb:	Outfits of all black, including dyed hair, eyebrows, lips. The chic French look, or anything that's weird.
Best-known fact:	Stephen Leacock taught here.
Least-known fact:	The money for the gym built in 1938 was raised by the sale of McGill cigarettes. Alumni were encouraged to smoke often to help build the athletic facilities.

If you had to put it in one sentence:	As long as McGill is in Montreal, it will always be a great school for happy-go-lucky college kids.
Alumni:	Sir Wilfrid Laurier, Leonard Cohen, Arthur C. Erikson, Irving Layton, Sir William Osler, Zbigniew Brzezinski, Violet Archer (composer), George and Jonathan Birks, Charles and Edgar Bronfman, Eugene Forsey, Herb Gray, Don Johnston, Michael Meighen, Stuart Smith, Alastair Gillespie, David Culver (president of Alcan).

DO'S AND DON'TS

DO check in at the fraternities and sororities when looking for a place to live. They often rent out rooms to non-members to fill the places up.

DON'T join a sports team in the hope of becoming a Big Man on Campus. No one cares about the teams, what happens to them, or who's on them.

DO attend the orientation-week residence street dance. It's the best party all year.

DON'T use matching sets of cutlery and china at any dinner parties you throw: unmatched sets are definitely more cool. Wearing mismatched socks is also cool. Being odd in general is cool.

DO volunteer to help out at the annual Winter Carnival Debating Tournament. It's the largest debating contest in North America, and an excellent way to meet students from other schools and far-away places.

DON'T develop phobias about wearing dead people's clothes. Unless you sometimes wear some second-hand clothing, no one will respect you.

I REMEMBER...

"I very much credit McGill for my career; without those houses on Peel Street, without those cafés on Stanley Street, without those spirits like Hugh MacLennan, Louis Dudek, Irving Layton, Frank Scott — without those men, I certainly would have taken a very different turn." — *Leonard Cohen*

McMASTER

Why do so many of Canada's funny people — Dave Thomas, Martin Short, Eugene Levy, Ivan Reitman, Doug Henning, and Gary Lautens — come from McMaster University? Perhaps because you have to have a sense of humour to go to McMaster. Or perhaps because humour is a form of escapism.

Humour is not the only form of escapism practised here at "Suitcase U." McMaster students spend amazingly little time on campus. The university helps them escape by running a cheap bus service between the McMaster campus and Toronto's York Mills subway station on the weekends.

McMaster may be dull, but it's incredibly efficient in some ways. The parking lots, for example, work brilliantly. At most commuter schools, students and faculty park in the next county, and then walk through howling winds, rain, sleet, and snow to the centre of campus. Not at McMaster! A shuttle bus between the campus and the parking lots delivers students to their classes, and then ferries them back to their cars warm and dry. There are six huge parking lots, and yet the wait for a shuttle bus never exceeds 10 minutes.

Apart from the easy parking, why bother with McMaster? For students who live nearby, it's convenient and cheap. Going to McMaster rather than U of T enables Hamilton and Burlington students to live at home. Of course, they could always take the GO train to Toronto, but the parking at the GO train station isn't nearly as good.

Besides, many McMaster students would never be admitted to U of T. "There's an underlying feeling here that we don't exactly fall into the 'top three' category," says a student thoughtfully.

Another reason to bother with McMaster is its surprisingly agreeable campus. The broad, parklike lawns between buildings are lush and lovely in the fall and spring. On warm days, students lounge on the grass, keeping their eyes on Mac's dignified, ivy-covered Gothic edifices, and ignoring the immense concrete hangars to which the scientists and engineers have been condemned.

The arts buildings are about a quarter of a mile from the science buildings. The theological department (Mac began as a Baptist seminary) is over the horizon. The distances at other schools may be much greater, but arts students at McMaster see a sinister significance in the separation. Giving them the nice buildings doesn't reassure them. A recent graduate worries that "Many feel that McMaster is abandoning its liberal-arts heritage to become a technical factory." Letting arts slide and courting the sciences is a tempting strategy to a fearful university that realizes it is known to the outside world only for its medical school.

Many students are lured to McMaster by the belief that they will be treated indulgently by the medical school's admissions committee. According to a member of that department, the strategy may work. "The selection process at McMaster is very idiosyncratic, so it helps to be close to it. It's helpful to ask successful candidates about it. You can pick up a sense of how it's done just by being near it." The essential difference between the admissions procedure at McMaster and medical schools elsewhere? McMaster emphasizes empathy, bedside manner, and character, rather than relying exclusively on grades and MCAT scores.

Perhaps the greatest blow to the pride of the ailing humanities departments was the news — headlined in *The Globe and Mail* — that over half of McMaster's freshman class had failed a basic literacy test. The figure was later massaged down to a 42 per cent failure rate. It is, however, possible to place a charitable construction on this dreadful performance. Take a look at one of the test's questions.

Reconstruct the sentence given below (mentally, if possible) by following the directions given. In doing so, retain the meaning in the original as much as the directions permit. When you have reconstructed the sentence, select from the options (A) to (E) the word or phrase that is included in your reconstructed version.
SENTENCE — The ship made little progress against the Polar ice, finally giving up its efforts.
DIRECTIONS — Change **little** to **so little**.
(A) consequently
(B) so that
(C) and so
(D) thus
(E) that

Stumped? Me, too. For better results, McMaster might consider having its literacy tests written by people who are fluent in English.

No school that feels it has to run shuttle buses to the next city is going to have a pulsating social life. Most McMaster students come from the 10 nearby high schools, and they don't extend their friendships much beyond their adolescent limits. "Groups don't cohere around common academic interests. The common denominator of my group was that we all played euchre," says an academically successful student. "What McMaster lacks," in the opinion of one professor, "is a group of bright students who make life interesting for the rest of the campus."

The Young Progressive Conservatives tried to make life interesting for the rest of the campus in spring 1987, by donating a princely $25 to the Nicaraguan resistance. Some students were outraged. A mocking, "Adopt-a-Contra" poster campaign provided the campus with the only exciting controversy of the year. Perhaps, to promote school spirit, the young Tories should send money to anti-Soviet guerrillas every year.

No additional excitement is needed in McMaster's dormitories. "They're a zoo!" to quote a satisfied customer. There are some co-ed dorms, but the wildest are all-male. The best parties are held in the residence quads, which are among the prettiest spots on campus. Super Pubs are held every Thursday in the residence commons. Since many residence students go home on the weekends (most are from Toronto suburbs or nearby towns), partying goes on during the week. "I go home on the weekends to rest," says one first-year student from Mississauga. "Five nights a week is about all I can take with these guys!"

Orientation for residence students can be pretty rough. A favoured gag: male students are taken to a downtown drugstore to buy condoms. They are then ordered to stand on the sidewalk of the main street, inflate their prophylactics, and hold them over their heads as respectable Hamiltonians pass by, snickering.

Residence students are greatly envied by students who live off campus, not just because they get to play with condoms, but also because the residences are about the only convenient housing near the university. If you don't have a car, be prepared for very long bus rides. On the other hand, rent in Hamilton is low. Students sharing a house usually pay no more than $150 a month each.

To improve life for non-residential students, the student council has created SOCS: the Society of Off Campus Students. SOCS runs its own orientation week, in which students learn the SOCS song: "We are SOCS — pity us/ The walks are long/ The bus ride's hideous." SOCS also has its own lounge. According to a regular user of the lounge, "It's always full. People are really friendly. And why not?"

As a college town, a native readily concedes that "Hamilton is a big BLAH!!" McMaster has three pubs: the Rat, the Phoenix, and the Downstairs John. "Lots of people go only to the John. It's the best place in town for students. There's just not much else, except maybe the strip joints."

McMaster is probably not the school many of its students wish it were, but there is no doubting that, in the areas of parking and humour, McMaster is tops.

THE FACTS

Founded: 1890 in Toronto,
                        1930 moved to Hamilton.

Address:	Hamilton, Ontario L8S 4L8
Tuition:	$1,263
Cut-off grade for general admission (per cent):	65–70
Average grade 13 mark of entering class (per cent):	73.7
Enrolment:	14,991
Undergraduate full-time enrolment:	approximately 10,000
Percentage of foreign students:	3
Percentage of students from outside the province:	2
Residence fees:	$2,670
Percentage of students in residence:	23
Male-female ratio:	52:48
Athletic facilities:	Excellent.
Team name:	Marauders. Hockey and swimming: Marlins.
Colours:	Maroon and grey
Coolest major:	Pre-med
Fraternities/sororities:	None.
Typical garb:	"This is a track-pant university."—*Student*
Campus political attitude:	Middle-of-the-road.
Best-known fact:	The place is dead on the weekends.
Least-known fact:	McMaster has produced more Hollywood stars, per capita, than any other Canadian university.
If you had to put it in one sentence:	"We're not the snobs of Queen's or the clones of Western. We're normal people."—*Student*
Alumni:	Robert Nixon (treasurer of Ontario), John Munro (former Liberal cabinet minister), Robert Welch (former

deputy premier of Ontario), Lincoln Alexander (lieutenant-governor of Ontario), Muriel Kauffman (owner of the Kansas City Royals), Lynn Williams (president of the United Steelworkers of America), Marian Engel, Lawrence Martin (journalist), Roberta Bondar (Canada's first lady astronaut).

DO'S AND DON'TS

DO use the shuttle bus service to Toronto on the weekends. It's $15 each way, departing at 2:00 and 3:00 p.m. on Fridays and returning at 7:45 p.m. from York Mills station on Sundays.

DON'T fail to visit the McMaster Art Gallery sometime before you graduate. It has a large collection of German expressionist prints and an antique-coin collection.

DO go to the Blue lounge in Hamilton Hall between classes to watch your favourite soaps and game shows. You'll find LOTS of people there.

DON'T miss the chance to view Bertrand Russell's personal library, desk, and chair, all housed in the main McMaster library.

UNIVERSITY OF MANITOBA

"Yes, We're Big!" gushes the enthusiastic admissions handbook of the University of Manitoba. "But Being Big Doesn't Mean We're Impersonal." Unfortunately, what we have here is a classic instance of protesting too much. With 23,400 students, the University of Manitoba is both big *and* impersonal.

No matter how much you're warned about the size of U of M, there's no preparing yourself for your first visit to a university that is easier to tour by car than on foot. The campus is spread out over 111 acres of land. If it weren't for the underground tunnel system, most students would freeze to death before they could get from one class to another.

Originally a school of agriculture, U of M is located on the outskirts of Winnipeg, or, bluntly, in the middle of nowhere. Perhaps once, when cattle and wheat were the main preoccupations of the students here, a location 30 miles from downtown might have made sense. But today, it is stretching it to call this place an urban university.

"There are a lot of similarities between a nice, quiet, affluent suburb and U of M," says the editor of the student paper, the *Manitoban*. "Everything goes on behind closed doors. There's not a lot of activity happening out in the open."

The trick to surviving at U of M, as at all big schools, is finding your own niche — a tall order at a school where students have trouble just finding their classes. "Yeah," says the editor, "you spend your first three months here just being lost. And after you've found where your classes are, you don't have much energy left to do or find anything else. The ideal way to get around this place is on snowmobile." He's only half-kidding.

But according to the vice-president academic, what makes U of M different from other big universities is its emphasis on undergraduate education. "We take undergraduates more seriously here than they do at U of T," he says.

The question is, do undergraduates take the U of M seriously?

"Most people arrange to spend as little time as possible here," says the student editor. "Since it takes most people at least half an hour to commute on the bus, they go home as soon as possible. People only do what's on their agenda. No one ever goes out of their way for anything. I have trouble getting people to work on the paper. At any place this big, a sense of alienation is involved. If you're not an outgoing person, it's going to be hard to make friends. This place can be an absolute hell for new students in their first term."

Naturally, these comments apply to all big Canadian universities, but somehow the sprawling campus, the distance from downtown, and the inescapable academic and economic impoverishment makes U of M more depressing and alienating than either UBC or the University of Toronto. Still, 23,000 students show up at U of M every day, so obviously the university is doing something right.

Most students agree that U of M has prestige. Although it may not be acclaimed in the rest of Canada, the University of Manitoba is certainly the leading educational institution in Manitoba.

"I know I would have had a better time at the University of Winnipeg," says one student. "But I am ambitious. You have to come to U of M if you are planning a career, if you need to impress an employer, or if you plan to apply to a good grad school."

The prestige of the old and respected U of M (founded in 1877, it is the oldest university in the west) also appeals to the many students who come here from northern Ontario. Says one student from Thunder Bay, "It's a better school than what we have up north and a good way to avoid southern Ontario."

Greater resources and facilities are other reasons why students choose U of M over other alternatives. In addition to all major fields of study, U of M also offers at the undergraduate level: agriculture (of course), architecture (a highly regarded faculty), dentistry, dental hygiene, human ecology, medical rehabilitation, nursing, and pharmacy. (U of M is one of only eight educational facilities in Canada to teach pharmacy.) But U of M's resources are great only when compared to those of Winnipeg, Brandon, or northern Ontario.

Poverty threatens many departments with loss of accreditation. One engineering and one medical program have actually lost their accreditation. The engineering program's status has since been restored, albeit on probation. The University of Manitoba professes unconcern. According to the university's vice-president: "U of M has been under a financial constraint longer than most schools. And yet we feel we have coped well, and have continued to deliver a high-quality education."

While Manitobans with a choice continue to choose U of M over Brandon and Winnipeg, most of its students understand the position of their school in the scheme of things. "You have to face it: there's a lot of other schools people think of before U of M comes into their minds. We know this isn't a status school."

Nor is U of M a romantic school. "Social life takes second place at this school. People work very hard. Some departments, like science, are very competitive, especially in the weed-out courses. [In pre-med, for example, the professors deliberately fail a certain proportion — sometimes as much as one-half — of the class.] People just want to do their work. If you're seeking As, you can spend a lot of time on it."

Not that the student council, UMSU (pronounced "um-soo"), doesn't try to get students to be a bit less pre-professional. "Nooners" — afternoon concerts in the student union building lobby — draw large crowds. Their organizers hope that meetings will result and beautiful relationships be formed. Men complain that it's hard to meet women at

U of M, but the women at least try. At lunch-time, the women's washroom in the student union is packed with girls who gather in silence to apply eye-liner, fix lipstick, spray on hair-spray, and check that their teeth contain no trace of recently consumed lunches. Great hope lives here.

Although the great majority of students commute (the place becomes very quiet at night), about eight per cent of students live on campus. They enjoy the normal social advantages of residence life. They don't know what the other students are talking about when they complain of "alienation." A lucky eight per cent! The most popular residence on campus is Taché, reputed to be a real party place. "If you can't handle a rowdy time, don't live here," cautions one student.

The architecture at U of M really defies description — "eclectic" is a nice word; "bizarre" may be more accurate. Taché, built in 1911, is a beautifully renovated Spanish-Chinese pavilion-style building in which many socials are held. (In Manitoba, "parties" are known only as "socials.") The socials here, and in the other residences, are open to all students, and are the best spots for meeting members of the opposite sex. "Let's say the social interaction there is high," says one resident.

For students who don't live with their parents and who don't live in residence, most off-campus housing is located downtown. "U of M is really an isolated place," explains an out-of-town student. "Once you leave University Circle, there's nothing out there for miles." The area around the University of Winnipeg is the U of M student ghetto, too.

Since there is no single area of town where U of M students live, there is also no single area where they drink and dance. Close to the university, the hot places are on Pembina Strip. Scandal's and Strawberry's are meeting places beloved of residence-dwellers. Times, Night Moves, Dayton's, and the Keg are favoured by those who live off-campus. Um-Zoo Club on campus, serves good food by day, and is a rowdy pub by night.

The University of Manitoba is not a lot of fun, but it won't kill you. This is a practical school for serious people. Glamour years will have to come later.

THE FACTS

Founded:	1877
Address:	Winnipeg, Manitoba R3T 2N2
Tuition:	$1,002

Cut-off grade for general
arts admission (per cent):   50

Enrolment: 23,319

Undergraduate full-time
enrolment: 13,326

Percentage of foreign
students: 8

Percentage of students from
outside the province: 13

Residence Fees: $3,069–3,525

Percentage of students in
residence: 8

Male-female ratio: 57:43

Athletic facilities: Excellent. Stadium (seats 10,000), new gymnasium.

Team Name: Bisons

Colours: Brown and gold

Coolest majors: Pharmacy and engineering

Fraternities/sororities: Yes, 10 of them.

Typical garb: Conservative, preppy. Kilts, designer jeans, and lots of jewellery for girls.

Campus political attitude: "None. People are too busy finding themselves." Not to mention their classes.

Best-known fact: This is the oldest university in western Canada.

Least-known fact: In 1986, the university raked in a surplus of $5,302. Wonder what they'll do with all that dough!

If you had to put it in one
sentence: "Going to U of M is the price you must pay if you are from Winnipeg and want to get into a good grad school." — Student

Alumni: Marshall McLuhan, David Kilgour, Brian Dickson (chief justice, Supreme Court of Canada), Fred Burbidge (CEO of CP), Edward

Schreyer, John Hirsh (Stratford
Festival), U.S. Senator S.I.
Hayakawa, Heather Robertson
(author).

DO'S AND DON'TS

DO check into "Simkin and Gallagher, Barristers and Solicitors" if
you run into legal trouble. Their well-appointed offices are smack in
the centre of the student union building.

DON'T run away if you see someone approaching you with the word
"Icebreaker" plastered across his chest. It's just an orientation
volunteer trying to make you feel welcome.

DO your best to stay cheerful during the month of January, when
average temperatures are around -15 degrees Celsius. Students
complain that avoiding depression in January is as difficult as pulling
off As in physics.

DON'T wait until the last moment to apply for a parking permit. The
best spots go fast and the worst spots are far, far away from
civilization. You want a good spot.

MEMORIAL

The campus pub at the Memorial University of Newfoundland is the
most profitable in the country. The Breezeway earns a quarter of a
million dollars a year from selling beer to the Munners. A $500,000
extension was tacked on in 1986, but the pub still can't hold all the thirsty
students. Hundreds line up on Wednesday through Saturday nights —
the Newfoundland weekend — hoping to get a seat.

In conversations about Memorial ("Mun" to the locals), smiling alumni and students all seem to pick on the same phrase again and again: "party school." "Very social," a third-year student shouts over the din in the Breezeway. "We have a lot of fun at this place," agrees his buddy, while ordering another beer.

Munners countenance no doubts about the social life of their university. No parties are louder, no dances wilder, no pub nights rowdier, they insist. And they may be right. Although there is something a bit weird about students having so much fun at a school located in a province with a 33 per cent youth-unemployment rate, fun they have.

Munners have more doubts about the academic quality of Memorial. They can't quite believe they have created something good. And even if they could believe it, they doubt that Mainlanders would. "I *think* I'm getting a good education here," says one hesitant business student.

It takes some struggling with one's prejudices to accept that Newfies have created a major Canadian university, yet, MUN has good facilities, wide course selections, and a strong faculty. A mandatory first-year general studies program helps students adjust to university life by postponing the need to declare a major. (The program also mitigates the consequences of spending your first year in the Breezeway.)

Of course, not every student falls instantly in love with the university. "Baymen," from coastal Newfoundland, often find St. John's bewildering, after having grown up in a town of 500 and attending high school in a two-room schoolhouse. Fortunately, they need never venture into the big city.

Night-life in St. John's is far from dull, but most students prefer to save their money and party on campus. The Breezeway's brew is the cheapest in town, and a weekend without several residence parties is like a weekend without rain. The courtyards and lobbies of residences must have been designed by an especially fun-loving architect: parties last all night and present great opportunities for "dragging off" someone new ("dragging off" is Newfie for "picking up"). MUN men invite MUN women to join them for a drive to Signal Hill — an historic fort offering a romantic view of St. John's — to "watch the submarine races." Which is just an elaborate way of asking a girl if she wants to go make out. It works.

The work week at Memorial begins on Sunday night and peters out by Wednesday afternoon. Then it's party time. Whee! The student council at MUN never worries about losing money on parties, even though with a budget of three and a half million dollars it can afford a lot of losses.

When they do venture out, discerning Memorial students prefer the cuisine of McDonald's, Burger King, and Harvey's as overture to a long night of drinking and dancing on George Street in the centre of St. John's. The Cornerstone is probably one of the nicest discos in the whole country. Pepper's, and Sun Dance, on nearby Water Street, are also popular. But take your pick. George Street is a street of nothing but bars. A very long street.

Dancing, drinking, and sex are the only truly accepted recreational activities at MUN. Poetry readings, opera, ballet, and *nouvelle vague* cinema are comparatively neglected. Tactful inquiries about sex at MUN get leering answers like: "Ohh boy! Are you kidding? There's not one girl here who isn't on the Pill." Or, "Well of course everybody does it, we're all adults here, aren't we?" A recent Decima poll showed that Newfoundlanders have sex more often than any other Canadians.

All that drinking and submarine-racing leave Munners little time for serious interest in politics or sports. Sports are especially unpopular because they lead to physical fitness, which interferes with smoking. But if the Munners lack political sophistication, they compensate with gracious sociability. Newfoundlanders may not actually be friendlier than other Canadians, but few campuses in the world can possibly be more warm, exuberant, and happy than Memorial's. It's hard to feel lonely at MUN. No wonder that its graduates, tossed into a crueler world, write letters to the school paper about how much they wish they'd never left.

This happy-go-lucky attitude sometimes bothers more activist Munners. The student council and the editors of *The Muse* worry that Munners never seem to get angry about anything, even issues that directly affect them. "Newfoundlanders have learned not to expect much," the student council president theorizes, "and they don't see the point in complaining."

Memorial is a relatively young university. It was founded in 1949 and unfortunately looks it. The campus's enormous red-and-yellow brick boxes look grotesque against the rugged beauty of the surrounding hills. Still, the university is not a total architectural disaster. The bold 1982 library uplifts the campus, and Paton College, (nine dorms done up in antique, New England-style — despite their construction date of 1960, the *annus horribilis* of Canadian university architecture) is even better.

Students who live off campus try to live as close to school as possible. Rent in St. John's is cheap, and rent on the outskirts near MUN is cheaper still. You can live in a rooming house for $100 a month. Shared apartments will cost about double that. Residences are a bargain, too, at about $264 a month, for a double room plus food. With a tuition of about

$1,000, MUN is a real buy, especially for foreign students. MUN is the only university in the country that doesn't exact extra fees from non-Canadians.

MUN gives little evidence that it's funded by Canada's most economically depressed province. A brand-new music building gave a big stimulus to the local red-brick and mundane-architecture industry. A new nursing school adjoins the hospital. Plans for a new earth-sciences building are well advanced. Memorial has also just acquired Atlantic Canada's only school of pharmacy. And the federal government has contributed the new Centre for Cold Ocean Resources.

Newfoundland's economic problems intrude, however, when 300 people are turned away from an already overcrowded introductory chemistry course. Or when all the best teachers desert the new music building because the university has no money left for their salaries.

In the old days, students of promise and students who could afford it escaped to Nova Scotia for university. Now, Newfoundlanders have a respectable educational institution of their own. They may go on to spend their graduate years at Dalhousie or in Ontario, but they will never be as happy again.

THE FACTS

Founded:	1949
Address:	Elizabeth Avenue St. John's, Newfoundland A1C 5S7
Tuition:	$1,056
Cut-off grade for general admission (per cent):	60
Enrolment:	14,529
Undergraduate full-time enrolment:	13,522
Percentage of foreign students:	1.3
Percentage of students from outside province:	6
Residence fees:	$2,220–2,480
Percentage of students in residence:	13

Male-female ratio:	43:57
Athletic facilities:	Sad.
Team name:	None.
Colours:	Maroon and white
Fraternities/sororities:	None.
Typical garb:	Jeans, lumberjack shirts, caps.
Campus political attitude:	Pro-parties.
Best-known fact:	It's the only university in Newfoundland.
Least-known fact:	It's the biggest school east of Montreal.
If you had to put it in one sentence:	"People come here for a good time. They don't care if they flunk out. There's always second year." —*MUN student*
Alumnus:	Brian Peckford.

DO'S AND DON'TS

DO check out MUN's Co-Op Programs in business, nursing, and engineering. They are among the most popular programs at Memorial.

DON'T use the women's field-hockey team's pitch under any circumstances. Yes, it's the only maintained pitch on campus. Yes, it's hardly ever used. And yes, you'll get thrown off it if you try.

DO refrain from burning *The Muse* in the tunnels. It makes a terrible mess.

DON'T think that you are going to get work done in the library. It is the favourite campus hangout after the Breezeway.

DO take a date for a drink at the nearby Playhouse Bar, if you want to get away from the hustle and bustle of the campus or if you don't want your best friend to know you are taking out his girl.

DON'T believe anyone who tells you the portables are temporary. They've been on campus for 15 years and are there to stay.

DO participate in the intramural ball hockey tournaments: they are an excellent way to meet new boys and girls.

MOUNT ALLISON

When you want to mail a letter to a friend at Mount Allison University, all you have to do is put your friend's name, "c/o Mount Allison U," on the envelope. Mount Allison is a very small university in a very small town.

There are only 1,769 students at "Mount A." People here say they prefer an intimate little college to a big, intimidating, impersonal institution like, say, Acadia. "That place is really getting huge," says one student in disgust. "They're more than twice our size now!"

The advantages of attending a small school are easy to think of: personal attention, accessibility, easy friendships, a sense of community, school spirit, and close contact with fellow students. Mount Allison has all these things. But some may feel they overdo it.

Take "close contact," for example. As one student recalls: "Last night at the pub, I realized I forgot to introduce the girl I was with to my friends. After she left, I said, 'I'm sorry, I forgot to introduce you guys to her,' and they replied, 'That's okay, her reputation precedes her.' "

Indeed, future Mount Allison students should be warned that from the moment they arrive on campus, everything they do will be noticed, remarked upon, and remembered by everyone else at Mount Allison. "It's very common for people to pick up nicknames on the first day of orientation week which last their whole college career," says the president of the student council. "Everybody knows what everybody else is doing, who they eat with, who they hang out with, and how they dress." And, warns a staffer who works with students: "Reputations are easily developed and they stick. If a girl comes and sleeps around a lot in the first few weeks of school, she's going to be stuck with that reputation the whole time she's here."

Despite its huge, hilly campus, cabin fever has been known to strike Mount A students. Happily, there's also a cozy awareness of superiority. "If there were an Ivy League in Canada, Mount A would be in it," says one student proudly. "Our image is very much like that of a private school," says another student. "Most students are from middle-class backgrounds, very few are on student loans, and we have a reputation for working hard."

Mount Allison has benefited greatly from the current heavy demand for university educations. With more students to choose from, Mount A can be more selective than most other schools in the region, notably UNB. It is certainly harder to be accepted by Mount A than by UNB.

Only 22 per cent of applicants make it. Over half of those chosen had at least an 80 per cent average in high school. Thanks to these statistics, the university has developed a relatively new reputation for academic seriousness.

"This used to be much more of a party school, a much more social place," says the student president. "But now, with the new stress on academic achievement in the admissions office, a new type of student is being accepted. Kids are a lot more serious than they used to be."

Along with the studious attitude come feelings of rivalry and academic jealousy. "There is a very competitive atmosphere here," says one confessedly average student. "Because students know each other so well, you know ahead of time how everyone else in the class will perform. Some people who always like to be at the top of the class check the class list before deciding whether or not to take a course. Depending on who they see, they will or won't sign up."

"At a school this size," says the student president, "you can't avoid competition. Anyway, I think it's healthy for standards. Sure, there is constant rivalry, and even sometimes a strange tension; but it promotes excellence and it's good preparation for the real world."

Not everyone loves the new, intense Mount A atmosphere. A men's group, the Polo Club, has declared war on what they think has been the undoing of the good ol' Mount A party spirit. The club hands out membership cards to those students who are committed to living it up the way college kids are supposed to. Their goal — "to wipe out apathy at Mount Allison" — by which they seem to mean "sobriety." In true Canadian fashion, the men of the Mount A Polo Club spend a lot of time worrying about how they can cease to be so dull.

No one in the administration building is terribly broken up over the excessive studiousness of their students. They kind of like the idea of teaching kids who want to learn. They think these kids have come to the right place. "The main advantage to studying at Mount Allison," says the dean, "is that you can tailor your degree to your own interests. There are no majors or minors, only concentrations, so that students can do a real mishmash of things." Everyone in arts and science has to take at least one credit in the humanities, social sciences, and sciences. But, says the dean of students, "we go for breadth and speciality here. We think you can do both."

At other universities, students complain about being treated like numbers. Mount Allison students don't even have student numbers — their teachers and deans make the effort to learn students' names. There is a 12:1 student-faculty ratio. Every student has a faculty adviser, who is usually prepared to take more than a passing interest in his charge.

Probably the most famous department at Mount Allison is the fine-arts department, where Alex Colville, Christopher Pratt, Steve Scott, and Paul Kelley got their start. Although these men are long gone from Mount Allison, their spirits remain. Music and commerce are also widely respected.

"What makes us special," says the dean of students, "is that we are involved in the total education of our students. We're not done with them at 5 o'clock. Students have the opportunity to experience many things." The student president, however, suggests that life at Mount A is not always exciting. "We have to make our own fun, since there's nothing here. You end up doing odd stuff, like playing party games. Last night we played charades." (*The Cosby Show* is also big.)

There are, of course, extracurricular activities on campus, and the university owns the only theatre in town, but it's not surprising that students are especially fond of their on-campus pub, the Tantramarsh Club. The pub is, in fact, a club in the true sense of the word. Only card-carrying members who have remembered to pay their dues get in.

Residence parties are another great pastime, especially because 65 per cent of the students live in residence. The McConnell Hall "beer gardens" are *le dernier cri* in Mount A entertainment. But, complains one student: "Someone came up with the beer garden idea about 10 years ago and that's the only kind of party we ever have. It's time for a new idea." In town, the favourite drinking spot is Steve's Tavern, and the favourite eating spot, Antonio's Pizza.

Luckily for the Polo Club, the old Mount A isn't all dead and gone: everybody still loves sports. Although everyone insists it's a fluke, the Mount Allison Football Mounties are the recent two-time winners of the Atlantic Bowl, and were second to the University of Calgary in the 1984 Vanier Cup. Most students participate on a team of some kind, whether varsity or intramural. And girls — the women's rugby team is the one to join if you're looking for attention. Reputed to have the brightest, most beautiful girls on campus, women's rugby plays to big crowds, "for reasons that don't always have to do with rugby."

Students love Mount Allison. The alumni are uncontainable. "Although it's corny, there really is such a thing as the Mount Allison family. I know my friends here are ones I'll keep forever." Mount Allison alumni are famous for their loyalty and largesse. Mount Allison receives more money from private sources on a percentage basis than any other school in Canada. "As a result of this," says the dean, "the school has acquired the reputation that it's rolling in money." Although the dean insists that in fact Mount A struggles along like every other Canadian institution, the struggle seems less cruel than elsewhere. But if the test of a university's success is its ability to make its students care about it even after they leave, then Mount Allison passes that test with a higher grade than any other university in Canada.

THE FACTS

Founded:	1839
Address:	Sackville, New Brunswick E0A 3C0
Tuition:	$1,530
Cut-off grade for general admission (per cent):	70
Average grade of entering class (per cent):	75
Enrolment:	1,769
Undergraduate full-time enrolment:	1,764
Percentage of foreign students:	.5
Percentage of students from outside province:	5
Residence fees:	$3,500–3,835
Percentage of students in residence:	65%
Male-female ratio:	47:53
Athletic facilities:	Good. Arena (seats 1,200).
Team name:	Mounties
Colours:	Garnet and gold
Fraternities/sororities:	None.
Typical garb:	"We're not terribly fashionable here." — *Student*
Campus political attitude:	Quietly and happily conservative.
Best-known fact:	It's hard to have a secret at Mount Allison.
Least-known fact:	The first woman to receive a

	Bachelor's Degree in the British Empire —Grace Anne Lockhart— graduated from Mount Allison in 1875.
If you had to put it in one sentence:	"They're filling this place with a lot of digit heads." — *Student*
Alumni:	John M. Buchanan (Premier of Nova Scotia), Christopher Pratt, Alex Colville, Harry Bruce (journalist), G. Wallace McCain (president of McCain Foods).

DO'S AND DON'TS

DO expect to be called a "freshette" if you are a first-year woman.

DON'T count on an extravagant orientation week. The theory here is, why meet everyone in your first week when, under your own steam, you'll meet them by your second?

DO expect to live in residence for at least two to three years if you are from out of town. Off-campus housing is very hard to get. There just don't seem to be a lot of extra houses in Sackville.

DON'T get too depressed about the lack of culture. The Owen Gallery, founded in Sackville in 1895, is the oldest painting gallery in eastern Canada. There's also Strut's Gallery, which is worth a visit, and a good place to go on a date.

I REMEMBER...

"Many people at Mount A have had a lasting effect on me, but two individuals in particular played a major part in my life while at university and made the university what it was. The first of these was the President at that time, Dr. Ross Flemington. He knew every student by first name, and was always available on campus, either for conversation, for an athletic event or any other situation that might arise. The second individual was Dr. Don MacLaughlin who was the dean of men. Dr. MacLaughlin spent most of his life at Mount A, and very little went on in residence or the university campus that he did not know about. He is fondly remembered by 'his boys,' individuals who went on to many positions of influence, not only within Canada, but in many parts of the world." — *John M. Buchanan*

MOUNT SAINT VINCENT

Mount Saint Vincent University wins the award for the most out-of-whack male-female ratio at a Canadian university: 84 per cent women, 16 per cent men. The president of the student council worries that "some women don't realize what they're getting themselves into. They know that women outnumber men but often they don't understand how radically."

Once upon a time Mount Saint Vincent, a former private Catholic school, was the only independent women's university in the British Commonwealth. Today, because it is a public university, it is unable to discriminate against either male or non-Catholic applicants, and so has a few of each. But if it can't refuse men and non-Catholics, it doesn't have to encourage them either.

The calendar makes it plain: "Although it now accepts men as non-resident students, Mount Saint Vincent University considers the educational needs of women to be paramount and therefore remains sensitive to the needs of women in an evolving society. Further, it believes there is a place for a university dedicated to promoting an environment characterized by a Catholic tradition."

Over half the 3,100 students are women 25 years or older who study part-time. "This is not a girl's finishing school," insists the student president. "Many women here are mature students. They live on their own or have families. They lead busy lives. They are trying to improve themselves in order to re-enter the work-force."

Mount Saint Vincent delicately blends its commitments to Catholicism and the rights of women. It calls the result "open-minded, conservative feminism." Margaret Fulton, the Mount's recently retired president, has formulated the school's complex political and religious position — a position which corresponds better to *Ms.* magazine than *Real Women.*

Take, for example, birth control. The school's health plan does not, unlike the plans at many other colleges, pay for contraceptives. But the Pill is not disapproved of at Mount Saint Vincent because the church forbids it, but because it's unhealthy. "Students are encouraged to use other forms of birth control," says one student. Non-doctrinaire feminism is every bit as much a doctrine as Catholicism.

Indeed, the school's position on sex was expressed thoughtfully by Sister Paule, who said in the school paper, *The Picaro*: "I hope the women of this university have the courage to say that while they don't deny the right of women to use contraceptives, that we, as a university dedicated to the education of women, want to project a different image [from that of sex object]. We want you to see us as human persons, with a great contribution to make, with an intellect, and a heart."

The ordination of female Roman Catholic priests, the place of women in the working world, the legitimacy of "women's studies," these are some of the other issues that the Catholic feminists of the Mount struggle with.

In a brochure sent out to prospective students, the Mount urges: "If you really want to succeed, get an IMPRACTICAL EDUCATION." But, although the university advocates a traditional liberal-arts and sciences education, and has solid departments in these areas, demand has impelled the school to aggressively lobby the provincial government for exclusive rights to professional training programs.

The most popular of these programs is public relations — the only PR degree in Canada. In this program you find the most men and the most non-Catholics. The school offers the only child-study degree in the Maritimes. And, in its most recent coup, the Mount won approval for the only Bachelor of Tourism and Hospitality Management degree outside Ontario.

The Mount is actually located not in Halifax, but in Rockingham, the area between Halifax and Dartmouth. The university's grounds are spacious, wooded, and peaceful. There is a nice blend of old and modern architecture. There is a limited number of residence spaces on campus, and they are fiercely sought after, despite the strict rules that accompany them. Most students must live off campus. The clever ones (who realize that Halifax is one of the worst places in the world to search for an apartment) opt for accommodation in Dartmouth. Some students commute all the way from Truro.

The campus bar, Vinnie's, is used during the week, but on weekends, girls from the Mount understandably prefer to go to Dalhousie or St. Mary's for fun.

The greatest problem facing women at the Mount is that people in Halifax refuse to take them seriously. "People assume there is a lower quality of education being offered here because it is a school for women," complains the student president. "And it's hard to get rid of that image." The image is indeed unfair. The Mount is a unique Canadian institution: a small, warm, modern university attempting to balance Catholicism, the promotion of women, and the liberal arts. How can that not be interesting?

THE FACTS

Founded: 1873

Address:	Halifax, Nova Scotia B3M 2J6
Tuition:	$1,550
Cut-off grade for general admission (per cent):	65
Average grade 12 mark of entering class (per cent):	72
Enrolment:	3,969
Undergraduate full-time enrolment:	2,176
Percentage of foreign students:	1.7
Percentage of students from outside the province:	13
Residence fees:	$3,300–3,651
Percentage of students in residence:	25
Male-female ratio:	16:84
Athletic facilities:	Fine.
Fraternities/sororities:	None.
Typical garb:	Sweats and billy-boots.
Campus political attitude:	Open-minded conservative feminism.
Best-known fact:	This used to be a women-only college.
Least-known fact:	It still is — basically — a women-only college.
If you had to put it in one sentence:	"We know this isn't a girl's finishing school. But we don't know how to convince the outside world of that." — *Student president*

DO'S AND DON'TS

DO keep abreast of events happening at Dalhousie and St. Mary's, as you'll be wanting to spend a lot of your free time there.

DON'T turn down your parents' offer of a car. Bus rides to the Mount can be long and slow.

DO order some dessert next time you eat at the Citadel Inn in Halifax. The pastry chef is a Mount grad.

DON'T despair about the Mount's library situation. Although the current one is small, a new one is on the way.

DO volunteer your services to the Women's Week Committee. They are usually desperate for help. "It's a bit embarrassing, a women's school with no one who ever wants to work on 'Women's Week.'"

UNIVERSITY OF NEW BRUNSWICK

In 1985 the University of New Brunswick celebrated the first bicentennial attained by a Canadian university. Sadly, at 202, UNB is academically inferior even to many of the instant schools of the 1960s. "Want to get an education? Then go somewhere else," quips an angry fourth-year student. "This is nothing more than a provincial technical school," quips another student. One UNB professor refers to his university as "a winter make-work project."

An indication of UNB's depressed state: at other schools, students and faculty become excited when discussing the university's researches into the causes of cancer, or its archaeological digs, or even its football team. At UNB, there is just one passionately argued topic: the flamboyant student council president, who was recently impeached by the administration and is now suing the university for wrongful dismissal.

"He's the most controversial student ever to attend UNB," according to the director of the alumni, and student opinions confirm this. "The question is, why isn't he in jail?" "He's a dictator." "He outclasses everyone here." "He's a great guy, best thing that ever happened to

UNB." "People are captivated by him." "All the little chickadees have a crush on him." The opinions about John Bosnitch and his lawsuit vary, but everybody at UNB — from the chancellor, to the janitors, to the newest freshmen — has an opinion about "The Boz."

"President Downey had a heart attack the day I was nominated for president for the third time," says Bosnitch rather cheerfully. "They had to rush him to the hospital, but he's okay now."

Bosnitch's detractors accused him of overspending, violations of the student council's constitution, power grabs, smear campaigns, and mismanagement. But what appalled them most was Bosnitch's plan for a party system for student council elections, requiring prospective student leaders to campaign in groups on detailed policy platforms.

Actually, it wasn't the proposal for a party system that caused the fuss so much as the character of Bosnitch's own party. Supporters of his "Students' Party" wore menacing red-and-black armbands. He himself took to wearing only black. His own remarkable charisma, the loyalty of his followers, and his naked but vague ambitions worried many UNB students, as well as the administration.

One day in April, 1986, Bosnitch arrived at his office to find that the locks had been changed, and another student installed student council president. He sued. His case has yet to be heard by the courts.

A defiant Bosnitch denies any bad intentions. "All we wanted to do was serve as an alarm clock for a very sleepy public. We wanted to shout: WAKE UP! We wanted to stir people into action, challenge them, make them think." Bosnitch sneers at the intellectual sloppiness of UNB, and complains that "the only word students at UNB can pronounce properly is the name of their brand of beer." This year, he leaves for McGill, where people can order their brand of beer in two languages, and UNB will never be the same. The loss of Bosnitch will be almost as debilitating as the loss, one year ago, of UNB's greatest love of all: booze.

"This used to be the best party school in the country," mourns one long-time student with a big memory. "But the administration is trying to change that. Too many people were getting killed in drinking accidents. One guy fell out of a window and killed himself just two weeks ago." "They've changed all the regulations," continues another student, "there's no more residence pubs, there's no drinking beer in hallways, all university-sponsored parties must be alcohol-free, orientation is a totally dry event, and any party with booze must have a licensed bartender. The campus bars aren't even allowed to advertise. There's great pressure to wipe out drinking altogether."

Students blame the alumni and the new president for the new sobriety. "President Downey has made himself very unpopular with his efforts to change the drinking rules at UNB," says a student journalist.

"The rules are stifling. You even need a permit to have a wine and cheese." Students suspect that the harsh new rules come from a sinister source. They claim that the power brokers of Fredericton, who also happen to own all the in-town drinking establishments, have pressured the administration into forcing drinking off campus. (I'm told you have to be from Fredericton to appreciate the plausibility of this argument.)

Still, the UNB administration deserves a great deal of credit for the more stringent academic requirements. "In the old days, if your GPA (grade point average) fell below a 2.0, you had a year to get it back up. Now they just boot you out. They're even getting rid of the bird courses. Russian Civilization 2040 and Psychology 1000 used to be the best. Not anymore. They've been toughened up. They actually give assignments now." Students say they notice a different kind of student at UNB these days: "The administration is trying to attract a student body that's here to study and do well."

Some programs at UNB are reasonably strong. The forestry program is generally considered to be one of the best in Canada, and engineering also has a good reputation. "Our survey engineering is the best in the world," the current student president maintains. "Our real strengths are in the technical and applied sciences. And history is probably our strongest humanities program. The main thing is that we're under-graduate-oriented, as opposed to a place like Dal."

UNB and St. Thomas together make up one of the loveliest campuses in this country. The remarkable feature of UNB is that all buildings conform to the original Georgian, red-brick design. There isn't one ugly building on the whole campus. It's a miracle.

The most interesting new building on campus is the Harriet Irving Library. Looming imposingly at the campus's main entrance, the library's impressive size and charming Georgian-style exterior would be a great monument to the munificence of the Irving family if the Irvings had had anything to do with the financing of the building. But they did not.

When the library was under construction, the university — in what it thought was a really clever move — decided to put Mrs. Irving's name on the building in an effort to embarrass the Irving family into forking out the dough to pay for it. But the Irvings are not easily embarrassed, especially since they have already given millions to the university for other projects. And so it stands there today, financed by taxpayers' money and named after the richest family in the province.

Some of the most wonderful-looking buildings on campus are the residences. They look like beautiful old mansions. Residence life can be very wild, and strong rivalries develop between houses. In fact, competition became so fierce that the university had to abolish inter-residence sports to prevent the violence. They also made residences co-ed so that the inter-dorm tensions would be of a more wholesome kind. And, complains one student, "there are quiet hours now. Gosh, we never had to have those before."

Is there any house spirit left? "Well," says one residence dweller, "sometimes the guys in Harrison and Bridges have rumbles. They yell nasty things to each other through their windows and then go out and wrestle. So that's spirit, I guess."

Most students live off campus, either with their parents or in nearby apartments. There is no student ghetto here, but Needham Street and the Skyline Acres apartments are popular choices. "But this is such a small community that no one ever has to be very far away," advises one student.

Although affordable housing is available close to campus, fashionable eating joints are not. "The closest place in town is a 20 minute walk," says the student president. The Deli on Regent, La Vie en Rose on King, and everybody's favourite, Pizza Patio are usually filled with UNB students. The student union building and pub also offer a wide selection of somewhat edible food and eminently potable drink.

One special attribute of UNB is its highly organized orientation week for freshmen. Modelled after the approach taken by many American schools, UNB's orientation week is a varied and tightly structured event that offers something for everybody: frosh, parents, foreign students, and the handicapped.

Although UNB does not remotely live up to its administration's academic claims, an education can still be had here. And, despite the clamp-down on drinking, UNB remains one of the wildest party schools in the country. Take a look at the window of a Jones House resident for proof. Posted in his window alongside a pyramid of 200 or more beer cans a hand-lettered sign reads: Looks good? Tasted great!

THE FACTS

Founded:	1785
Address:	PO Box 4400 Fredericton, New Brunswick E3B 5A3
Tuition:	$1,575
Cut-off grade for general admission (per cent):	70
Enrolment:	7,809

Undergraduate full-time enrolment:	6,339
Percentage of foreign students:	6
Percentage of students from outside the province:	21
Residence fees:	$3,140–3,385
Percentage of students in residence:	25
Male-female ratio:	58:42
Athletic facilities:	Excellent. Arena seats 4,000.
Team name:	Ironmen, Red Blazers, Red Shirts … depending on the sport.
Team colours:	Red and black
Fraternities/sororities:	None.
Typical garb:	Lumberjacket shirts, jeans.
Campus political attitude:	Never trust student politicians.
Best-known fact:	UNB students love to party.
Least-known fact:	This is the oldest university in Canada.
If you had to put it in one sentence:	"This used to be a beer and pizza campus, but someone is trying to turn this place into a serious school." —Angry student
Alumni:	Thor and Fredrik S. Eaton, John Bassett Jr., Anne Murray, Dalton Camp.

SAINT THOMAS

In theory, St. Thomas University is distinct from UNB, but in practice, St. Thomas is simply UNB's Catholic college. Located on the grounds of UNB, the school was originally founded to educate high-school-age Catholic boys. Today it serves an almost exclusively female undergraduate student body. "The relationship is much like King's at Dalhousie, or Huron at Western," explains St. Thomas's female student president. "When I first got here, I spent a lot of time trying to convince people that St. Thomas was different from UNB. Most people think it's the same, but it's not."

Unlike King's or Huron, St. Thomas is a full-fledged university, offering its own degrees. But St. Thomas and UNB share a library, a student union building, a pub, a gymnasium, a bookstore, and, from time to time, residences. The distinctions blur. St. Thomas students may take courses at UNB and vice versa, but, warns the student president, "there's a limit to how many."

Over half the students at St. Thomas are Catholic, and these students must take a religious-studies course before they graduate. "The great thing about St. Thomas," says the student president, "is that we get all the advantages of bigness from UNB, added to the advantages of smallness that any school of 1,266 is going to have. When you go in to see your prof, it's 'Hi, how are you,' not, 'Do I know you?'"

The other great advantage of St. Thomas, say cynics, is that it is the easiest school in Canada to get into. "I know someone who got in with a grade-nine education. People go to STU if they can't get in anywhere else. All you have to do is go see Father Martin. If he likes you, he'll take care of you." STU's student president concedes that people at UNB love referring to St. Thomas students as "STU-pid."

The best-known character at STU is not a menacing student leader but an eccentric professor. Philosophy professor Leo Fererra founded and runs the "Flat Earth Society of the World." Professor Fererra believes that the theory the earth is round is "the most incredible hoax in the history of the world." He begins his class each year by asking how many of his students believe in the fraudulent theory. When all the students put up their hands, Professor Fererra shakes his head and exclaims, "Oh boy! Do I ever have a lot of work to do this term."

St. Thomas has its own newspaper and its own student council. Occasionally they throw their own parties, but with a student population that is two-thirds female, no St. Thomas party is a success unless a lot of UNB boys show up.

Although it is generally recognized that UNB is more prestigious, students say that for education and social work St. Thomas is the better (and in the case of social work, only) choice. "People transfer back and forth between the two schools all the time," says the student president. "Each school has its specialities and so sometimes a student needs to transfer."

The other favourite joke about St. Thomas is that it is "the high school on the hill," but many "Stewies" feel that the school's similarity to a high school is its best attribute. "The spirit here is contagious," says one student. "People are so supportive of each other, it's so easy to make friends. It's a great atmosphere."

THE FACTS

Founded:	1910
Address:	PO Box 4569 Fredericton, New Brunswick E3B 5G3
Tuition:	$1,355
Cut-off grade for general admission (per cent):	60
Enrolment:	1,569
Percentage of foreign students:	1.5
Percentage of students from outside the province:	9
Undergraduate full-time enrolment:	1,269
Residence fees:	$2,740–3,390
Percentage of students in residence:	40
Male-female ratio:	35:65

UNB/ST. THOMAS DO'S AND DON'TS

DO be careful who you have in your room after midnight. St. Thomas residences fine girls $25 for having male visitors after hours.

DON'T worry if Fredericton makes you stir-crazy. Many students make weekend trips to Montreal (6–8 hour drive), Halifax (4–5 hours), Boston (6 hours), and Bangor (3 hours).

DO be sure to witness the great Pumpkin Sacrifice on Hallowe'en night... a top partying evening at UNB.

DON'T ask where the football team is. It's a very sore subject around here. UNB used to be a football great until budget cuts ended all that.

I REMEMBER...

"When I first went to UNB, I thought "These people are really smart, they know what school I went to before UNB." They'd all come up to me and say: 'You're from Upper Canada, eh?' I soon learned about the Maritimes and Maritimers and I learned to appreciate the differences that make Canada great. UNB was great for me. I'd recommend it for anybody who wants the friendliness and openness that a smaller university offers. Some of the best days of my life were spent there!" — *Fredrik S. Eaton*

UNIVERSITY OF OTTAWA

At the University of Ottawa, bilingualism is not just a cheap political gimmick. It *is* that, of course, but it's also a cherished principle and a thoroughly implemented ideal. Unfortunately for the university, bilingualism seems not to be cherished by anyone else. Prospective Québécois students assume that a bilingual university in Ontario must be an artfully disguised English university; wary English Canadians read "bilingual" as code for French.

"We have a phenomenal image problem," concedes the director of admissions. "Students don't understand what we're about. It's difficult to persuade them to apply."

Confusion over what Ottawa is about is not unique to prospective students. The administration can't make up its mind. On the one hand, it propounds as its goals: "the furthering of bilingualism and biculturalism" and "the preservation and development of French culture in Ontario." On the other hand, it also makes sure that possible applicants get a copy of its brochure, *Bilingualism and You*, with the following reassuring message: "APPLICANTS [the capitals are theirs] NEED NOT BE BILINGUAL TO BE ADMITTED TO THE UNIVERSITY OF OTTAWA. SECOND LANGUAGE COMPETENCE DOES NOT ENTER INTO THE ADMISSION DECISION. EXAMINATIONS, REPORTS AND ASSIGNMENTS CAN NORMALLY BE SUBMITTED IN THE OFFICIAL LANGUAGE OF YOUR CHOICE."

The University of Ottawa has even retreated from its old demand that its students prove proficiency in a second language by graduation. The language tests have not, it is true, been formally abolished, but "they're so simple they're just a joke." "Yes, I passed my French proficiency exam," admits one young man from PEI, "but can I speak French? No."

Any student who does attempt to become bilingual will find Ottawa an easy place in which to succeed. The admissions director proudly claims that "a student can come here with not one word of French and three years later he can carry on a French conversation — no problem."

If exposure to French (or English) doesn't persuade you to come to Ottawa, not much else will. Blame economics. U of O teaches virtually every course twice, once in English and once in French — an expensive way to run a university. And so, Ottawa finds excelling in anything other than Canadian linguistic ideals prohibitively costly. "Bilingualism," a student explains, "is the reason this place exists. We want to get into all that high-tech business and science stuff, but not at the expense of bilingualism." If you seek modern labs and nationally known professors, look elsewhere. One program, however, is acclaimed: translation. Lucky translation graduates find their employer right down the street.

Many students choose Ottawa because of the wonderful career opportunities it offers to aspiring bureaucrats. And not only will there be jobs after graduation, but in Canada's only recession-proof city, it's easy to work through college. "There is such an enormous service industry here that you just have to knock on the door of any restaurant and you'll get hired on the spot."

A school full of future civil servants is not likely to be a flamboyant place. One disappointed student describes his classmates as "sedate." At five minutes past five, this campus in the middle of downtown Ottawa looks a little like Dawson City the day after the gold ran out. Be prepared for a social life that will develop only slowly. Can you study here for four years and not make one friend? "Oh yeah, it's been done," acknowledges a student journalist. Another dissatisfied customer says: "It's not that I expected them to roll out a red carpet for me or anything, but I did expect more. If you want anything on this campus, if you want to meet people, you have to go to them. They won't come to you." A woman who has since transferred to Carleton says: "I tried being friendly at first. When I was in the bookstore line the first day of class, I tried talking to the people around me. But they were all French and I can't speak anything but English. So right away there was this brick wall. Boom. It was frustrating that we couldn't communicate, and I know they felt the same way." A Maritimer concludes: "This university is very much like the city itself. It's very cold, very closed, very inaccessible. You come here because you are attracted to the idea of being in the nation's capital, but that world is very hard to penetrate."

It is true that during your years at U of O it is unlikely you'll ever get invited for cocktails at 24 Sussex Drive or to a garden party at Rideau Hall, but there is still much about Ottawa that is ideally suited to student life. The Rideau Canal flows through town just a few steps from the downtown campus; in fact, during the winter, some students skate to school. The National Arts Centre, the National Museum, the Sparks Street mall, Byward Market, and Parliament Hill are just blocks from the campus.

The University of Ottawa was a Catholic university until its forced secularization in 1965. Because of the abrupt transformation, a student journalist believes "it's unfair to judge us as an old school." Even though Ottawa's predecessor, Bytown College, was founded 138 years ago, "this university feels, and, of course, looks very new. It began fresh in 1965. The sad part is we lost a lot of our great traditions. The most beautiful building on campus, the chapel, had its pews removed and it's now used for French tests. The special requiem masses aren't put on anymore. Graduation ceremonies are now conducted in English, rather than in Latin like the old days."

But Catholic remnants persist. There is no anthropology department. The United Way did not campaign on campus until 1985. The smoke-stack atop the university's physical plant (built the year after secularization) is transversed by concrete slabs, to make the chimney appear to be a crucifix from every angle.

Secularization and bilingualism have not entirely extirpated old animosities. When asked his opinion of Carleton, a student just smouldered. "What do I think of Carleton? You mean what do I think of a university that was built so that a bunch of Protestant, Anglo, rich preppies could be spared the experience of going to school with a bunch of French Catholics? Is that what you mean?"

Still, most of the rivalry between Ottawa and Carleton is friendly. The recruiting officers from the two schools even travel together. "We each have a different clientele. We're not in competition with each other for students."

The rivalry erupts once a year, during the annual Panda Trophy Football game, when the Ottawa Gee-Gees play their arch-rivals, the Carleton Ravens. Ottawa aggressively insists that "this is the best university party in Canada. Queen's, Western, McGill can hide their heads in the sand." (For details see the chapter on Carleton.)

The best recent news at Ottawa is that a new residence is planned. It's too early to know whether new dormitories will enliven the ghostliness of the campus after five, but at least they will release several hundred students from the hell of looking for an apartment in one of the hottest neighbourhoods in one of the country's toughest rental markets.

In fashionable Sandy Hill, Ottawa students must battle wealthier yuppies, civil servants, and speculators for shelter. Be warned: "With all the gentrification going on around campus, don't expect to find anything reasonable any closer than 10 miles away from school." There are over 3,500 applications for the 1,300 dormitory rooms, and those rooms are reassigned every year.

For entertainment, the most famous whooping-it-up spot in Ottawa is, of course, not in Ottawa but in Hull, Quebec. Ottawa and Hull, it is said, "have clubs for every sort of person. There's Hoolihan's for swingers, Zeebra and Zink for the self-consciously hip people." This informant adds that "the Equinox [on campus] is popular for those who like to throw it back during the day. There are even those who go to the Chateau Laurier to sip tea. I also have it on very good authority that this is a good campus on which to be gay."

Despite its age, sophistication, complicated history, and linguistic politics, the University of Ottawa, like everything in this town, "has an inferiority complex like you would not believe. The richest and brightest kids from Ottawa go away to Queen's. The ones who stay feel put down."

To make up for the psychological toll it inflicts, the University of Ottawa gives you the Rideau Canal, a chance to learn a second language, and a whiff of power in the air.

THE FACTS

Founded:	1848
Address:	Ottawa, Ontario K1N 6N5
Tuition:	$1,428
Cut-off grade for general admission (per cent):	70
Average grade 13 mark of entering class (per cent):	73.5
Enrolment:	20,687
Undergraduate full-time enrolment:	11,312
Percentage of foreign students:	2.7

Percentage of students from outside the province:	21
Francophones:	41.6
Anglophones:	47.2
Residence fees:	$1,318–1,550
Percentage of students in residence:	11
Male-female ratio:	50:50
Athletic facilities:	Good.
Team name:	Gee-Gees
Colours:	Garnet and grey
Fraternities/sororities:	None.
Typical garb:	Slight French influence: dangling earrings for men and women, lots of bracelets, short haircuts.
Campus political attitude:	Pro-French, pro–civil service.
Best-known fact:	This is Canada's oldest and biggest bilingual university.
Least-known fact:	The team name, "Gee-Gees," comes from shortening "Garnet and Grey" (or "Grenat et Gris").
If you had to put it in one sentence:	"I think everyone who had no school spirit in high school came here."—*Student*
Alumni:	Hon. Jean-Luc Pepin, Maureen McTeer, Paul Desmarais, Hon. Robert de Cotret, Roger Hamel (president of Canadian Chamber of Commerce), Mary-Lou Finlay, Alex Trebec.

DO'S AND DON'TS

DO come to U of O for the unique opportunity to study common and civil law at the same time.

DON'T expect a lot by way of orientation-week events. "Frosh week knocked my socks off . . . because there wasn't one."

DO conduct your business with the administration in French, if you can. Things go much faster that way (especially at registration), since most U of O staffers are native francophones.

DON'T worry about how to transport your heavy groceries to your residence kitchen (Ottawa residences have no meal plan). A free shuttle bus runs every Thursday from Stanton and Leblanc residence to a Loblaws store in Vanier.

DO go to the engineers' TGIF pubs. They are the most lively events on campus and people line up to get in.

DON'T bother running for the student government unless your French is up to scratch. By tradition, most student council business is conducted in that language.

UNIVERSITY OF PRINCE EDWARD ISLAND

At UPEI, your body is incomplete unless the letters U, P, E, and I appear on it somewhere. Don't worry about finding the insignia — the bookstore may not stock T.S. Eliot's poems or Creighton's histories, but it is crammed with UPEI sweaters, UPEI shorts, UPEI tee-shirts, UPEI jewellery, and UPEI sweatpants, as well as UPEI mugs, UPEI bumper stickers, UPEI paperweights, UPEI pens, UPEI stationery, UPEI plates, and UPEI key-chains — all so you can tell the world that you're damn proud to be at Prince Edward Island's only university.

When asked whether the bookstore sells more books or clothes, a saleswoman responds with amusement: "Definitely clothes."

UPEI calls itself a "teaching college." What that means is that the university does not do any research, or development, or experimental work. It simply teaches students what's in the textbooks. According to an Ottawa-based student organizer: "UPEI is a classic picture of under-funding. They don't have the money to be any better than a high school."

An ambitious physics professor once tried to change that with a nifty project that would at the same time be academically exciting and financially profitable: he would build Atlantic Canada's first planetarium at the gate of UPEI. He succeeded in raising the money, only to discover once his planetarium opened that no one else on the island had the slightest interest in such a thing, not even the tourists. The planetarium now stands empty at the entrance to the college. One must say, however, that it looks very sharp in the promotional brochures.

UPEI is an ambitious university struggling to do a decent job on a small, poor island. The legislature created it in 1969 by forcing Protestant Prince of Wales College (founded in 1834) and Catholic St. Dunstan's University (founded in 1855) to merge into a single non-sectarian university located on the beautiful, historic St. Dunstan's campus. Neither school was thrilled, and to this day it is unsafe to argue religion or politics with the many professors who even now think of themselves as either St. Dunstan's or Prince of Wales men.

UPEI students, on the other hand, could not care less about either religion or politics. "We're not completely apolitical," insists a former student president. "We did raise $2,000 for Ethiopia this year. But the motto around here is just smile and have a good time."

People at UPEI do like to talk about sports, especially soccer, basketball, and hockey. School spirit, or "Panther Pride," as it is called here in "the home of the Panthers," is tremendous. Many students can remember when it seemed that the Panthers never won a game — ever. But today, for reasons which no one seems to understand, they are winning all the time. "UPEI is now known for its sports teams," says the current student president proudly. "The whole community comes to watch us play hockey — we play in the Charlottetown arena. That's partly because the town loves us and partly because our own arena is about to be condemned."

Most of the Panthers' fans are women. Many of these women are at UPEI for reasons that have nothing to do with education. "A lot of the girls come here just to get married, especially the ones from the rural areas who want to do better for themselves. I don't know if they get what they want," says one young man.

The urge to marry may explain why UPEI women are such sports fans. But what can explain the predilection of UPEI men for dressing up as women? At the annual "Kloset Queen Contest," dozens of otherwise normal — and, one assumes, sexually confident — young men compete in a bizarre beauty contest, wearing panty-hose, padded bras, dresses, high heels, and lots of Cover Girl. Don't despair if you lose, boys! You can always try out for a position with the Pantherettes, a male cheerleading squad, that, yup, dresses up as girls. If you fail even at that, there's the annual Hallowe'en party, to which men are pretty much obliged to wear lingerie.

Looking good in lingerie, while important to a young man's social life at UPEI, does not even begin to compare with going to the right high school. Rural students resentfully describe UPEI as "Colonel Grey North" — Colonel Gray South being Charlottetown's high school. Colonel Grey graduates seem to run almost all organized student life. Rural and suburban students avoid each other.

The faculty societies mitigate these social divisions to some extent. The business and biology students are the most active, but the engineers (as usual) have the most fun with their "corn boils" and lively pub nights. The cliques meet in "Carrelville" on the second floor of Robertson Library. Here, in the long orange rows of study carrels, students gather to gossip and goof around. A "mayor" of Carrelville is elected annually. The true centre of excitement at UPEI, however, is an old barn, now renovated as the student union. Since only one-quarter of the students live on campus, the Barn is vital to student life. At the Barn, students drink, watch movies, discover the joy of victory and the agony of defeat in lip-sync contests, celebrate Panther wins, or simply hang out when they have nothing better to do. There are some residence parties during the year but the really big bashes are thrown in the Barn.

Ninety per cent of UPEI students are from PEI. Most either live at home with their parents or in an apartment in Charlottetown. (Lucky ones find an apartment in the Mary's Field area.) There are three residences on the campus: for women, big, modern, Bernardine Hall; for men, Marion Hall, small and Georgian; and for both, apartment-style housing in Blanchard Hall or on the "quiet floor" of Bernardine.

Just beyond the residences lies fast-food heaven. The choice — A & W, McDonald's, Arby's, Burger King, Mothers, Pizza Shack, Tim Horton Donuts — is bewildering. Although it is hard to believe that anyone would ever get tired of this selection, students do sometimes eat at restaurants with menus, especially Caeser's Italy, Casa Mia, or Smitty's. For drinking, dancing, and meeting new people ("Sometimes you get desperate to see new faces," says one senior) there's Gentleman Jim's in the K-Mart Plaza, and Father's Lounge close to campus. Students with cars, who are eager to escape from campus, frequent bars near the harbour, especially Myron's Pub, the Trade Winds Lounge, and the Hideaway.

Until 1986, UPEI only bestowed undergraduate degrees. Now there are two graduate degrees available: a two-year Master of Science degree and a seven-year Doctor of Veterinary Medicine degree. The new veterinary school — one of four in the whole country — is the pride of UPEI, even though it was financed by the federal government and belongs to the whole Maritime region. UPEI won it after fierce lobbying. Places at the school will be distributed among students from all the Atlantic provinces.

Despite the new vet school, arts remains the most popular faculty. UPEI also offers the usual assortment of majors, including business administration, Canadian studies, education, home economics, and music. UPEI knows its limits, but its fortunes, like those of its athletic teams, are on the rise. Someday, maybe the whole country will know about the Kloset Queen contest.

THE FACTS

Founded:	1969
Address:	Charlottetown, PEI C1A 4P3
Tuition:	$1,480
Cut-off grade for general arts admissions (per cent):	60
Enrolment:	1,837
Full-time undergraduate enrolment:	1,785
Percentage of foreign students:	1.4
Percentage of students from outside the province:	10
Residence fees:	$2,942–3,344
Percentage of students in residence:	25
Male-female ratio:	47:53
Athletic facilities:	Poor.

Team name:	(M) Panthers (F) Lady Panthers
Colours:	Green, white and rust
Most popular major:	Home ec, Canadian studies
Fraternities/sororities:	None.
Typical garb:	Jeans, sportswear, anything with "UPEI" blasted all over it.
Campus political attitude:	What are politics?
Best-known fact:	UPEI is located in one of Canada's favourite vacation spots.
Least-known fact:	Canada's youngest B.Sc. ever, Tony Lai (age 14), is a UPEI graduate, class of '86. (He also received the school's Governor General Award for top grades.)
If you had to put it in one sentence:	"I have no problem communicating with other students, since no one communicates with me anyway." — *Tony Lai*
Alumni:	**St. Dunstan's:** Mike Duffy (CBC National News), John MacDonald (CEO, Nabisco Foods), James Lee, **Prince of Wales:** Lloyd MacPhail.

DO'S AND DON'TS

DO bring your ladies' attire, men. You'll want to compete in all the exciting transvestite events.

DON'T fail to be seen hanging out at the "Pit Stop" in the basement of Robertson Library. You can bring or buy your lunch and can be sure to spot lots of your friends avoiding work there.

DO remember to bring flattering formal wear with you to school, so you can compete in the Winter Carnival King and Queen contest.

DON'T bother applying to the UPEI vet school if you are not from one of the Atlantic provinces. Although the differential fee of $26,685 has been withdrawn, upper Canadians are still not very welcome.

QUEEN'S

"Cream of the crop," "Canada's élite," "young achievers," "a cut above": these are the phrases Queen's students use when asked to describe themselves. Queen's students have never been known for their modesty. "As far as I am concerned," says one typical Queen's freshman, "there's no other university in Canada."

Queen's students are absolutely head over heels in love with their school, not to mention themselves. But while one may admire the profound loyalty and blind adoration Queen's students have for their alma mater, it's harder to be enthusiastic about their arrogance and snobbery. Ask a Queen's student and he'll tell you earnestly that people at Queen's are smarter, prettier, stronger, happier, friendlier, livelier, and smell better than people at other schools.

"Face it," says one recent graduate, "no other school in Canada has what we've got." Okay, okay, she's got a point. Queen's is certainly one of Canada's best universities. Founded in 1841, Queen's is a wealthy school with old traditions, high standards, and a powerful group of alumni who treat each other as members of a private club.

Perhaps the greatest advantage of Queen's is that there is a truly collegiate atmosphere here. Queen's is a unified, self-sufficient, isolated community in the tradition of America's pastoral colleges, which explains why you'll often hear Queen's students refer to their school as "the Princeton of Canada." (Let's hope Princeton doesn't find out about this.)

The chief attraction of Queen's to most students is its reputation for élitism. Not academic élitism but social élitism. Since this social élite can be oppressive, it is important to know if you are the real "Queen's type." To help you decide, here are some questions you should ask yourself.

Number one: Am I blonde? (It doesn't matter how you do it, naturally or with chemicals, but it is important to have an overall look of whiteness and brightness.)

Number two: Did I go to private school? A private-school education is important. For one, it will ensure that you already know the fundamentals of preppy dressing. Two, it will mean you can join the private-school clique (which admits students from any private school found in Vancouver, Toronto, or Montreal), thereby avoiding the trauma and/or boredom of making new friends.

Question number three, which is connected to question number two, is: Am I rich? "Having lots of cash," as one Queen's student puts it, is very key. Queen's is the kind of place where people jog in sweat-shirts that promote Midland Doherty (I swear), and have "Poverty Sucks" posters on their walls.

Of course not everybody at Queen's is blonde, from a private school, rich, and obnoxious. It only seems that way. As the editor of the *Queen's Journal* (the student newspaper) explains: "That group is simply more visible because they're louder, drunker, better looking, and spend less time in class than other people. But the fact is, there are more people who don't belong to that group than do, and I think they are just as happy here."

He's got a point. It sure is hard to find an unhappy Queen's student. Whether you ask the group of Chinese students whose separate, and sparsely attended, Saturday night dances seem to place them on the fringe of Queen's society, or the hippyish, granola-eating, peacenik folk who hang out at Tara's Whole Foods, they're all willing to talk about just how much they love the place.

One reason for this is that the Queen's administration is very good at promoting the idea of Queen's superiority. When the associate dean of arts welcomes freshmen by stating, "You are part of a highly select group of fifteen hundred students who will begin their studies this September in our faculty," Queen's students feel reassured. They feel that their uniqueness has been recognized.

Yet, students would be wrong to get carried away. Not everyone is of the same mind as the dean. It was the chairman of Queen's English department who reported to the *Queen's Journal* last fall that, "...remarkably few students are fully literate. In fact, fully one third of first-year students at Queen's have serious writing problems when they enter university."

But even if it turns out that Queen's students are just as illiterate as students in all other Canadian universities, they shouldn't feel too let down. There are, in fact, some areas in which Queen's students are legitimately superior. School spirit, for example. Any Canadian student, no matter how loyal to his own university, will respectfully acknowledge that Queen's fans are unsurpassed in the areas of rowdiness, vivacity, and general enthusiasm. It doesn't matter that Queen's' football stadium is a good mile from main campus. Nothing short of a nuclear war would prevent thousands of purple-painted, jumpsuit-clad Queen's fans from watching the Golden Gaels trounce or be trounced: it really doesn't matter. The Golden Gaels enjoy unconditional love.

Wherever a Golden Gaels game is played, you can always count on hundreds of bussed-in fans, all looking forward to a good "sports hump." The sports hump is a Queen's invention whereby innocent and unsuspecting spectators are grabbed, tackled, and tossed onto a huge mound of squirming bodies.

Another area in which Queen's leads the way is in its legendary rough-and-tumble orientation festivities. In orientation week Queen's students go all out to emulate summer camp. The campus is decorated with bed-sheets reading "Kiss your virginity goodbye," and the fun just never ends. Students are blasted with gushing fire-hoses, their heads are shoved into huge reusable bowls of Jell-O and aren't freed until they blow bubbles into it. (Good thing Queen's students are too clean to have communicable diseases.) And then there's the famous grease pole: engineering students attempt to climb a slime-covered telephone pole that has been erected in a pool of cold water, paint, mud, and marshmallows. (In past years, some dead animals have been thrown into the mixture.) There is even a special organizational group called "Trash" who make sure transfer students aren't left out of the fun.

Another terrific advantage of Queen's is Kingston itself. While most people know it as Canada's criminal incarceration capital, it is in fact a beautiful, graceful, and lively college town. There are many more interesting restaurants, bars, food, and bookstores here than in some of Canada's larger cities (Ottawa, for example). And, with RMC and St. Lawrence College in town, local proprietors have an interest in meeting student tastes and needs.

Some favourite hangouts are Dollar Bills in the Prince George Hotel; the Tap Room, an old haunt of John A. Macdonald's; Whiskers; and the new, neon Cocamo's. For eating out — something most Queen's students can afford to do — the list includes the Copper Penny, Stoney Street, Minos, Poor George's and Ruby's. Prices at these restaurants are reasonable and the decor is up-to-the-minute urban. For special occasions, such as a visit from parents, or when, to quote a campus journalist, "Buffy and Janie want to celebrate the first blissful year of their meaningful relationship," Chez Piggy's, Kingston's most elegant dining room despite its name, is always the choice.

No place is more popular, however, than the three on-campus pubs: Alfies, the Quiet Pub, and the Clark Hall engineer's pub. "We are very campus-centric," says a student explaining their popularity. You can always expect line-ups at these pubs, especially on weekends, but that's all part of the experience. In fact, when there isn't a queue, students can be heard to complain: "Hey! What happened to the line-up!"

But what most students seem to love best about Queen's is its giant playground atmosphere. Since over 90 per cent of its students come to Queen's from someplace other than Kingston, almost every one of Queen's' 10,000 undergraduates lives away from home, from parents, from rules.

Almost all freshmen live in residence during their first year. There's room for 2,600 in the 10 campus dormitories, which range in size from

Victoria Hall for 769 women to 152 Albert Street, which houses 11. After first year, students group up and move into one of the hundreds of charming, wooden-porched houses that make up the student ghetto (radiating east and west from University Avenue).

Ghetto life is the focal point of all social activity. On weekends, dozens of house parties are thrown, and hosts are easy about who walks in. It is perfectly okay to roam the ghetto with your friends searching for a good party. You will probably be welcome whether the hosts know you or not. The biggest and best parties are the street parties, when whole streets full of ghetto dwellers combine forces.

Queen's has strong departments in almost all arts and science fields. In addition to the usual concentrations (at Queen's you don't have a "major," you have a "concentration"), programs are offered in drama, classical studies, computing and information studies, health, Greek, Latin, and something called "Image of Man in Modern Literature," which is separate from plain old English.

The commerce department is the most exclusive, and graduates are considered to have credentials equal to those from Western's School of Business. The Queen's engineering department, notorious thanks to the boisterous reputation of its students, is considered inferior to that of Waterloo and U of T.

More than anything, Queen's has long been famous for its intimate relationship to the Canadian civil service. The university has supplied manpower, research, and expertise to all parties for many years. As a result, the political-studies and economics departments are enormously prestigious.

Queen's has very competitive entrance requirements. While their calendar stipulates a minimum grade of 60 per cent, the truth is that few students with averages lower than 75 per cent are admitted. In the case of the commerce program, nothing less than 82 per cent will do. Some students who are especially eager to attend Queen's but lack the marks, apply for part-time status or to the music or fine-arts programs, which are the only departments for which a 65 per cent average may suffice.

Queen's' rich endowment is obvious to any observer. The campus is densely packed with facilities, modern and antique. Everything about Queen's, its gym, library, labs, classrooms, bookstore, student centre, art gallery, recreational facilities, is of excellent quality. The only problem is that you have to like grey. The whole campus is constructed of Kingston limestone, which, on a rainy day, can turn even the most cheerful soul melancholy.

Queen's is one of the few places in Canada that students choose to attend, not because it's close, but because they *want* to be there. "We all feel we're so damned lucky to be here, and Queen's does a good job of making us all feel special," sums up the editor of the *Queen's Journal*, who happens to be from Vancouver. "This isn't just some place where I got my degree. Queen's was my home and the place where I will always feel welcome."

THE SPORTS HUMP

1.   2.   3.

"The sports hump is a Queen's invention whereby innocent and unsuspecting spectators are grabbed, tackled, and tossed onto a huge mound of squirming bodies."

THE FACTS

Founded:	1841
Address:	Kingston, Ontario K7L 3N6
Tuition:	$1,264
Cut-off grade for general admission:	mid-70s
Average grade 13 mark of entering class:	78.8
Enrolment:	15,000
Undergraduate full-time enrolment:	9,700

Percentage of foreign students:	4
Percentage of students from outside the province:	12
Residence fees:	$3,730–4,976
Percentage of students in residence:	26
Male-female ratio:	50:50
Athletic facilities:	Excellent. Stadium merely okay. Arena.
Team name:	Golden Gaels
Colours:	Red, gold, and blue
Coolest major:	Commerce. (We're going to be rich!)
Uncoolest major:	Film. (They'll never get a job.)
Fraternities/sororities:	None.
Typical garb:	Expensive casual clothing. Queen's gold-leather jackets for engineers.
Campus political attitude:	Let's ease into our conservatism slowly.
Best-known fact:	Queen's is Canada's snootiest school.
Least-known fact:	The first student AM radio station was started at Queen's in 1921.
If you had to put it in one sentence:	"Queen's is about as far removed from the real world as you can get." — *Graduate*
Alumni:	Lorne Greene, Gerald Bovey, Isabel Bassett, John C. Crosby, Hon. James Kelleher, Fraser Elliott (of Stikeman, Elliott), Robertson Davies.

DO'S AND DON'TS

DO drop the name of Sandi Ferran, the second-year Queen's history major who became Miss Eastern Ontario 1986, when boasting about how Queen's has the prettiest girls. (Need I mention she's a blonde?)

DON'T fail to spend as much time as possible hanging out at the nearby beachfront of lake Ontario. There is a paved footpath for romantic, moonlit walks, and lots of green grass for Frisbee tournaments.

DO look for the Moosehead beer cap on the head of the Socrates bust in the library...an example of a witty Queen's joke.

DON'T pretend you never read the engineers' paper, *The Golden Words*. Yes, it's vulgar and crude, but isn't that why you read it?

DO visit the "Jock Harty Arena." Do you think it was named after a real person?

DON'T leave Queen's before you have memorized the words to "Oil Thigh", the Queen's school song. You'll be singing it for the rest of your life at reunions and weddings.

I REMEMBER...

"My years at Queen's occupied me from 1949 to 1953. I have to admit that my memory is very positive. I have many memories of political debates, I was then somewhat misguidedly adhering to the Liberal party, which just goes to show how ill-directed one might be in one's younger years. The model Parliament was always fun. Both at Queen's and Dalhousie Law School I had time to indulge myself, following up everything that I was interested in. Who could ask for more than that?" — *John C. Crosbie*

UNIVERSITY OF REGINA

In 1974, the Regina campus of the University of Saskatchewan broke free, to assume proud and independent status as the University of Regina. "I don't believe the University of Saskatchewan has gotten over the shock. I think they still feel it was rather uppity of Regina to do that," says a former Regina student, now at U of S. Thirteen years later, Regina is also beginning to wonder whether liberation from Saskatchewan was such a great notion.

"Do you want to know what I really think of this university?" asks a student journalist. "I hate it. I think it stinks. There isn't one person here who wouldn't rather be in Saskatoon."

It's alarming to get such a reaction. Most students are ready to defend their alma mater at least briefly, no matter how terrible they really think it is. Most schools inspire a little loyalty. But everybody seems to hate Regina.

It's hard to love a school in which the hallways are lined with buckets ready to catch the rain and snow that seeps through the roofs of buildings "that have been neglected for years," and where "the microscopes in the biology classes are at least 40 years old."

It's hard to love a university that doesn't seem to love you back. Recently, the board of governors recommended — for the good of the university — "increasing student fees by fifteen per cent, closing the sculpture studio, cutting funding to the Norman MacKenzie Art Gallery, closing the Department of Extension, cancelling the inter-varsity athletic program (the Cougars and the Lady Cougars), and closing the Conservatory of Music."

The university is in a desperate plight. "This place is really depressing," according to several students. "School spirit?" jeers one student. "You want to know if there's school spirit? Ha! Don't make me laugh. I haven't heard the expression 'school spirit' since I was in grade eight."

Perhaps the situation at U of R would not be quite so galling if the University of Saskatchewan in Saskatoon weren't so dramatically better off. "Everybody knows that this is the inferior school, and that a lot more money goes to U of S. Nobody with any talent stays at U of R any longer than they have to."

In a depressed province, with a $956 million debt, it is simply not possible to support two universities. Instead of depriving both, the government has apparently chosen to starve U of R while sustaining the older U of S.

What will be the result? "I think the university is going to be closed down," says a worried student. "I think we are going to be injected with a large amount of funding soon," says an administrator hopefully. "I think we're going to revert back to being the second campus of the U of S," says a campus reporter. "Whatever the plan, something dramatic has to happen soon. We can't go on like this much longer," a member of the fine-arts faculty concludes ominously.

Passions run particularly hot about the fine-arts faculty. The Regina Five, who brought "New York derived, post-painterly abstractionism" (one critic's label) to Canadian painting were associated with this department. It is one of the university's best.

"We do the best we can. We manage. There has been a promise of a new building," says the drama director. He resists the suggestion that the U of R fine-arts faculty will simply be moved to Saskatoon. "If you know anything about politics, it seems difficult to believe that the government will do that. They always prefer the path of least resistance. They'd like to do nothing if they could."

Perhaps Regina's gravest problem is an administration with a weak grip on reality. It has been insisting for years now that the provincial government will hand over some money. Perhaps because they actually believe their own soothing assurances, they have, in the last few years, created new programs in computer science, administration, social work, journalism, and human justice — *without any significant increase in the university's budget*. To cap this brilliant planning, the university has permitted student enrolment to rise by 50 per cent between 1980 and 1986, again without any increase in funding.

The university's president, Lloyd Barber, explains this apparently inexplicable policy by offering an analysis of his own psychology. "I've indicated," he told the student newspaper in a recent interview, "that I'm a builder, not a buster. If the University of Regina is facing a major winding down, they'll have to find somebody else to do it, because I'm not capable of doing it. Temperamentally, I'm not suited."

Evidence abounds that U of R's resources have been stretched much, much too thinly. Consider some examples:

- The engineering department, which only teaches one branch of engineering while most schools teach five, has been decredited many times and is currently on probation.
- Education students who graduate from U of R usually lose out on teaching positions to education graduates from U of S, even when the jobs are in Regina. The stigma is not peculiar to the education department. A science student complains: "Just the name 'University of Regina' is a drawback when you're looking for a job."
- The university library closes at 8:00 p.m. on week-nights and has one of the smallest inventories of any Canadian university library.
- The arts and science departments have frozen spending. They have been forbidden to buy any new equipment, indefinitely.
- During busy times — between 8:30 and 11:30 — 110 per cent of classroom space is used on campus. This means that some classes are

taught not in classrooms but in offices, seminar rooms, and any other available, uncomfortable space that can be found.

Still, nearly 5,700 students attend U of R every day and not all of them are weeping in the hallways. They get by. Some even have a good time. "One great thing is the small size of this school," says the vice-president of the student council. "You can take your prof out for a beer, visit him in his office, or just strike up casual discussions with people, no problem."

Unfilled rooms in residence impose a further strain on Regina's finances. Only 280 of the 350 are used. Students don't mind that the rooms are located on top of mathematics classrooms but do protest that "they have too many rules and regulations. All friends must be signed in and out. You have to pay $8 if you want a friend to sleep over, and, even at that, no guest can stay more than four nights. You can only sign in three or four people at once, so parties with off-campus people are pretty much impossible. The best thing is that rooms are apartment-style. You cook your own food."

Students say Regina is a pleasant place to live and that there are enough interesting hangouts. The B-Bop is for the trend watchers and the Unwinder for heavy-metal types. But most students stick with the same bars they frequented as high-school students. No one place pulls U of R students exclusively, except, of course, the Lazy Owl pub in the Student Union Building (which really ought to be called the Student Union Shack).

U of R students, according to student organizers, are political, especially when the politics consist of a demand for more government money for their university. The student union often sponsors forums in the lounge area of the Administration-Humanities Building (known as the Ad-Hum Pit). These deal with current issues such as South Africa, and nuclear disarmament. Routinely, 500 students show up. "There's a great deal of tolerance here for left-wing ideas," says the student vice-president.

Although no one can be sure what will happen to Regina, students are steadfastly continuing their studies, planning careers, and hoping for the best.

THE FACTS

Founded: 1974 as independent university.
                                1910 founded as Regina College.

Address:	Regina, Saskatchewan S4S 0A2
Tuition:	$1,192
Cut-off grade for general admission (per cent):	65
Enrolment:	9,731
Undergraduate full-time enrolment:	5,410
Percentage of foreign students:	5
Percentage of students from outside the province:	11
Residence fees:	$1,028–1,328
Percentage of students in residence:	5
Male-female ratio:	45:55
Athletic facilities:	Good. Arena (seats 700).
Team name:	So long as they last... Cougars, Lady Cougars
Colours:	Green and gold
Fraternities/sororities:	None. "We're against anything élitist."—*Student*
Typical garb:	Down-to-earth wear.
Campus political attitude:	"You couldn't say Ronald Reagan was a very popular guy around here."— *Student*
Best-known fact:	Regina is the best place to major in Canadian Plains Studies.
Least-known fact:	Regina offers conversation and grammar courses in: Cree, Dakota, Dene, Ojibwa, and Hebrew.
If you had to put it in one sentence:	"You get the feeling someone's decided to slowly pull the plug on this place."—*Professional student organizer*

Alumni: Pamela Wallin, Arden Haynes
                            (president of Imperial Oil), Claude
                            Breeze (painter), Ken Mitchell
                            (author).

DO'S AND DON'TS

DO eat lunch as often as possible in Campion College, especially on
Wednesday, which is Perogie Special day. All the rest of the week they
serve the best home-cooked, "Saskatchewan-style" food in Regina.

DON'T think of bringing a car to school if you are on a tight budget.
Parking will cost you $99 a year, even though U of R claims to have
more parking spaces per capita than any other Canadian university.
"A commuter school that charges a hundred bucks a year for parking.
I love it!" says one student ironically.

DO try to park your car as close to civilization as possible if you do
decide to drive. The outer parking lots are plagued by vandals and no
car stereo is safe.

DON'T fail to check into the Lazy Owl pub on campus for the cheapest
beer and burgers in town.

DO try to get an apartment on 13th Avenue if you are going to live off
campus. It's Regina's "own little Greenwich Village."

I REMEMBER...

"When I was there, the University of Regina was a fledgling campus,
seeking autonomy from the more traditional administration in Saskatoon. Many of the professors were young and radical, and we had our
share of American draft dodgers, who sought refuge in a province
where socialists (Allan Blakeney's NDP) flourished. There were protest marches, sit-ins, and countless other manifestations of student
militancy — all carried out in the bitter cold of a very bleak and barren
campus ground. I remember a second-year class in oohming and
levitation offered by a professor who had been involved in the early
testing of LSD (clearly it had taken its toll). Perhaps the single most
important thing I learned was from a brilliant American Marxist
named Bill Levant. The text for his "psychology" class was Darwin's
Origin of the Species. He analyzed both our political and social culture
in terms of the 'survival of the fittest' thesis. I have not to this day
found a more succinct description of the most fundamental aspect of
politics." — *Pamela Wallin*

ROYAL MILITARY COLLEGE

Pretty much all that's standing between you and communism are the graduates of RMC. And, of course, the American, British, and West German military. But do they ask for thanks? No. Just free tuition and an income of $30,000 a year, guaranteed for five years after graduation.

But an RMC career is not all spit 'n' polish and free dental plans. RMC students give up almost every pleasure of the undergraduate's life. They must shave every day. They must make their beds. They may not have telephones or televisions in their rooms, and cars are forbidden until second year. They have no privacy: their bedroom doors must be open whenever they leave, so that they may be inspected at whim. Squadron leaders may open their drawers and closets and poke around as much as they want. Slouching is regarded as worse than plagiarism — first-year students must trot around with their elbows pressed into their rib-cages, and their backs locked. They must polish their black boots every night, and they have to wear goofy-looking polyester uniforms — short capes and pillbox hats that make them resemble the old Paris traffic cops. There's no sleeping in. There's no talking politics.

RMC is the only college in Canada that makes high school look like libertarian heaven. "RMC isn't meant to be fun," says a reservist, "it's meant to train young men and women to be leaders in Canada's military." "A lot of people don't realize what they are getting themselves into," says an RMC recruitment officer. An alumnus recalls: "It doesn't matter how prepared you think you are for the place. As much as you think you understand, you still can't know what it's like until you go through it."

The Royal Military College is one of three military colleges in Canada, but RMC is the only one to offer an engineering degree. Consequently, almost every cadet at Royal Roads College in Victoria, BC, and at College Militaire Royale de St.-Jean in Richelian, Quebec, has transferred to RMC by the beginning of third year.

RMC is small: only 860 students in all. And attrition wears away each class. "In my year," the alumnus says, "there were 144 of us at the beginning, and only 70 left four years later. Sixty percent left after their first year."

RMC tries to educate the "total man," or, now that RMC accepts women, the "total woman." Students receive "a comprehensive education that stresses academic achievement, military leadership, and physical fitness," says the recruitment officer. But that doesn't mean that RMC is turning out Renaissance men. Its job is to produce military officers — a strange, hard-to-understand human type.

Training at RMC begins with basic training the summer before first year. Ten to 20 per cent of the prospective cadets jump ship during this mutual testing period. "Students must complete basic training before they are allowed to continue. They spend approximately seven weeks in Chilliwack, BC, in a weed-out course. They are tested under various conditions, just like military basic training. They run up and down the mountains of British Columbia. It's a chance for both sides to check things out, to check suitability. We always encourage students to have another university in mind, just to keep their options open," says the recruitment officer.

After their summer of running up and down mountains in combat boots, the cadets are flown by the government to Kingston, Ontario, for the academic year. During the school months, the only military training is drill, although military discipline is maintained at all times. "Of course, military discipline is not the Kingston pen." In the summer after first year, the cadets are taught the other official language; in the two following summers they jump out of airplanes, shoot guns, run up and down mountains some more, and learn to fly planes and drive tanks. The summer after graduation is devoted to preparation for the cadet's first posting.

RMC does not pussyfoot on bilingualism. The cadets are told to become bilingual, and RMC cadets do what they're told. In addition to compulsory language classes (compulsory is a word you hear a lot at RMC), every first-year student is assigned a bunkmate who speaks the other official language. A French Canadian cadet says warmly: "In first year I had one room-mate from Ontario, and another room-mate from Newfoundland. We were forced to communicate. We are now very close. You make bonds when you have to work so hard to communicate."

The worst communications difficulties are not linguistic, but sexual. Women were admitted to RMC in 1980, and today compose 11 per cent of the school. Today's cadets say that women are a welcome addition. Alumni seem more upset. "Women interfere with male bonding," says one. "I think most graduates agree that the addition of women has not been a good change," says another. "The point of the military is to teach people how to prepare for action. When push comes to shove, aims must be accomplished. The aim is not to look after your little sister in combat."

At lunch-time, the female cadet in charge of supervising the Dining Hall calls the hall to order to make the day's announcements. She ends with the joke of the day: "Why do cadets wear their shorts in the shower? [Pause] They don't like to look down on the unemployed." Loud guffaws. As she sits down, I ask her what she thinks of her male class-mates. "They're bastards," she says. When asked if women are treated equally, she replies: "That's not what I'm talking about. Yes, we're treated equally; it's just other things." She won't say more. An observer suggests, "what she probably means is that those guys would jump on her in a minute, and then tell everybody about it after. This is probably not a good place to be looking for a relationship. I don't think there's a lot of loyalty." Still, it is not utterly unheard of for cadets to fall in love. There's been more than one marriage between RMC graduates.

Just as much is expected of women at RMC as of men. They follow the same routines as the men. The only exceptions are in the standards of physical fitness. For example, while a man must do 16 chin-ups, a woman need only do eight.

The RMC day is strictly regimented. Cadets are up by six. They shower and prepare their rooms for inspection. (A quarter really would bounce off these beds.) Breakfast, and then classes begin at eight. Lunch at noon. Afternoon classes. Work-outs. Drill. Dinner. Compulsory study hours from seven until 10. Boot-shining and sword-polishing. Lights out by 11. Patriotic dreams.

RMC cadets must wear their uniforms even during their brief escapes to town. They don't all love them. "Nerd suits," in the words of one.

RMC men care rather more about impressing Queen's women than old ladies. The admiration seems to be mutual. Throughout the year, social conveners at Victoria Hall — a women's residence at Queen's — are called upon to arrange dates for RMC formals. Probably no college formals in Canada are more formal than RMC's. It must be pretty exciting to date a man who wears a sword. Says a Vic Hall social convener: "The RMC formals are really great. The girls have a lot of fun and it's never a problem getting anyone to sign up. And sure, a lot of heavy relationships develop." A less-romantic observer notes, "RMC guys have no problems getting laid."

As graduation approaches, not all RMC cadets are puffed up with martial excitement. Those who decide that five years of being shot at in Cyprus is a sub-optimal way to spend one's youth can take advantage of a little-known option called "buying out your education." They pay the government a set sum, and return to civilian life. I suspect they never make their beds again.

"There's been more than one marriage between RMC graduates."

THE FACTS

Founded:	1874
Address:	Kingston, Ontario K7K 5L0
Tuition:	They pay you! All expenses are covered, including travel and clothing. Students also receive an allowance.
Cut-off grade for admission:	There isn't one, but usually two-thirds of the class have averages of 80 per cent or more.
Enrolment:	860
Undergraduate full-time enrolment:	750

Percentage of students from
outside the province: 44

Residence fees: Fees paid from student allowances.

Percentage of students in
residence: 100

Male-female ratio: 89:11

Athletic facilities: Good.

Coolest major: Engineering

Uncoolest major: Anything in the humanities.

Typical garb: Hasn't changed in 100 years: funny
                            red suits with pillbox hats.

Campus political attitude: Anything for King and country.

Best-known fact: Graduates of RMC have good
                            posture.

Least-known fact: The Canadian flag — designed in
                            1965 by an RMC man — is a thinly
                            disguised variation on the RMC flag.

If you had to put it in one
sentence: "There's no life like it."

Alumni: Billy Bishop, Walter Gordon,
                            Desmond Morton (principal of
                            Erindale College), Graham Gibson,
                            Jack Granatstein (historian), George
                            Hees, Gordon Wotherspoon, Jack
                            Morrow (Senator), General E.L.M.
                            Burns.

DO'S AND DON'TS

DO give your mom a big hug goodbye when you leave for school.
Cadets get only two weeks off for Christmas and two weeks off in
summer.

DON'T bring a lot of stylish casual clothing with you. First-year cadets
must wear their uniforms both on and off campus.

DO bring an alarm clock. Sleeping in is a punishable offense.

DON'T expect to move off-campus after first year. Students must live
in residence until they graduate. Single rooms are available after first
year.

DO follow the RMC gentleman's code: never talk about religion, politics, or women ... by name.

I REMEMBER ...

"The greatest help of RMC to me was the constant emphasis on the importance of everyone working together for a common goal. This was drilled into cadets constantly: on the sports field, in our military training and through the team approach in our studies. The emphasis on the 'honour' system created a keen sense of values during those very formative years. I would not have missed the experience for anything!" — *George Hees*

"My father had bitter memories of his recruit year at RMC of quite malignant cruelty — such as the entire recruit class, in full winter order, greatcoats, fur hats, overshoes and all, marched into the furnace room because a senior considered them "slack" and ordered to mark time until they began to drop, or being beaten by senior cadets for reasons he was never told. Absolutely none of that happened to me at CMR. RMC and CMR left cadets very little time to themselves or their thoughts and I believe that this is still true. [However] the intensely crowded schedule at RMC left me with a rare capacity to manage time productively. If I have any success that I could directly attribute to the military college experience, I suspect that it is time management." — *Desmond Morton*

RYERSON

In the old days, it was a disgrace, a total embarrassment, to study at Ryerson. "What's the matter," you'd hear people sneering, "not good enough for a real university?" But today things are different. In our practical era, Ryerson is the quintessential Canadian university. It offers no frills, no thrills, just practical, modern, sensible programs that lead directly to practical, modern, sensible jobs. Ryerson is the People's Express of Canada's universities.

"This is not the kind of school people come to just to bum around," explains one recent graduate. "No one wants to hang around Ryerson. The school wants you in and out in four years. You're not allowed to take eight years to do a four-year program. You have to do your work in ordered phases. There's an expression we use here: out of phase, out of luck."

Education at Ryerson is relentlessly practical. Ryerson's promotional material promises "a firm foundation for success." "You don't come here to get an education, you come here to get a training," explains one student. Training is what you get — often training that is unique, or at least unusual.

Students may earn a Bachelor of Technology in aerospace engineering (the only such degree in Canada), applied computer science, architectural science, chemical engineering, electrical engineering, graphic-communications management, industrial engineering, laboratory science, mechanical engineering, or survey engineering.

A Bachelor of Applied Arts is available in applied geography, early childhood education, environmental health, fashion (again the only such degree in Canada), food, nutrition, consumer and family studies, hospitality and tourism management, interior design, journalism, nursing, office and administrative studies, photographic arts, public administration, radio and television arts, social work, and urban and regional planning.

There's also a Bachelor of Business Management and non-degree programs in theatre, landscape architectural technology, and arts. Like I said, no-nonsense.

The reputation of Ryerson has been revolutionized in the last 10 years. It is no longer lumped together with Ontario's community colleges. Modern students consider Ryerson right along with other "real" universities. "I got into U of T, Western, and Ryerson," claims one student. "And I wanted to come here." Most students credit Dr. Segal, the school's dynamic president, for the transformation.

Dr. Segal is proud of his accomplishments. "When I started here in 1980, 25 to 30 per cent of our students graduated with degrees instead of diplomas. Now nearly 70 per cent are graduating with degrees. We now require graduation from grade 13 rather than grade 12 for admission."

Some programs, like the journalism, fashion, radio and television, photography, and hotel management, are in fact highly prestigious and keenly competitive. "For these programs," says Dr. Segal, "we have great demand. Often 900 people will apply for 120 places, 700 of whom are qualified. Many individuals with high grades get rejected."

If you know what you want to do with your life, and are ready to start right now, come to Ryerson. But be warned that a decision to study at Ryerson can be irreversible. "Because it's Canada's only polytechnical university," explains a student, "Ryerson's credits are not always accepted at par with those from other universities. This means you can't transfer to another university without starting all over again from scratch. Once you choose Ryerson you're stuck. If you're in second year and you realize you've made a mistake, that you don't really like what you're studying, your investment of time and money is a total write-off."

Furthermore, since the degrees offered are not full B.A.s or B.Sc.s, but rather B.A.A.s and B.Tech.s, many Canadian universities will not accept them as prerequisites to a Master's program. Ryerson students often have to go to the United States to pursue graduate degrees. "It's true," explains Dr. Segal, "that with, for example, a Ryerson degree in architecture, you cannot get a Master's in architecture in Ontario. But some of our students go on to get Master's degrees at places like Berkeley or the University of Michigan. The barriers exist only in Ontario." For students planning on paying for their graduate work in Canadian dollars, however, Ryerson is probably not the wisest choice.

Social life at Ryerson is not only dampened by the careerism of the students but also by the sorry fact that Ryerson programs usually appeal exclusively to *either* men or women, but rarely to both. "What happens," explains one knock-'em-dead blonde in the fashion program, "is that you get stuck in a class with the same twelve people for four years. And *none* of them are guys. If you take a female-dominated course — like fashion, family studies, social work — it means no men. It's the same thing for the engineers. You walk through their cafeteria and you can tell by the way they heckle that they haven't seen a woman in a *very* long time."

So what's a poor, beautiful girl to do? "You go to Brandy's a lot. No, I'm kidding. Actually, you go to the York University library. The Ryerson library is so quiet. People go because they *want* to go to the library. At York, the place is so noisy. It's a great spot to meet guys. In my first year at Ryerson I took the bus to York every day after class." The other problem with Ryerson, explains another young knock-out, is "the serious shortage of attractive men. It's a well-known fact that attractive women at Ryerson outnumber attractive men by a long shot. You go to U of T or York and your eyes fall out of your head, they're so good looking. Here, yuck." Because they appeal more equally to both male and female students, hotel management and tourism, and business are known as the most "fun" faculties.

What there is of social life at Ryerson occurs in the Ryerson Thursday night pubs, in intramural sports, and at the annual fall picnic on Toronto

Island. The picnic is the vortex and turning point of Ryerson social life. "It's held the first Wednesday of the year. There's a march down University Avenue and then a boat ride to the island. It's a great time, several thousand people show up every year. There's a barbecue, dancing, and we drink a lot of beer."

There is only one residence at Ryerson and it holds 38 men, or about .5 per cent of the Ryerson population. All other students must find apartments of their own. One co-op apartment building across the street from Ryerson, Neill-Wycik, functions as an unofficial residence — almost all the tenants are Ryerson students. Students try to live as close as they can to campus. Unfortunately, Ryerson is situated in one of Toronto's grubbier neighbourhoods. "You have to dodge the prostitutes to get to your front door." Ethnic neighbourhoods in the southwestern part of town are popular because they're cheap. Nobody in Toronto, though, is likely to be fussy.

Ryerson may be as urban as it gets, but the school does have some interior quadrangles that are green and shady. Unfortunately, they're not very secluded. "In four years here I've only eaten lunch outside once," says a student. "You have to step over bums to get to the lawn and then they're probably going to ask for your lunch anyway. It's more peaceful to eat inside."

When students want to eat lunch out, they opt for the Big Slice pizzeria. "It's a big Ryerson hangout. Ryerson students helped build that place from a hole in the wall to three locations." The Mug, a cheap eatery with too many plants in the Eaton Centre, and Nuts and Bolts, a nearby disco, are other favourites.

Ryerson is not a university where students explore their characters, read Hegel, make friends for life, or accumulate trophies for the mantelpiece. So what? Ryerson graduates know what they want. As they say smugly: "We're going to get jobs."

THE FACTS

Founded:	1945
Address:	350 Victoria Street Toronto, Ontario M5B 2K3
Tuition:	$913
Cut-off grade for general admission:	No cut-off grades.
Enrolment:	19,323

Undergraduate full-time enrolment:	7,695
Percentage of foreign students:	Not available
Percentage of students from outside the province:	Not available
Residence fees:	$1,260
Percentage of students in residence:	.5
Male-female ratio:	52:48
Athletic facilities:	Okay.
Team name:	Rams, Lady Rams
Colours:	Royal, blue, and gold
Fraternities/sororities:	None.
Typical garb:	Career-oriented: either high-fashion couture or sensible working clothes.
Campus political attitude:	Ever since Mulroney promised "Jobs, Jobs, Jobs" he's been a popular guy on campus.
Best-known fact:	Ryerson offers "career education."
Least-known fact:	70 per cent of Ryerson students earn a university-level degree.
If you had to put it in one sentence:	"This is not the sort of school where people wear the word 'Ryerson' all over their bodies."—*Student*
Alumni:	Brian Linehan, Chris Makepeace.

DO'S AND DON'TS

DO listen proudly to Ryerson's radio station, CKLN-FM (88.1 on your dial). It is the favourite station of Toronto's hip cats and dogs.

DON'T worry if you forgot to bring your cheque-book to the cashier's office. Ryerson accepts VISA cards for payment of tuition.

DO go to Oakham House Campus Community Centre on Tuesday and Thursday at noon. There is always some sort of presentation or lecture or concert going on. Hanging out here may give you a sense of community you might not feel otherwise.

DON'T bring a car to school. Parking couldn't be worse, and, besides, public transit is mega-convenient on this campus.

DO take advantage of the 100 computers available for students on the third floor of the library. Be aware, however, that there are only seven printers, so line-ups for that part of the process are loooong.

DON'T be startled by all the mounted ram's heads all over campus. "Eggy the Ram" is the school's mascot.

ST. FRANCIS XAVIER

You might suppose that a university that has among its graduates the prime minister, a Supreme Court justice, the Liberal leader of the Senate, the Conservative leader of the Senate, three other senators, and the president of the National Research Council of Canada would be fabled in song and story, and perhaps be featured prominently in conspiracy theories. But it's not.

St. FX (properly slurred as "Sain-of-ex"), if it is known for anything at all, is known as a school for Catholics. And because of its low profile, many Catholics and non-Catholics alike dismiss this lovely old college as nothing more than a parochial school for the devout. That's a mistake. Yes, it's true that all the statues of the Virgin Mary, St. Francis, and Jesus Christ, not to mention the conspicuous priests, nuns, and crucifixes, give the impression that students here are holier than average. But the impression is misleading. Not only do they go to class and play sports, but they even have heterosexual sex and smoke soft drugs. "There are just as many animals here as at any other school," says one business student, startled that anybody would think anything else. But while there are animals, they're tamer than the wild beasts found in Wolfville.

Statistics about the proportion of Catholics at St. FX are not available because the administration likes to pretend that it is uninterested in such matters, but a good guess is about 75 per cent. Students and faculty, however, insist vehemently that the predominance of Catholics does not matter. "You definitely don't have to be Catholic to have a good time here," says the Protestant president of the student body. His own popularity indicates that he's right.

But Catholicism is never far from anybody's mind, and even the student president jokes that he's the only one who doesn't genuflect before student council meetings. Sunday mass is to students at St. FX what football games are to those at Acadia. Almost everybody, including non-Catholics, attends at least one of the three services offered on weekends, and many go to daily afternoon mass. Even students who don't go to church at home attend services at St. FX, because, they say, services are just too much of a social event to miss.

There are other differences. Art students are not allowed to hire nude models for drawing class. The student health centre is neither permitted to promote the use of birth control, nor to advertise its availability on campus. (It is, however, available.) And the first-year women's residence is staffed by a coterie of nuns who strictly enforce a "no male visitors ever" policy.

But why has no one heard of St. FX? Well, for one thing, St. FX doesn't need much publicity to recruit new students. Perhaps more than any other school in the country, St. FX relies on its "community" to spread the good word. Most St. FX students have a parent, an aunt, a cousin, or a friend who attended and loved St. FX.

St. FX graduates wear their school rings for their whole lives. Many a friendship or marriage has started with: "I see that's a St. FX ring you're wearing. You know, I went there too." "You often hear about St. FX graduates who have met and married each other long after they've left the college. St. FX people are always on the look-out for each other," says one still-single girl.

The atmosphere at St FX is warm and cheerful — a reasonable reaction to the serene beauty of a huge and manicured campus. (Some students complain that the grounds are so well maintained that they eat, drink, sleep, and study to the sound and smell of lawn-mowers, snow-ploughs, and burning leaves.) The university's Georgian residences are copies of those at Lake Forest University in South Carolina. With unusual sensitivity, the administration has carefully tucked all modern extensions and additions out of sight, so that the campus is beautiful from every vantage point. On the majestic grounds of St. FX you feel more "at college" than almost anywhere else in the country. Perhaps this is why students at St. FX have a reputation for being slightly more serious than students elsewhere.

One St. FX student who has also studied at Dal and Acadia claims, "St. FX is the only place I've been where you can talk about book reviews, politics, and what you've learned in class. At St. FX, people actually seem interested in what they're learning."

St. FX is a tiny school of 2,300. Not only do students know their peers, they know their professors as well. Everyone knows everyone else: a walk across the campus involves an exchange of greetings with all who pass by. Some of the more friendly professors invite students to visit them at their homes, share a meal, watch home videos, and become friends. (Of course, professors in Antigonish have little better to do.) But even if you don't become pals with your professors, they will probably know your first name, and many will be pleased to be addressed in the same way. The faculty, like the student body, is primarily Catholic.

Location hinders St. FX in recruiting faculty. While Antigonish (pronounced with the stress on "Anti") is charming enough, it is tiny, and, unlike Wolfville, it's hours away from Halifax. "Who would want to be stuck in Antigonish?" asks one student who rejected St. FX in favour of Acadia. "It's not much of anything."

What there is in Antigonish tries to cater to undergraduate tastes. The Orient Lounge is a drinking hangout for music students, English majors, and other weirdos. It is very popular, crowded on weekends, and known for its jazz. The Library Lounge in the Wandlyn Hotel on Main Street suits those in a romantic mood. The Triangle Tavern on College Street is a rowdy, beer-swigging type of bar. And, no matter what mood you're in, the Gael Lounge is every student's last stop, since it doesn't close until 3:00 a.m.

To the irritation of the local merchants, however, no establishment in town approaches the popularity of the campus hangouts. Very few students bring cars to school, because student life at St. FX takes place on the university's 40 acres. The Golden X Inn and Jack's, in the Bloomfield Centre (the Student Union Building), are everybody's favourites.

St. FX's residences are wonderful. Although the rooms tend to be small, the structures themselves are nicely laid out, and architecturally beautiful. Each residence is made up of "houses" that foster a close, familiar feeling among housemates. Most rooms are doubles, and all students on the lower campus share the same dining hall. Students interested in living in Brian Mulroney's old room should apply to Aquinas House.

For first-year women, the only option is "The Mount." Mount Saint Bernard, once an affiliated Catholic school for women, is now the university's main female dormitory. Female students insist the place is better than it sounds. It sounds terrible. Located in the most remote upper part of campus, it is linked to the lower campus by a dark and unwelcoming passageway. There are no residence parties, at least none that include men, and there is strict supervision inside the dorm and regular room inspection. After one year at The Mount women can move down campus to one of the more conveniently located female dorms. Sixty per cent of St. FX students live in residence, an unusually high proportion for a Canadian university.

For the 40 per cent who do not live in residence, however, finding adequate housing is probably the hardest thing they have to do all year. There's not much housing available in Antigonish; and much of what is available is nasty and expensive. Students begin their search as early as March for September occupancy. No matter how hard you try, you may still end up in a trailer or sharing a bachelor apartment with seven friends.

Since almost everybody who attends St. FX is from out of town, the housing problem affects everybody. Most St. FX students, about 60 per cent, are from Nova Scotia and Cape Breton, although many come from central and western Canada. Usually the students who travel great distances to come to St. FX are the children of alumni. There are very few foreign students at St. FX (about seven per cent), and those who do attend are usually enrolled at the separate Coady International Institute.

The Coady Institute was named after a St. FX professor and activist, Dr. Moses M. Coady, who was the central figure in the important Antigonish Movement. The movement attempted to combat poverty and social unrest in the Atlantic provinces during the late 1920s by creating one of the first fishing co-operatives in Canada, as well as the first Maritime farmers' and fishermen's credit unions. Today, in honour of Dr. Coady, the St. FX International Institute recruits officials from developing countries for mid-career education.

The Antigonish Movement, now decades old, continues to influence the political atmosphere at St. FX. Students display an unusual awareness of community and charitable concerns, and they have an impressive record of community involvement. Dozens volunteer every year to tutor underprivileged native children in the "X-project." In 1985, St. FX music students recorded their own Band-Aid–style fund-raising long-playing album, "It Takes More Than One," and sponsored a 16-hour Live Aid concert on campus.

Above all other political subjects, St. FX students like to talk about the reconciliation of the Church's doctrines with modern social attitudes on sex and authority. In this, the St. FX administration has proven that it can bend with the times. In 1971, students went on strike for two days to protest the policy of sex-segregated dormitories. Finally, when some radical students threw a fire-bomb into the library, the university relented and created three of them.

The modern age was not satisfied, and it has continued to throw hard questions at the uneasy weld between St. FX's religious and political principles. Should pro-abortion speakers be allowed on campus? So far, no one has dared to invite one. Should condom ads be permitted in the student newspaper? The last time an editor tried that, the ad was pulled by the student government and replaced with cartoons. Should homosexuality be tolerated? Students maintain that there are no homosexual students at St. FX, and that if there were any they wouldn't last long.

Students at St. FX like to believe they are just normal Canadian college kids. That's mostly true. But there's a distinctive intellectual and political seriousness to the university that should be congenial to young Catholics interested in exploring their spiritual, political, and social beliefs. And non-Catholics who want a solid education, a cheerful campus, and a warm and spirited student body will always feel welcome.

THE FACTS

Founded:	1853
Address:	Antigonish, Nova Scotia B2G 1C0
Tuition:	$1,540
Cut-off grade for general arts admissions (per cent):	60
Enrolment:	2,500
Percentage of foreign students:	7
Percentage of students from outside the province:	30
Residence fees:	$3,050–3,615
Percentage of students in residence:	60
Male-female ratio:	48:52
Athletic facilities:	Excellent. Stadium (seats 4,000), arena (2,700), and a new gym.
Team Name:	(M) X-Men (F) X-Ettes

Colours:	Blue and white
Most popular major:	Business administration
Coolest major:	Music, jazz studies
Fraternities/sororities:	None.
Typical garb:	Very casual: rugger shirts, sweat-shirts, jeans, hockey jackets.
Campus political attitude:	"Everyone is a MOR: Middle of the Road. No extremists on either side." —*Student*
Best-known fact:	It's a Catholic school.
Least-known fact:	St. FX was the first Catholic co-ed school in North America.
If you had to put it in one sentence:	"Everyone's virtues and vices are more or less public here." —*St. FX faculty member*
Alumni:	Brian Mulroney, Gerald LaForet, Alan MacEachen, Lowell Murray, Larkin Kerwin.

DO'S AND DON'TS

DO attend Winter Carnival and Fall Fest — the biggest, bestest parties all year.

DON'T try to take a shower in your dorm after 11:00 p.m.: there are rules against it, and you'll get hauled out of there by your floor resident.

DO be sure, if you are an athlete, that your high-school grades are up to scratch. The administration insists on an equal-admission standard for athletes.

DON'T tell your feminist friends that the first St. FX woman to serve as the president of the student union wasn't elected until 1985.

DO make sure your girlfriend turns up to watch you when you play for the varsity hockey team. Every member of the team has to have a girl watching him, or he's not a real man.

DON'T think you'll be lonely if you're coming all the way from western Canada. In 1986 there were 80 students just from Calgary.

DO bring lots of blue and white clothing with you. Those are the school colours, and there will be many events where you'll want to be covered in school spirit.

I REMEMBER...

"For a boy from a small town, St. Francis Xavier was the big time. This, like any university, was the place where ideas were percolating, and where friendships that would last a lifetime were being made. At St. FX, politics was all-pervasive, particularly the social activism of professors such as Dr. Moses Coady. I became involved, not only with the campus Conservative Club, but also with the student co-op, where I gained my first managerial experience. I had political ambitions before I got to university, but the highly-charged atmosphere at that school provided a strong stimulus, and immeasurably increased my desire to become involved." — *Brian Mulroney*

ST. MARY'S

If Canada has a jock college, this is it. The little St. Mary's campus is overwhelmed by an enormous, expensive, spanking-new, 10,000-seat stadium. Almost all of the academic and residence buildings overlook it. There's no mistaking what this university cares about.

St. Mary's has a reputation for great teams — football and hockey teams especially. But it also has a reputation for cheating. In 1985, St. Mary's hockey and basketball teams were suspended from the CIAU — Canadian Interuniversity Athletic Union — when they were caught with ineligible players.

St. Mary's recruited a basketball player from Florida who already had a college degree. Since CIAU athletes must be undergraduates, and this fellow was indisputably a graduate, he adopted the identity of his high school-aged brother. When this was discovered, St. Mary's was booted out of the league for two years. The co-ordinator of inter-collegiate athletics says now: " We want to leave that incident in our past. Our current mood is onwards and upwards. This year we indicated to everyone that we are 'up front'. The basketball team is all local talent. And we even managed to get into the CIAU national championships."

Almost 70 per cent of St. Mary's students play on an intramural or varsity team. The new St. Mary's sports complex, also located in the middle of the campus, will — boasts one enthusiastic jock — make Dalplex (Dalhousie's new sporting complex) "look sick." St. Mary's fans are zealous. "The teams get great turnouts when they do well, and great turnouts when they don't do well. And the alumni come no matter what."

Athletics don't necessarily teach St. Mary's students the virtues of clean living. "They really go wild at St. Mary's," says a Dalhousie student with disgust and envy. A St. Mary's enthusiast gloats: "This is not an academic school. It's a jock school. And a party school."

St. Mary's was once a Catholic school. Officially secular now, Catholicism still affects university life, if only because St. Mary's is a family tradition for many Haligonians. "A lot of kids here are the sons or daughters, nieces or nephews of someone who was already here," explains one student. The school continues its regular Sunday mass in the on-campus Canadian Martyrs' Church. "It's a very popular thing. A great place to pick up girls. Everyone goes." But St. Mary's clerical traditions are fading fast. "The religious element used to be a lot stronger. There is only one Jesuit left on the faculty."

Academically, St. Mary's is known for its commerce program. Some say this is the best place in Nova Scotia to study business — certainly better than Dalhousie. As for everything else, St. Mary's students seem to find the programs and faculty adequate. One disappointed student complains, "I have no respect for our engineering faculty. So many of the profs are just terrible."

St. Mary's is hoping to make a name for itself in Asian studies. The campus is the headquarters of the Canada/China Language and Cultural Project, a program sponsored by the Canadian International Development Agency to teach managerial skills in China.

To the extent that St. Mary's is known for anything besides athletics and partying, it is known for its dedication to undergraduate teaching, and for fostering a feeling of community. Over 40 per cent of the 3,000 students live in residence. Apply early — there are simply no vacant apartments in Halifax, and anyway, students in residence have the most fun. "It's just a zoo in residence on Saturday night, and it's even worse on Sunday when all the bars in town are closed." Thanks to the tunnel and overpass system, a res student never need go outside. "You can always tell a res student in winter. He's wearing a Hawaiian shirt, shorts, and shoes with no socks. Everyone else has to lug around heavy winter coats all day."

A potentially disagreeable legacy from the Catholic era are the tough residence rules. But residence students cheerfully report: "They're never enforced. Residences at Acadia are much stricter."

For fun, if you can bear to cover up that gorgeous Hawaiian shirt, go to downtown Halifax. Current favourites on the downtown strip are Rosa's Cantina, Cheers, My Apartment, and Scoundrel's. "The nice thing about downtown Halifax is that all the bars are within walking distance of each other. If one place is dead, just go right next door," says a knowledgeable native.

For the athletic and the sociable, St. Mary's could be paradise. It has loads of school spirit, everybody loves sports, everybody loves drunken parties, and the community is dramatically centripetal. St. Mary's takes accessibility for the handicapped extremely seriously: few schools anywhere do more to meet their needs. Degrees from some other universities may be more prestigious, but there are worse ones, too. Only remember — bring your running shoes.

THE FACTS

Founded:	1802
Address:	Halifax, Nova Scotia B3H 3C3
Tuition:	$1,540
Cut-off grade for general admission (per cent):	60
Enrolment:	3,234
Undergraduate full-time enrolment:	3,141
Percentage of foreign students:	5

Percentage of students from outside the province:	4
Residence fees:	$2,720–3,075
Percentage of students in residence:	40
Male-female ratio:	61:39
Athletic facilities:	Excellent, of course.
Coolest major:	Commerce
Fraternities/sororities:	Most Dalhousie frats and sororities welcome St. Mary's students. The two schools are within walking distance.
Typical garb:	Sports paraphernalia. Team jackets and windbreakers.
Campus political attitude:	Doesn't matter which side you're on, so long as you win.
Best-known fact:	St. Mary's is home to some great teams.
Least-known fact:	St. Mary's has outstanding facilities for the handicapped.
If you had to put it in one sentence:	"This place is great for jocks, not so great for intellectuals." — *Student*
Alumni:	Louis Comeau (president and CEO Nova Scotia Power Corp.), James Radford (president and CEO, N.S. Savings and Loan), Terry Heenan (CEO, BC Tel), Terry Donahoe (minister of manpower), Arthur Donahoe (speaker of the provincial house).

DO'S AND DON'TS

DO bring a good Hallowe'en costume with you to wear to the Halifax Mardi Gras, Hallowe'en night. This huge, city-wide parade is the biggest event of the year.

DON'T be cavalier about where you "grow your stone." Although many in residence are known to have their own personal plants for winter use, the police occasionally visit to throw the plants (and you) out.

DO watch out for flying tennis balls. "Ball-tag" is a favourite St. Mary's game. If you get hit in the head with the ball, you're "it".

UNIVERSITY OF SASKATCHEWAN

Boring. Numbingly boring. If universities were people, then the University of Saskatchewan would be the polite, handsome, well-dressed man you want desperately to meet, only to discover he talks about nothing but his curling team. Although the University of Saskatchewan is one of the oldest, most reputable universities in Canada, it has one of the lowest profiles... and blandest personalities.

Students seem pleased enough, but not thrilled, to be here. "Yeah, I like it," "It's okay," "It'll do," "Better than Regina" are typical unpassionate responses to the question, "What do you think about this place?" Maybe it's too cold to get excited; maybe nobody cares about the institution; or maybe U of S students simply refuse to boast. There is a lot to boast about.

The campus, though blemished by modern academic buildings, remains one of the most attractive in the West, adorned by a mock-Gothic core, and decorated with charming, tree-lined paths and big stone gateways.

Sadly, the most central and beautiful of all the university's buildings, the Adminstration Building, has recently been condemned. University planners decided it was cheaper to build a replica than to fix the original. The twin will be directly behind the now boarded-up original. Saskatchewan insinuates that when the provincial government finally gets the nerve to close down Regina —and spends the money on them instead — the grand old building will make a dandy fine-arts department.

The University of Regina resentfully and correctly complains that the provincial government loves U of S best. "Luckily for us," one student journalist says, "the government always worries about Saskatoon first. But they're trying to finance two universities on the taxes of only one million people." So while U of S is favoured over Regina, it's not exactly rolling in dough. "We have space problems galore," says the student body president. "Some classes are absolutely packed," says another student. The agriculture department has been housed in the same building since 1912. Corners are cut everywhere.

The University of Saskatchewan is a medium-sized school of 16,000. But because of the university's college system, students maintain that the numbers don't bother them. Each faculty is also a college, but whether this is meaningful or not depends on which faculty you're in. With 5,000 students and no single building of its own, Arts and Science doesn't feel like much of a club. Neither does the faculty of Education. "If anybody feels lost at this place, it's the people in Arts and Science," says the student president. But Agriculture, Engineering, Nursing, Home Economics, and Commerce are tightly knit colleges in which students feel a strong sense of identity.

There are 14 different faculty colleges and three colleges with religious affiliations. Each has its own personality. A Roman Catholic philosophy student would have to choose between St. Thomas More College and Arts and Science College. It is the colleges, not the student council, that throw the parties. The biggest and best party each year is the "Ag Bag Drag" (sponsored by the Agriculture College), which is "a huge party held around Hallowe'en, with *lots* of drinking. Students begin to line up around the bowl (an interior lawn which is the main hangout when the weather is good) for tickets at six in the morning."

Because some colleges are predominantly either male or female, traditional alliances between the Home Economics and Agriculture colleges, and the Nursing and Engineering colleges, have developed. (Things are looking a bit dicey for the Home Ec–Aggie alliance, now that girls are signing up for Swine Psychology 101 too.) The Health Sciences College is reputed to be one of the tightest, whereas the Medical and Dental Colleges are the least socially active. (What a surprise!)

The smaller colleges run big brother/big sister programs to ease freshmen into the university. But the student president warns: "People in the small colleges tend to be very cliquey. Although it may be harder at first to be in one of the bigger colleges, you'll meet more people in the end, and you'll work harder at exposing yourself to more things. It's important to remember that this is a very friendly, down-to-earth campus."

The most newsworthy of the University of Saskatchewan's departments is engineering. A team of mechanical-engineering students, under the direction of Professor Barry Hertz, designed a car that won the 1986 Esso "Super Mileage" race. The U of S car gets 5,691 miles to the gallon, which is a world record. (Just why a gasoline company would sponsor such a race is unclear.)

A new engineering building went up in 1984 (there's a wind tunnel in the basement to help with the car competition), but students are already complaining. Although the building is well equipped, it was designed to accommodate only 700 students. The average class size over the past few years has exceeded 1,000.

The heart of the U of S is agriculture. Before the founding of U of S, Canadian universities assumed that liberal-arts students from the cities should not have to associate with agriculture students from the farms. U of S was the first Canadian school to teach both agriculture and the liberal arts: the university's arts faculty was founded in 1907, and agriculture in 1912. Allegedly, the Saskatchewan agriculture department is second only to Guelph's. But then, all Canadian agriculture departments say they are "second only to Guelph," which merely confirms that Guelph is number one. The faculty is famous for its contributions to the development of rust-resistant strains of wheat.

Agriculture students are desperately awaiting a new building of their own. A promise to fund a new facility was a minor campaign issue in the last provincial election.

According to the staff at the U of S student newspaper, the *Sheaf*, U of S students "just want to have fun. They would certainly be just as happy if we left out all the political reporting stuff, and doubled our coverage of sports and entertainment."

Many students complain that U of S is located far from any good restaurants and bars. "It's very isolated out here. There's no place to go out and get a nice lunch. And the food in the buffeteria is always the same, and really bad." The food is better at Louis's, the U of S student pub named after Louis Riel, the legendary Métis leader. (The Place Riel student centre is also named for him.) Louis's "has a really nice atmosphere — it's a great place to relax," says one regular. When they go into town, students favour the Pat, the Senator, Sliders, Hop House, Park Town, and Kelsey's. All are casual and inexpensive.

If you've always fantasized about being in a Brönte novel, living in U of S's Voyageur Place dormitories may be a good substitute. There's nothing scary about the inside of these dormitories (other than your neighbours), but from the outside they look like haunted baronial castles. The residence director suggests that students who want a place in residence "should apply by mid-March, since we get enough applications to fill our dorms three times over." There's room for 572.

Students with more modern taste (the majority) prefer McEown Park, a convenient apartment complex where they can prepare their own meals rather than buy a meal plan. Waiting lists for September vacancies can be 18 months long, but you may be able to jump the queue by renting an apartment in May.

One potential irritant at U of S is the secretive, even paranoiac, administration. When I asked a staff member for the names of prominent University of Saskatchewan alumni, she nervously replied, "I'll have to check with my superior to see if I can release that information." She retreated into an inner office. Through the door I could hear the superior bark, "NO!" She returned.

"I'm sorry," she said, "we don't give out that kind of information."

"What's the big secret? I don't want their telephone numbers."

After a great deal of thought, she said: "Well, if you tell me who you want to know about, I could confirm or deny whether the party went here." She was willing to confirm that John Diefenbaker *did* attend the University of Saskatchewan.

THE FACTS

Founded:	1907
Address:	Saskatoon, Saskatchewan S7N 0W0
Tuition:	$1,075
Cut-off grade for general admission (per cent):	65
Enrolment:	16,520
Undergraduate full-time enrolment:	12,229

Percentage of foreign students:	4.9
Percentage of students from outside the province:	5.4
Residence fees:	$2,778–3,021
Percentage of students in residence:	5 (off-campus apartments are available)
Male-female ratio:	52:47
Athletic facilities:	Good. Stadium (seats 3,500).
Team name:	(M) Huskies, (F) Huskiettes
Colours:	Kelly green and white
Fraternities/sororities:	None.
Typical garb:	Urban cowboy.
Campus political attitude:	"Can't we talk about music instead?" —*Student*
Best-known fact:	"It's cold here, but it's a dry cold."
Least-known fact:	Dry cold is every bit as cold as wet cold.
If you had to put it in one sentence:	There is a certain lack of excitement at U of S.
Alumni:	John Diefenbaker for sure. The rest are classified.

DO'S AND DON'TS

DO visit the U of S Observatory on Wednesday evenings, when it's open for star-gazing.

DON'T miss the movies in the Place Riel Theatre. There's one every night, and they rarely charge more than $3.50.

DO be patient when it comes to learning how to use the U of S library on-line computer catalogue. It's very new, very complicated, but, in the end, very efficient. It is one of the few on-line academic catalogues in North America.

DON'T just wonder about what life is like in Umea! Go there! U of S operates a student exchange with "Umea U," which, just in case you didn't know, is in Sweden.

SIMON FRASER UNIVERSITY

It is so hard to get to the isolated campus of Simon Fraser University, you have to figure that anyone who's here *really* wants to be. Located forty minutes from downtown Vancouver, on top of Burnaby Mountain, the drive to SFU — and you have to drive — is an endless, uphill affair. Once here, civilization and its discontents seem far away. The Coast Mountains rise around you. The air is clean. All is still. All is at peace. Somehow, a Himalayan spiritual retreat has been transposed into Vancouver's outer suburbs. In all this beauty, serenity, and tranquillity, the human mind can dwell on only one thing. God? No. Money.

Yes, money. In the 1960s, when universities on mountaintops an hour from anywhere struck nobody as implausible, it could not be imagined that the money might ever run out. It has, and especially painfully in British Columbia. For Simon Fraser, poverty has destroyed two beautiful dreams.

The first, the utopian curriculum, which would teach students a little of everything because all knowledge was one great whole, is kaput. Arthur Erickson, the school's guru/architect, put his expectations of Simon Fraser in writing: "I believed that above all a university should express universality of knowledge; that the fragmentation into faculties and departments, each isolated in its own world, was artificial; and that indeed the usual campus, where forestry or commerce, chemistry or law had each a building to itself, created mistaken intellectual boundaries in the student's mind. Knowledge was freer than that and transgressed such arbitrary boundaries; higher education had to be more than the sum of its parts. I suppose I wanted to realize at Simon Fraser a true community of learning."*

A psychology professor saddened by Simon Fraser's failure to create a "true community of learning" laments: "We built our own walls. There's no need for masonry. Any money the philosophy department gets, we don't get. It makes for an invidious environment. We are in competition, and it all relates to money."

The other dead, beautiful dream is the dream of a new kind of student. Erickson wanted unusual, mature, experienced, some might even say, fringe, students. But today, at Margaret Trudeau's alma mater, 60 per cent are either majoring or minoring in business administration.

Students and — especially — the faculty at SFU sense guiltily that they are not living up to the lurid expectations of the gaudy era in which

* *The Architecture of Arthur Erickson* (Montreal: Tundra Books, 1975.)

their university was founded. It was so easy for the students of the 1960s. The only question for them was how to make the world worthy of SFU.

Three student strikes at Simon Fraser between 1967 and 1969 were SFU's earliest contributions to an improved global village. During the second strike, in the fall of 1968, Simon Fraser became the first Canadian university to ask the RCMP to remove students from an occupied administration building. The third strike, in 1969, had the students and faculty of PSA (Politics, Sociology, Anthropology) — the largest department on campus — striking in the name of Democracy. "Democracy" meant putting students in charge of hiring, firing, and tenure. Raucous picket lines surrounded the university's main buildings. Eight teachers were suspended for joining the strike. Eventually the strike dwindled away and the teachers were reinstated.

Twenty years later it is interesting to speculate how the martyred eight would react to the new Simon Fraser — the Simon Fraser, where the *Junior Entrepreneurs* are one of the school's most visible clubs, the Simon Fraser that operates a "Student Business Advisory Council." Would they hurl rocks and Molotov cocktails at the extremely successful young Socreds — militant Vander Zalm enthusiasts to a man — which claims to be the biggest club on campus and which funds its own newspaper? Would the stoned advocates of non-linear thinking be pleased that Simon Fraser students score the highest national averages on the MCAT (Medical College Aptitude Test)? Would they be chagrined that the median SFU student uses marijuana only twice a month?

At least Erickson's mystic campus hasn't changed. The university is a long, low-rise, concrete structure built in pillared quadrangles around open malls and connected with flowing outdoor walkways. As you drive up Mount Burnaby, your first glimpse of Simon Fraser makes you think of what the Athenian acropolis would have looked like if they'd known about poured concrete and hadn't hired Phidias. And as you park your car, it occurs to you that Erickson cares as much about the convenience of drivers as Phidias did.

In defense of the school's isolated location Erickson wrote: "In the ordinary university it is too easy to escape from one's fellows to a faculty enclave or refuge off campus, but at Simon Fraser one would encounter the whole university community. But in the late sixties, the architecture of Simon Fraser was blamed for student unrest, because the design turned the student body inward and made them socially conscious!" Today the campus is blamed for turning the student body into apathetic commuters.

If Simon Fraser hasn't changed physically, it's turned upside-down intellectually. The interdisciplinary emphasis has been lost. Politics, sociology, and anthropology are now separate departments, and students can specialize to their heart's content.

Academically, the modern Simon Fraser tries to offer as much flexibility as possible to its students. The school operates on a trimester system so that students are free to study all year round to get their degrees quickly, or they can take courses every other semester according to their needs. The school also has a huge number of co-op programs and few schools offer such a range of work/study options. They include: computer science, mathematics and statistics, management, chemistry-biology, bio sciences, physics, engineering sciences, kinesiology, accounting, marketing and finance, and communications.

Another example of how much the school has changed is in student politics. While left-wing politicians still dominate SFU, they are no longer unopposed. When, for example, the student council decided to spend $3,400 of its student fees to run an anti-Socred election campaign, a great number of students protested the misuse of their money.

Defending the spending, the council's external relations officer (at any other school he would be called vice-president-external, but, as he insists, while staring fondly at a poster of Che Guevera, "hierarchical titles went out with the snuff-box") says: "It was a non-partisan campaign. We were pro-education, not *anti-Socred*. It was partisan on behalf of students." He adds, in response to the student anger over the campaign: "There certainly has been an increase of conservative students here. And it's hard to get them interested in issues. Still, compared to UBC, we're like anarchists."

The external relations officer is onto something here. A recent special lecture entitled, "AIDS, Censorship and The Right Wing," (everything terrible in the world in one comprehensive lecture) is a typically Simon Fraser-ish form of entertainment. And Simon Fraser is the only university in the country whose student handbook is loaded with large ads for things like:

• Past Life Regression Therapy
• Tarot Card Readings and Tutoring
• Living Visions: Wholistic Health Practitioner, Iridologist, Herbalist
• Ingrid Pincott, Naturopathic Physician
• Elly Roselle, Core Belief Engineering
• Relaxation Therapy
• Rima Levine, Deep Energy Work and Transformational Healing
• Olaka'a Therapy, Transpersonal Psychotherapy and Acupressure
• Norma Myers, Consultant Ethnobotanist

It is important to remember that, as conservative as Simon Fraser may get, it will always be on the west coast.

Simon Fraser will also always be isolated, and this presents students with a difficult choice to make when it comes time to decide whether or not to live in residence. The idea of spending at least two hours on the bus to get to and from school does not appeal to most people. And an obvious solution is to live in residence. However, spending two hours on the bus to get from residence to a downtown bar is also unappealing. It's a question of lesser evils. At least in Burnaby the apartments are cheaper than downtown. Residences at SFU are convenient during the week and miserable on the weekends. It's a hard choice. The crucial bit of advice is that a car is *de riguer* even for those who plan to live in residence. Vancouver does have a public-transit system but it closes down at 12:30 at night.

Residence students who don't mind suburban night-life can take the 15- or 20-minute bus ride to Coquitlam to see a movie, have dinner, or buy groceries. But Vancouver, with its rich downtown atmosphere, is irresistible, and students are inevitably drawn to it.

There are no identifiable, off-campus drinking or eating hangouts unique to SFU, since most students are scattered all over the Vancouver area. The on-campus pub is probably the most popular spot. On Thursdays the place is always packed. But all on-campus facilities are popular and well used, since one has to go dozens of miles to find anything to compare them to.

There is no central student union building, but one isn't really needed; the unified architecture makes the whole university feel like a giant SUB. There are, however, two good bookstores, a movie theatre, a dance studio, several cafeterias, a zillion vending machines, a good library, and an excellent gym facility.

SFU, in fact, is quite a jock school. Its sporting accomplishments are not well known in Canada, because SFU plays in an American college league (the NAIA). Simon Fraser is the only Canadian university that awards athletic scholarships — something the Canadian league forbids — which explains their banishment to the American field. One sports fan insists: "We are one of the top schools in our league. We won the women's national championship for skiing. Our men's soccer team is two-time champs. Our football team is really good. I think we have the finest athletic program in Canada. SFU athletes are like a who's who of Canadian sports."

But while SFU is a jock school with a loyal core of fans, it is not a party school. There are, naturally, dances and mixers on campus, but for whatever reason, perhaps because of the infectious calm of the mountaintop, this is a very sedate campus. This is the university Mohandas Gandhi would probably have chosen if he were a Canadian college kid.

"The favourite joke people at UBC like to make about SFU," confides one SFU student, "is that we are 'the kindergarten on the hill,' or 'SFSS: Simon Fraser Secondary School.' No one comes to Simon Fraser for the prestige. They come because it's nicer here. It's small, friendly, cozy. It's nice to come up against real, live faculty members, and to have small tutorial groups."

Small discussion and lecture groups, accessible professors, diverse pre-professional training programs, comfortable enrolment size, a flexible semester system — these are the academic benefits of Simon Fraser. The personal benefits are found in the school's sense of community and intimacy. And, let's face it, any place that helped mould Margaret Trudeau is going to have a certain amount of sex appeal.

SIMON FRASER
STUDENT MEDITATING
1960S

SIMON FRASER
STUDENT MEDITATING
1980S

"In all this beauty, serenity and tranquility the human mind
can dwell on only one thing..."

THE FACTS

Founded:	1963
Address:	Burnaby, British Columbia Y9A 1G8
Tuition:	$1,432
Cut-off grade for general admission (per cent):	C+ (or about 63)
Average grade 12 mark of entering class (per cent):	B (or about 70)
Enrolment:	12,869
Undergraduate full-time enrolment:	5,857
Percentage of foreign students:	6
Percentage of students from outside the province:	14
Residence fees:	$1,584–1,800
Percentage of students in residence:	10
Male-female ratio:	56:44
Athletic facilities:	Excellent.
Fraternities/sororities:	None.
Typical garb:	Levis, sweaters, mountain-climbing gear.
Campus political attitude:	Left-wing faculty, left-wing student council, right-wing students.
Best-known fact:	Simon Fraser was Canada's biggest hippie school.
Least-known fact:	Simon Fraser is the only university in Canada that offers athletic scholarships. There are 22 awards available.
If you had to put it in one sentence:	"This used to be a progressive school. Now SFU students want the student council's activities restricted

to organizing softball games."
—*External relations officer*

Alumni: Margaret Trudeau, Terry Fox, Debbie Brill, Terry Bailey (B.C. Lions), Dave Cutler (Edmonton Eskimos).

DO'S AND DON'TS

DO take advantage of the hour-and-a-half bus rides to school by using the time to do your homework.

DON'T panic if your car runs out of gas after the long trek up Burnaby Mountain. There's a service station right on campus.

DO come to SFU if you're looking for an older man or woman. The average age of students is 26 years.

DON'T bring your wallet with you when you go to the Images Theatre. Their films are free to students.

DO escape to SFU's cabin in Whistler when you want to get away from it all. It's open all year round. Rooms are $6 per person during the week, and $8 on weekends.

DON'T let your Chinese slip. SFU runs an academic exchange program with Jilin University in Changchun, China. SFU students can spend six weeks there during the summers.

UNIVERSITY OF TORONTO

In the cavernous lobby of the Robarts Library, I run into an old friend who has transferred to Toronto from McGill. "How do you like it here," I ask. "I love it," she says, "everything is so professional. The course outlines state clearly what will be expected of you. Required and additional reading are plainly listed, and the professors are even more accessible than they were at McGill." "Wonderful," I reply. "And how's your social life?" "It's great," she answers, "but you know me, I hate people."

To be happy at the University of Toronto, you must have no illusions. This is the university with the best faculty, the best library, and the greatest number of intelligent undergraduates in Canada. But nobody here cares whether you live or die. With 55,000 students, 225 buildings, 3,600 full-time faculty members, 387 teaching assistants, 2,883 administrative staff, 30 libraries, 10 student councils, 15 newspapers, 3 radio stations, and at least 300 departments, it takes a long time to track down a missing person.

In 1984, the university commissioned a study of its students — not because it repents its traditional indifference to its students, but because too many talented students were actually turning Toronto down. Students were asked to what, if anything, they felt a sense of loyalty: 29 per cent mentioned to their college, 7 per cent to their residence, 6 per cent to the U of T generally, 5 per cent to athletics and Hart House, 5 per cent to a department, 2 per cent to frats, 2 per cent to a club, and 1 per cent to the international students' centre. The largest group, 42 per cent, felt "alienated," with "no sense of affiliation." The report concluded that "the undergraduate experience, for at least half our students, means tensions about being overworked, worry about marks, an unsatisfactory social life, and loss of personal identity in this large institution. But the corollary to this is that, for the other half of our undergraduates, life is not too bad." As far as the University of Toronto is concerned, not too bad is plenty good enough.

A student at the Scarborough campus explains bluntly why he prefers the suburban campus to downtown: "On the St. George campus, if you asked to borrow notes from the guy next to you, he'd probably say 'fuck you.'" A student at Innis complains: "It takes three years to make some personal associations." The two-thirds who commute to class — who neither live in residence or nearby — suffer most from alienation and loneliness. "Going to the University of Toronto to me," reports a recent graduate, "was like having a series of appointments downtown." A manager of the radio station warns that the University of Toronto is not for the meek: "It's a tough university to be shy at. It takes a real toll on people who don't have nerve." The university's Kremlin-like bureaucracy can crush even the most obdurate soul: "You constantly need the signatures and stamps of individuals who may not even exist." On the bright side, the hours you spend in line will be a rare opportunity to make friends.

The contempt the university feels for the convenience of its undergraduates is legendary. A student says: "You want to hear a classic University of Toronto story? Last week, I had two tests back to back: one from 1 to 2, the other from 2 to 3. Only, the two classrooms were twenty minutes apart. I had to leave one exam ten minutes early to get to the other ten minutes late."

So why would anybody subject himself to this nightmare? Because the University of Toronto is the only university in Canada with a Nobel prizewinner on the faculty. Because this is where Northrop Frye teaches, and where E.J. Pratt once composed poetry. Robertson Davies was master of the graduate college. The University of Toronto Press is publishing the collected works of John Stuart Mill. The history department may be the country's most prestigious. This is where almost every Canadian you've ever heard of went to college. This is where the most advanced research in computers, astronomy, medicine, engineering, and chemistry is undertaken. The Pontifical Institute may be the best place to study the Middle Ages in North America. Toronto has the best law school, the best medical school, the best dental school, and the best school of pharmacy in the country. Typically, 50 per cent of Ontario Scholars (students with high-school averages over 80 per cent) choose U of T each year. The presidency of the University of Toronto is one of the most powerful academic jobs on the continent: John Evans, president from 1972 to 1978, was offered and rejected the presidency of Yale.

From an academic point of view, there can be no doubt: the University of Toronto is far and away the best teaching and research institution in Canada. This is an intellectual community — the sort of place where people discuss books and ideas in sleazy coffee-houses and baronial common-rooms.

A Chinese girl is sitting alone, reading, in the dingy and noisy foyer of Sidney Smith hall, the main teaching building. She has studied at the University of Victoria, UBC, McGill, and now the University of Toronto. Which did she like best? "The University of Toronto, for sure. The students here are serious, they actually want to learn." But doesn't she mind that it isn't very homey? "Who wants homey?"

The whole point of the University of Toronto, after all, is to get *away* from all those folks at home who used to beat you up for being smart. The comic side of this intellectual seriousness is the common habit of dropping intellectually impressive names: Nietzsche is always a big crowd-pleaser, but Levi-Strauss, Virginia Woolf, F.R. Leavis, Leo

Strauss, and, of course, Marx are also popular. The predilection for
Nietzsche seems fitting — he was no doubt thinking of registration at the
University of Toronto when he wrote "whatever doesn't kill me makes
me strong."

Seriousness alone can't pay the bills, and don't think that Toronto, the
wealthiest university in Canada, can afford to spend lavishly on its
facilities. The Farquharson commission reported that it had "seen
students writing Christmas examinations in the Drill Hall while wearing
hats, coats, scarves, and gloves. The Drill Hall is notorious among
students for very high noise levels and painful lighting, and not least
because a squirrel once fell from the rafters to its death on a student's
examination paper." Even the university's pride, Robarts Library, has
serious gaps in its collection. Worse, one student worries that "its
bathrooms are so filthy that I'm afraid that I'm going to get a communicable disease before I graduate." And then, of course, there's the legendary Psych 100 course: 1,000 students crammed into Convocation Hall.
Students, a fair-minded bunch, don't object so much to classes of
1,000 — they object to classes of 1,000 with 800 chairs.

You might think that playing musical chairs with 999 others would be
a nifty way to make friends. It doesn't work. Many students complain
that the acquaintances they make in class somehow never become
friends. They may drink coffee together before class and walk to the
subway with you after class, but they would be startled to be asked to go
to the movies with you on the weekend. Real friends, for most U of T
students, are either inherited from high school, or met in student
organizations or in the colleges.

To make friends, you must join clubs. Sadly, few students do. In fact,
according to an editor of *The Newspaper* — *The Varsity*'s competitor —
"it's the same 10 per cent who run everything. Another 10 per cent
participate only occasionally. At *The Newspaper*, we're sometimes down
to three staffers, at a university where there are 55,000 people who all
complain that there's nothing to do."

It isn't just apathy that deters students from involving themselves in
university life. *The Varsity*, the largest newspaper on campus, prints
25,000 copies twice a week. The university's FM radio station can be
heard, as it boasts, from Cobourg to Kitchener and from Barrie to
Buffalo. For most students, signing up for *The Varsity* feels like applying
for a job at *The Globe and Mail*; the radio station seems as daunting as the
CBC. Nor do the editors of *The Varsity* and the managers of the radio
station — who often fantasize that they *are* running *The Globe and Mail*
and the CBC — exactly welcome newcomers. "You must instantly de-

monstrate talent. Nobody's going to nurture potential talent," says a defector from *The Varsity*.

The hundreds of other clubs—drama societies, debating teams, athletic teams, fraternities and sororities, political parties—do genuinely welcome new members. But, in a university where nobody knows anybody, clubs inevitably look cliquey, and, again, the timid are frightened away.

For those who are not bold enough to throw themselves into the clubs, the colleges are the last resort. Every arts and science student belongs to a college; all others are affiliated with a department. As usual, engineering and forestry are worlds unto themselves. Those who like that sort of thing will find that it is exactly the sort of thing they like. Generally, however, the colleges serve only as identifying marks: upper class, lower class; smart, not so smart; Catholic, Jewish, Anglican, or United Church.

University and Victoria are, respectively, the second- and third-hardest colleges to get into. University, founded as the only secular college, has become largely Jewish. Victoria, founded by Methodists, now teaches English and art history to the pearl-and-sweater set. Usually, any important club or organization at Toronto is run by students from University or Victoria colleges.

St. Michael's remains fiercely Catholic. Rules in the dormitories are zealously enforced. The politics that excite students at St. Mike's—and it's said to be the most political of the colleges—are the politics of the Catholic Church: birth control, abortion, and Nicaragua.

Innis College and New College form a sort of academic buffer zone. Virtually all their students would rather be at one of the four old colleges, but all are hugely relieved not to be condemned to Erindale or Scarborough.

Trinity College, founded by the Church of England in 1851, did not accede to the University of Toronto until 1904. It still remains aloof. Tuition and entrance requirements are higher than anywhere else in the university. Obtaining admission to Trinity is about the hardest thing a Canadian high-school student can do. Trinity is small, incestuous, and physically beautiful. Forty per cent of its students live in residence—the highest percentage at the University of Toronto. Nowhere else are old customs so lovingly maintained: academic robes, high table, a formal dinner hour with waiters every night, teas, the annual champagne ball, weird rituals like "pouring out," and the festival of Father Episkopon. Trinitrons, as they are disparagingly nicknamed by the 90 per cent of the university that finds them absolutely unbearable, care deeply about distinguishing themselves from all those slobs out there. This is every Anglophile Upper Canadian's idea of what college should be.

One-sixth of the students on the downtown campus of the University of Toronto live in residence; one-sixth live nearby; and the rest live with their parents. The grandest residences belong to Trinity, University College, and the men at Victoria. (Victoria has two women's residences —one's decrepit, the other's charmless.) Considering their location, all are tremendous bargains. To live nearby, remember this simple advice: bring money. There seems to be no upper limit to the price of one-bedroom apartments in downtown Toronto. Thanks to rent control, you probably won't be able to find one anyway. Still, with luck and determination, you might find a not-too-unreasonably priced apartment in the Annex or Kensington Market area. Your friends will be sick with envy if you do.

Every U of T student goes to the Brunswick House *once*. It's a little surprising that a bar this vile has retained the patronage of an entire university for so long, but there it is. The Madison, a three-storey pub which unlike the Brunswick, is cleaned occasionally, and Rowers on Harbord Street are eroding the Brunswick's dominance. Beyond that, you're on your own in Canada's swankiest city. Explore Harbord and Queen streets. Queen Street West has the greatest concentration of used-book stores this side of the Atlantic Ocean. College Street West is filling up rapidly with bars, restaurants, and other fun spots that recognize that dinner for two with wine can cost less than $25. Bloor Street West has cheap, chic restaurants and even cheaper goulash joints, in which schnitzel with a mountain of fried potatoes may cost $5. Just to the east of St. George on Bloor is "death row," the "zit strip," where Country Style Donuts, Mr. Submarine, the Fire Pit, Harvey's, Swiss Chalet, Mother's, Pizza Hut, and McDonald's are, as one student puts it, "just a short slide from the subway."

The University of Toronto is a ruthlessly Darwinian school. It has more to offer you than any other school in Canada. Success here requires nerve, energy, self-confidence, and a willingness to introduce yourself to strangers. If you find classes you like, congenial friends, a suitable club or sport, the right college, a decent place to live, then you're at the top of the greasy pole. You'll have the best education, the best degree, and the best time that Canadian academia can offer. Most people, however, fail. And failure means loneliness, unhappiness, and gnawing resentment at being surrounded by people having a much, much better time than you. Know yourself, and decide accordingly.

THE FACTS

Founded:	1827
Address:	Toronto, Ontario M5S 1A1
Tuition:	$1,518
Cut-off grade for general admission (per cent):	(These are approximate figures only): Trinity and University, 85; Victoria and St. Michael's, 80; New and Innis, 76.
Enrolment:	51,059
Undergraduate full-time enrolment at all colleges:	28,859
Percentage of foreign students:	1.8
Percentage of students from outside the province:	3
Residence fees:	$2,900–3,600
Percentage of students in residence, St. George campus:	10
Male-female ratio:	47:53
Athletic facilities:	Among the best in Canada. Varsity Stadium is the perpetual host of the Vanier Cup. Arena, super-modern gym, indoor track, Hart House.
Team name:	Blues
Colours:	Royal blue and white
Fraternities/sororities:	Yes. A good place to look for housing — 303 rooms are up for grabs — and friends.
Typical garb:	Everything goes. U of T leather jackets are popular.
Campus political attitude:	Every point of view is fully represented.
Best-known fact:	Drs. Banting and Best discovered insulin at U of T in 1921.

Least-known fact:	U of T is the fifth-largest university in North America, after Penn State, Ohio State, Texas, and Illinois.
If you had to put it in one sentence:	At U of T orientation, you play musical chairs with 2,000 people: either you like that kind of thing, or you don't.
Alumni:	Mackenzie King, Lester Pearson, Arthur Meighen, Norman Bethune, Ed Broadbent, Norman Jewison, Knowlton Nash, John B. Aird, Adrienne Clarkson, Peter C. Newman, Barbara Amiel, Margaret Atwood, Bob Rae, Barbara McDougall, J.J. Robinette, Pauline McGibbon, Northrop Frye, William Davis, Michael Wilson, Stephen Leacock, Barbara Frum, Ernest MacMillan, Keith Davey, Donald Sutherland, Christopher Plummer, Glenn Gould.

SCARBOROUGH

"Once you get here — put that in bold, italics, bold *and* italics — once you get here, you'll like it," a proud Scarborough student urges prospective applicants. The humiliation of being assigned to the Scarborough campus of the University of Toronto stings. The university seems to want the sting to last forever. Toronto is now hotly debating whether it should resume putting the signature of the master of each student's college on his degree. Students at Trinity like the proposal. So do some students at Scarborough: "I'm all for having my degree signed by a college master — Trinity's."

Yet Scarborough remains a reasonably selective institution. It's harder to get into Scarborough than York, for example. The difference between New College downtown and Scarborough may well turn on fifteen minutes of studying before your grade 13 French exam. Many professors teach both downtown and at the two satellite campuses. And serious students report that the very isolation of the campus promotes a more hard-working attitude.

Which is better: Scarborough or Erindale? "If you consider Yonge

Street the center of the universe," says a Scarborough student, "Scarborough's better because it's slightly closer." It's still 33 kilometres from the St. George campus, though. One mathematically acute Scarborough student computes that he has spent the equivalent of 56 days of his life on the bus over four years.

An increasing number of students actually select Scarborough as their first choice, to be close to home. Some socially conscious students refer to the student housing around the campus as "the upper, upper, upper, upper Beaches." Students resent the downtowners' vague notion that Scarborough lies somewhere near Moncton. "It's not exactly four days by caravan to downtown." While you may have to pay more for gas to get to Scarborough, you can save a lot on your clothing budget. "In a concrete jungle, the more hip clothing you put on, the more you look out of place. So we just wear grey."

THE FACTS

Founded:	1964
Address:	1265 Military Trail Road, Scarborough, Ontario M1C 1A4
Tuition:	$1,518
Cut-off grade for general admission (per cent):	Approximately 74
Enrolment:	4,804
Undergraduate full-time enrolment:	3,441
Percentage of foreign students:	1.6
Percentage of students from outside the province:	1.4
Residence fees:	$2,900–3,600
Percentage of students in residence:	8
Male-female ratio:	47:53
Athletic facilities:	Very good. Triple gym. 11 tennis courts.

ERINDALE

Erindale, understandably, answers the question, "which is better, Scarborough or Erindale?" a little differently. They point out that 30 per cent of Scarborough students fail the University of Toronto's compulsory English proficiency test, compared to a mere 11 per cent of students at Erindale. Erindale's campus is bigger and more opulent than Scarborough's, and heads of downtown departments, like zoology, biology, and psychology, have been lured to Etobicoke. Josef Skvorecky, Canada's best shot at a Nobel prize for literature, teaches literature at Erindale. On the other hand, a student from Calgary who wanted to live in Toronto, and had no idea where Erindale was, says bitterly that it took him a full year to get over the shock of his banishment to the suburban campus.

Erindale does attract slightly spiffier undergraduates than Scarborough, because it's located near more elegant, established suburbs. "A lot of milk gets drunk, a lot of mayonnaise gets eaten out here." Erindale guarantees every first-year student a place in residence. It also operates the single best orientation week of any college at the University of Toronto. Students camp on the luxuriant lawns near the Credit River for a week. (A Scarborough student notes sardonically, "we tried it too, but it just ruined the grass.")

"I'm jealous of the people downtown," says a representative Erindale student. "I mean, here you are getting this degree that says you went to the University of Toronto. But nobody's grandfather went here. You can't help feeling gypped."

THE FACTS

Founded:	1967
Address:	3359 Mississauga Road, Mississauga, Ontario L5L 1C6
Tuition:	$1,518
Cut-off grade for general admission (per cent):	Approximately 74
Enrolment:	4,804
Undergraduate full-time enrolment:	3,441

Percentage of foreign students:	1
Percentage of students from outside the province:	1.4
Residence fees:	$2,900–3,600
Percentage of students in residence:	10
Male-female ratio:	49:51
Athletic facilities:	Good outdoor facilities, modest gym.

U of T DO'S AND DON'TS

DO join at least one club or organization in your first week. Although students at all universities should do this, nowhere is this advice more crucial than at U of T.

DON'T ever expect speedy service in your dealings with the administration. Going to school with 51,058 other people means line-ups.

DO become a film buff by attending all the free films offered on campus. Innis has a regular free series. The student council offers free movies at Scarborough on Thursdays; Erindale on Fridays; downtown on Saturdays. There are also three good repertory cinemas near campus.

DON'T take a course without first consulting your *Anti-Calendar*. This is an underground publication produced by arts and science students that evaluates profs and their courses.

DO buy your lunch from the food trucks that line St. George Street. They are reputed to sell food that is tastier and cheaper than U of T's cafeterias.

DON'T worry if you need to make a copy of your year-end essay at 6:00 a.m. Kinko's — just off campus — is a copy shop open all day and all night. (This is why you go to school in the city!)

DO use Sigmund Samuel's library (Sig Sam) if you want to socialize, and Robarts if you want to be left alone.

DON'T graduate before you visit Erindale's pub — the Blind Duck. It's the number-one money-making pub at U of T.

DO read Josef Skvorecky's *The Engineer of Human Souls* to get an inside look at Erindale College.

I REMEMBER...

"I went to Victoria College at the University of Toronto between 1957 and 1961. In those days there were two kinds of students — those who wore camel's-hair coats and pearl-button earrings, and those who wore black and sweaters and were interested in the arts. There were about five of those at Vic. It was wonderful. You felt you had been given a big white piece of paper on which you could draw anything." — *Margaret Atwood*

"The University of Toronto was a perfect mix: an intellectually challenging faculty in the centre of a vibrant great city." — *Ed Broadbent*

"I went to the University of Toronto in 1941. The country was at war, and every day one heard of friends either killed, wounded or missing. For me and most of my friends, therefore, the university was a stopping place before we could go to the war. That is not to say that we did not have a good time but, the real truth is, we did not gain much from university life, as such. One of the reasons that I decided to allow my name to stand for Chancellor of the University of Toronto was in order to, in some small way, pay a debt to my many friends who never came back." — *John B. Aird*

"The notion that when you're in university you should know exactly what you want to become, and feel guilty if you don't, is crazy. I certainly never did. I was so worried about not knowing what I wanted to do I went to a professional vocational guidance institute and took three days of tests. At the end of them, they declared I should become a meteorologist! Some of my critics have said they were right. I certainly had no intention of being a writer. I spent most of my time in the library reading books. I had one professor in economic history, and he didn't like my economics very much, but he thought I could write. Nobody had ever told me that. So I started writing, just as part of a process of elimination." — *Peter C. Newman*

"Most of my college days at Victoria were spent in frantic production meetings, writing sessions, and rehearsals for either the 'Vic Bob' or the All-Varsity Revue. In those years 1946 to 1950, the spirit and energy were extremely high. Hart House Theatre was an exciting place to be; Wayne and Shuster, Don Harron, Keith Davey, Joe Potts were all highly visible. Political arguments went on for hours in the KCR at the Park Plaza as the returning veterans taught all the Vic students how to consume vast quantities of beer...a talent, I understand, which has been passed down through the years." — *Norman Jewison*

"I cringe to recall that I was 'a big man on campus,' not overly endowed with academic prowess. Astute old Victoria College Dean Harold Bennett quickly assessed the situation, suggested I would not win any gold medals and that perhaps 'you should cultivate some eccentricities.' I did. I joined the Liberal Party of Canada." — *Keith Davey*

"University gave me lifelong respect for those who labour to produce a book." — *Barbara Frum*

TRENT

Do you believe in magic? Do you think Frodo lives? Do you wear John Lennon glasses? Ripped tee-shirts? Birkenstocks? Levis? Do you love the colour black? Do you hate to shave? (This question is for both men and women.) Hate make-up? (Women only.) Do you like carrot juice? Whole-wheat muffins? Have you considered Trent?

Trent University is for the nostalgic, young and old. Not everybody at Trent is nostalgic for the same things, however. The administration, stuck in some weird colonial culture of its own, has tried to make Trent Canada's Oxford. They are responsible for Trent's college system, its high tables (which nobody sits at), the rowing, the increasingly meaningless adviser system. Until 1970, they managed to impose forest-green academic robes on students during classes and meals.

Nostalgic students and faculty members, on the other hand, want to make Trent a caricature of Berkeley circa 1968. They claim to want some new, mutant form of democratic, anti-patriarchal, anti-hierarchical, anti-establishment education. Alas, the student radicals resent the radicalism of their faculty: where's the fun of hating the system when the system thinks you're right? "It's a drag when the people you want to be radical against agree with you," complains one would-be rebel. The female student council president passionately declaims: "I see a contradiction in what our feminist professors preach and practise. How can you try to smash definitions using the same structures as the other disciplines? Even the feminist professors make you write exams, and produce essays that have an introduction, a middle, and a conclusion. I don't think this is consistent with post-modernist feminism."

Of course, the great majority of students at Trent do not share the student president's dedication to post-modernist feminism. They, like students all over Canada, study "administration and policy," Trent's euphemism for...business. They also wear preppy clothing, use deodorant, and avoid drugs. Still, the business students do not set the tone at Trent; "the 10 per cent of students who are active, and vocal, and concerned about planet Earth do."

That 10 per cent manages to infect even the most straight-laced kids. According to one student from Brampton, suburbanites often "come here as conservatives and leave as socialists." He adds: "This often has an ill effect when they go out into the world looking for jobs. It's very hard to chat with an interviewer from a multinational corporation when all you've heard in college is how that company exploits and tortures innocent peasants in the Third World."

None of Trent's academic departments is particularly good, but the lively atmosphere of Trent makes it more intellectually stimulating than some of Ontario's other small, second-tier universities — Guelph, Wilfrid Laurier, and Brock. The best thing about Trent academically is its low student-teacher ratio, a ratio that economic stringency is forcing up. Trent's founders hoped to mimic Oxford's tutorial system. The only vestiges left of that idea are the three meetings a semester each student has with his adviser — a member of the faculty who may or may not, but usually does not, belong to the same department. If the Oxonian tradition is dying, so too is the 1960s experimental curriculum. All that is left is cultural studies, a grab-bag of subjects which, once upon a time, were described as "relevant": anthropology, sociology, nude drawing, psychology, and political theory.

While many Trent students were rejected elsewhere, many others picked Trent first. "Next time I go to visit my friends at Queen's," says one first-year student, "I'm having an 'I REFUSED QUEEN'S' tee-shirt made up. It's obnoxious the way those people think the only school in the world people would want to go to is theirs."

Trent's college system works. There are five colleges at Trent, three on the rural Nassau campus and two downtown. The two downtown colleges, Peter Robinson College and Catharine Parr Traill, are considered the radical ones. "They're the places for the commies and the fags," says one hostile student. Miles away, on the Nassau campus, Lady Eaton College is "for prissy, preppy girls." Champlain is "the biggest party college and a favourite of the jocks." Otonabee is "the biggest, the least cohesive, but rather jocky."

The extracurricular life at Trent is surprisingly lively. Bad Art Night is the year's most eagerly awaited event. Students bring their worst paintings, poems, and songs to an evening of jeering and laughter. "It's great, a must-see," says one bad artist. Trent students also amuse themselves at the Salvador dance-a-thon (sort of like the Western Charity Ball, but different), the Amnesty International fund-raisers, and shows at Theatre Broad-minded.

Students also run a very with-it radio station, Radio Trent, and a newspaper, *The Arthur*, named after George Harrison's hair-do. (When a reporter asked Harrison what he called his hair-do he reportedly said "Arthur.") The newspaper almost had a name change two years ago, when a lesbian editor decided that a paper named after a man was not consistent with post-modernist feminism. She dropped it, but the name has since been restored.

The Arthur's current editor is very proud that her paper has "the only weekly, signed, gay column in the country." (Waterloo's paper also has a homosexual column, but it is written under a *nom de plume*.)

Perhaps because of their university's vast and wintry campus, Trent students love sports, although they prefer intramural to varsity sports. The colleges organize co-ed teams at three ability levels. "The worse your team, the more fun you have," says one hockey player. The-Head-of-the-Trent boat race is the biggest sporting event of the year. Dozens of crews from all over North America come to Peterborough to row.

For murky reasons, Peterborough is packed with musicians. As the student's handbook quaintly puts it, "one of Peterborough's great phenomena is that there are more musicians per square foot than anywhere else in the world. I don't know if that's really true but for some reason 'Pitaburrow' attracts some fantastic tunesters, and even grows a few of its own." The best bars in which to hear bands are: the Red Dog Tavern for country and western — go on Wednesdays, so you don't miss the Red Dog Howl; the Underdog, which features local talent as well as new Toronto bands; Clover's, for the latest in Euro-disco; and the Pig's Ear, which is better known for selling 20 drafts for $14 than for its music.

Many Trent students, especially those in the downtown colleges, live in the Peterborough student ghetto between Park Hill Road and Hunter Street, and Water and Reid. Although dilapidated downtown houses abound, students are finding that, as the Peterborough economy slumps, the competition for cheap housing increases. Still, there is no shortage.

Living in residence on the Nassau campus may be picturesque, but it is a little inconvenient for students who think there's more to life than cross-country skiing. One resident of Lady Eaton College complains: "You are stuck here with nowhere to go. All there is to do, sometimes, is take a walk. If it's cold, there's not even that." The only hangout close to the Nassau campus is a Kentucky Fried Chicken outlet. "Residence is not the place for hyper social life," confides one student.

Women students say dating at Trent is "really bad. There's a lot more girls here than men, and when you add in the gay factor, it doesn't look too good. But I don't know any girls who are looking for a boyfriend anyway. This is not the place to come for an M.R.S. If you're into that, you should be at a place that has engineers, and go for the really big bucks."

"When I think of social life at Trent," her friend chips in, "I think of the reggae night we had last week. It was so typically Trent. So relaxed. Just a major haze. No one cared what anybody else was wearing and no one said stuff like, 'Oh! Look at her! She can't dance.'"

Trent is an interesting and vibrant place. True, its politics are kind of goofy, but at least it has some. Trent is like some kind of hideous experiment gone wrong, in which a stuffy, colonial Toryism has been spliced onto a retirement home for radicals, with a mutant strain of political homosexuality blended in. The resulting creature may not be for everybody — but remember, as always, the vast majority of students are wholesome Canadian boys and girls looking for true love and management training.

"It's a drag when the people you want to be radical against agree with you."

THE FACTS

Founded:	1964
Address:	Peterborough, Ontario K9J 7B8
Tuition:	$1,264
Cut-off grade for general admission (per cent):	65
Enrolment:	4,445
Percentage of foreign students:	3
Percentage of students from outside the province:	Not available
Undergraduate full-time enrolment:	3,243
Residence fees:	$3,187–3,346
Percentage of students in residence:	34
Male-female ratio:	45:55
Athletic facilities:	Okay.
Team name:	Trent Excaliburs
Colours:	Green and white
Coolest major:	Cultural studies
Fraternities/sororities:	None.
Typical garb:	Black anything. Army fatigues.
Campus political attitude:	Women, gays and lesbians, members of minority groups revered above all.
Best-known fact:	Trent's founders intended the university to be "Oxford on the Otonabee."
Least-known fact:	Trent students have the lowest grade 13 averages of any entering class to any Ontario university.
If you had to put it in one sentence:	Everybody here is desperate to return to some bygone era.

DO'S AND DON'TS

DON'T give money to Trent. Thomas Bata did, and they named the library after him in thanks. But since Bata used to invest in South Africa, the university decided it was immoral to have his name on the plaque. They did, however, deem it moral to keep his money.

DO visit Artspace, a local gallery that displays the work of local artists. They take themselves ver-ry seriously.

DON'T come to school before you figure out how you feel about homosexual rights. This is a big topic of conversation here.

DO buy your "Empire cheese, Astro yogurt, dried fruit and nuts, nu-life, tea and coffee substitutes, Swiss Herbal vitamins, minerals and supplements, seeds and other staples, fresh ground peanut butter, bulk honey (bring your own container)" from Kelcey's Nutrition Centre, or any one of the other plentiful Trent health-food stores. Yum-yum.

TRINITY WESTERN

Trinity Western University is owned and operated by the Free Evangelical Church. If you choose to attend, the university will require you to sign a contract, in which you consent to follow the university's rules. You must:

> refrain from practices which are biblically condemned. These include drunkenness, swearing, or use of profane language, all forms of dishonest practice including cheating and stealing, abortion, involvement in the occult, and sexual sins including premarital sex, adultery, and homosexual behaviour.

> You must abstain from the use or possession of alcoholic beverages, tobacco in any form, marijuana and drugs for non-medical

purposes, social dancing, and to maintain discreet, inoffensive behaviour in relationships with members of the opposite sex.

You must exercise careful judgment in the choice of entertainment including television, movies and live productions.

You must regularly attend classes, chapel services, and university events.

Sound like fun? The kids at Trinity Western certainly seem to think so. Every year, each of the school's 1,100 students happily agrees to abide by these rules, and pays the highest tuition in the country — $3,700 a year — for the privilege. And the school has grown by 20 per cent over the past three years.

"Students and their parents like this school," according to one of its vice-presidents, "because it is the only university in Canada which takes a hard-headed, critical look at our culture. We are a refreshing alternative for a society increasingly concerned with values."

The popular misconception about Trinity Western is that it is a Bible college. It is not. Trinity Western is a liberal-arts university which integrates the teachings of the Christian faith with a normal university curriculum. Christian universities "are a dime a dozen in the States," explains the school's student president, "but in Canada, we're the only one."

Trinity Western calls its style of education the "whole person approach." What that means is set out in TWU's academic calendar: "The dual emphases of Christian integration in the classroom with total personal development provides an excellent atmosphere for nurturing qualities of Christian character, of using one's abilities to further God's plan and purposes for man, and of thinking creatively and biblically about the world."

Professors at Trinity Western are also required to sign an annual contract of faith, affirming their belief in Christ and his teachings. There are no non-Christians, atheists, evolutionists, or Marxists on the TWU faculty. And, like their students, TWU professors make considerable financial sacrifices to be here: when the coach of the football team deserted the University of Winnipeg for TWU, he took a 40 per cent pay cut.

Trinity Western is Canada's only private university. It gets no money from either the provincial or federal governments. School legend claims that the institution was begun on a $500 donation (and, of course, a prayer). Today, 25 years later, Trinity Western, with its small collection of two-storey red-brick buildings, still looks more like a fancy summer camp than a developed university. The school still lacks a decent library, a gym, a student centre, science laboratories, and many other amenities that even the most destitute, government-owned universities consider indispensable. Rudimentary facilities are just another sacrifice that the students and faculty of TWU are prepared to accept for their faith.

"Academics are important here," says the student president, "but the emphasis is on the total development of a person. Intellectually — yes, but socially and spiritually, too. You're not a student and a Christian separately. Whatever you do, you are always doing it as a Christian. Here we learn to question, test, and understand our beliefs." Another student puts it even more directly: "We are here because we believe in God and the Bible."

The atmosphere at Trinity Western is certainly filled with Christian love. Although these students may be very chaste in their personal lives, in public they touch, hug, squeeze, and smile at each other more than their counterparts at Canada's non-Christian schools.

You see warmth wherever you go. In a hallway, a girl who had been sick thanks a friend for some muffins with an enormous bear-hug and a profuse outpouring of gratitude. In the cafeteria, students compliment the staff on the food (!). Between classes, students walk around in chatty groups, and a stranger on campus cannot pass without friendly students stopping her, eager to welcome a newcomer.

As far as extracurricular activities go, TWU students forego normal student diversions — dances, pub nights, wine and cheese receptions, panty raids — in favour of higher entertainment. As long as you don't get bored with Christianity, there will always be lots to do at TWU.

The TWU campus is plastered with flyers advertising every possible Christian event:

- The latest Rebecca Pippert Films, *Learning to Love*, and *Sharing the Message*, sponsored by the Evangelistic Outreach program.
- Music with a mission, with Scott Wesley Brown and Ruby Duke.
- A lecture with Joanne Wallace — America's outstanding Christian authority on inner-outer beauty — speaking on self-worth.
- Wednesday Prayer Breakfast in the lower café.
- An afternoon of Billy Graham Training Films.
- A Missionary Pavilion featuring 100 missionaries from around the world.
- A travelling Christian Theatre troupe.

The only diversion at TWU that can compete with God for popularity is sports. Almost everybody participates in intramural sports. The Varsity teams are improving each year, and gather enormous crowds. There is no arena on campus, but there is a hockey team, as well as men's and women's soccer, basketball, and volleyball teams. Trinity Western competes in the Totem Conference, so that they play against community colleges rather than universities.

Because of TWU's situation in small-town Langley, BC, where the householders keep sheep and horses in their yards, finding a place to live off campus can be hard. Fortunately, half the student body are able to live in residence. For the others, it's tough. "Sometimes landlords don't want to rent an apartment to three girls from Trinity Western," complains a young editor from the student newspaper. What landlord wouldn't love to have three God-fearing young people as tenants? "Don't fool yourself," she replies, "people here can be rude too."

In fact, despite their image as goodie-goodies, students at Trinity Western are not the passionless creatures one might suppose them to be. On the contrary, students here spend more time thinking about love and marriage than young adults who are free to dally with s-e-x.

Dating goes on in a big way here and students feel the pressure to marry young. There is no other Canadian university student handbook, for example, that contains an advice section on engagements and marriage. "In the best interest of students as they begin their life together," says the TWU handbook, "it is recommended that they not get married during the academic year. Students planning to marry should notify the Student Affairs Office at least one month in advance. Name changes should be made with the Registrar."

Dating at Trinity Western is a highly organized, centrally-planned event. Each term, every dorm has its chance to go on an "all star" date: One of the dorms is designated, and its residents are required to ask the man or woman of their choice out on a date. There are also more loosely structured "dorm dates," on which entire dorms date each other *en masse*. Vancouver, which is only 45 minutes away, is the favourite dating ground.

Unlike many Christian universities in the States, TWU students may date without chaperones. And students say that although their contract does not allow premarital sex, there's a lot of room for interpretation in the section that reads: "you must maintain discreet, inoffensive behaviour in relationships." "It's a safe bet that not everyone here is a virgin," says a student. He adds, "the stupid thing is to do it in your residence room. I mean, you share the place with four other people. You're going to get caught." A blind eye is turned, however, towards people who do their "heavy mashing" (TWU for "necking") in the co-ed residence's lounge, or the "passion pit," as it is also known.

If marriage is important, so is getting an education. Academics at Trinity Western can be demanding and the university has a very structured program. Every student must satisfy a core requirement consisting of courses in the following subjects: two English, one fine arts, two humanities, one philosophy, three natural science or mathematics, three religious studies, one Bible content, three social sciences, one history, two physical education, and one course in interdisciplinary studies.

The content of all these courses is always discussed within a biblical framework. Explains one philosophy professor who teaches at Trinity Western during term, and at UBC in the summer, "the reading list for the courses I teach at UBC and Trinity Western are identical. The only difference is that at Trinity Western I try to show the relevance of my topic to students who embrace a religious faith. The content is the same, but I know my students worry about religious topics. It's a question of *additional relating.*"

The most unusual program available at Trinity Western is aviation. TWU offers a two-year diploma in aviation and a four-year degree with an aviation minor. While the course attracts students purely interested in commercial flying, its goal is the training of missionaries.

Although Trinity Western does not deny admission to non-Christians — they had two Sikh students last year — this would be a very difficult school for non-believers. Students applying to Trinity Western must write admission essays answering these questions: "Who is Jesus Christ to you and describe your relationship to Him at this time?" "Describe your involvement in your local church," and "Why do you want to attend a Christian university?" Those committed to evangelical Protestantism will find a TWU congenial. Others should steer clear.

"In the cafeteria, students compliment the staff on the food."

THE FACTS

Founded:	1962 Trinity Junior College 1972 Trinity Western College 1984 Trinity Western University
Address:	7600 Glover Road Langley, British Columbia V3A 4R9
Tuition:	$3,664
Cut-off grade for general admission:	C+ recommended
Enrolment:	1,109
Undergraduate full-time enrolment:	933
Percentage of foreign students:	8 — half of whom are American
Percentage of students from outside the province:	22
Residence fees:	$3,048
Percentage of students in residence:	48
Male-female ratio:	49:51
Athletic facilities:	Adequate.
Team name:	The Spartans
Colours:	Gold and scarlet
Fraternities/Sororities:	None.
Typical garb:	Wholesome, modest.
Campus political attitude:	There is only one political club on campus: the Young PCs.
Best-known fact:	Students here tend to be religious.
Least-known fact:	The school offers a degree in aviation.
If you had to put it in one sentence:	"This place is too expensive for me to be here without believing in everything it stands for." — *Student*

DO'S AND DON'TS

DO bring your ghetto-blaster to school. Although you're not allowed to dance, "rocking out to Bruce Springsteen" is okay.

DON'T decide against TWU because you think you can't afford it. The loan program here is outstanding. If you want to come, they'll help you.

DO bring some hillbilly clothing so you can attend the annual Harvest Fest. You don't want to miss the pumpkin-seed-spitting contest, the dunking booth, or the marrying booth.

DON'T forget to bring a few cases of Coca-Cola with you to school. It's all you'll be drinking for the next four years.

UNIVERSITY OF VICTORIA

When the natives say that the city of Victoria belongs to "the newly wed and the nearly dead," they mean that if you need rip-roarin', fire-breathing, non-stop fun, you had better look elsewhere. The student who has come to college to read poetry under the trees by himself, however, won't find prettier trees anywhere than at the University of Victoria. "To me," says a dreamy U Vic student, "this place is like a Never Never Land."

The campus lies on a huge expanse of park, and while its buildings don't add anything to the park's beauty, they don't detract from it much either. And just a few hours from school is an individualistic sportsman's paradise: salmon fishing, mountain climbing, skiing, windsurfing, sailing, canoeing, water-skiing, beaches, swimming, trekking. "The great outdoors, that's what this city, this university are all about," claims the president of the Ski Club. He adds that "there are winter days when all you need is a tee-shirt. Minus four is about as cold as it will ever get."

The university itself, sad to say, is undistinguished. The library, gym, stadium, residences, cafeterias, student centre, and bookstore don't sink too far below average, but for intellectual wattage the two big schools across the straits overshadow Victoria.

Victoria draws most of its population from the interior and the island. "What other university recruits in Spuzzum, BC?" asks a native of Spuzzum, BC. A substantial minority, about one-quarter, come from Vancouver. But while the students at Victoria come from all over British Columbia, they do not come from all walks of life. Victoria, "is really WASP," according to someone very WASP himself. "You don't see many non-white faces, not at the university and not on the island. And the majority of students come from pampered, upper-class backgrounds. Most students here don't need to work in the summer."

Victoria is one of a handful of universities in Canada where enrolment is declining. The university's admissions director looks on the bright side: "We have an extensive [junior] college system in this province, and students are finding it cheaper to spend a couple of years at college and then transfer to university for their third and fourth years. So, although our first-year enrolment has dropped by 14 per cent, the number of transfer students is up."

What does that mean for the tone of the campus? "This place is getting more goddamned élitist every day," complains the vice-president of the student council. "It's getting to be like the old days, when a college degree was a status symbol because only the rich could afford one."

The students at Vic, however, don't feel so rich that they can study whatever they want. Vic, like so many other universities, is gripped by grim pre-professionalism. The visual-arts department makes shift in "temporary" tin huts built during the second World War, but brand-new engineering and computer-science facilities have just been built. "They're trimming all the arts and turning Vic into a job-training centre," mutters one embittered artsy. But the admissions director disagrees. "It is still appropriate to describe this university as a liberal-arts school. There was a need for another engineering program in this province, since UBC had the only one and there is such a great demand. But there's been no deliberate cut in the arts; it just happens that fewer students are interested in them. We address student needs."

Artsies can console themselves that Vic continues to offer an ambitious fine-arts program. "Our Phoenix Theatre is probably one of the best places in the country to get technical theatre training," insists one happy fine-arts student. A hopeful writer adds, "The writer-in-residence program is what I like best. We've had some beautiful people here — Jack Hodgins, Lawrence Russell, Dave Godfrey, and Phyllis Webb. Now Phyllis, she's *really* beautiful!" Each year the fine-arts students put on a festival of fine arts which is "totally student-organized and -funded." It is a major event of the year.

There are also good co-op programs at U Vic in biology, chemistry, computer science, creative writing, engineering, geography, health information sciences, mathematics, and physics. The co-op system is a good program for students who need or want to work while going through school. It is especially helpful to have the assistance of the university in a city like Victoria, where jobs can be hard to come by.

"Victoria? Careers? No!" says one ambitious native Victorian who plans to move after graduation. "The only industries in this town are tourism, politics, and education." Still, the choice of Victoria can be justified in practical terms, at least in the opinion of another ambitious young woman. "I came here from Vancouver because it's easier to get good marks. When it comes time to apply to med school, I know my transcript will be better than if I had gone to UBC."

A little easier than finding a job, but not, apparently, as easy as finding good marks, is finding an affordable place to live. Students say rents of $300 are normal. U Vic is located in a spacious suburb. Students take apartments as near to campus as they can get, which is not very near. Having a car at school would be an extra bonus, since the campus is quite far from the downtown and on-campus parking is plentiful.

Life in residence is convenient, potentially cheaper, and more fun — more fun, that is, by the undemanding standards of Vic. "This really isn't a party campus," says one student. "It's nothing like the schools out east, for sure."

Vic students don't look to their downtown for excitement either. "Night-life in this town is non-existent," complain most students. Although this is one of Canada's best tourist spots, the restaurants and watering holes are not geared to rowdy, beer-bashing, college-style fun.

Three restaurants, Pagliacci's, Harpo's, and Julie's are the favourites, in order of preference. "You do get tired of always going to the same places," says the president. "I mean, the people who can still afford to be here are people who can afford to eat out. There's just nowhere to go." Of course, in a town as romantic and developed as Victoria, that's not strictly true. There really is no shortage of quiet, candle-lit, corner tables in this city. Students do say, however, that Victoria's best season is summer — a time when most students have left.

Romantics, introverts, sun seekers, sportsmen, athletes (Victoria's teams are outstanding), and environmentalists should think hard about Victoria. Dedicated academics, wild party-goers, and those who think that life begins at midnight should stay away. Victoria offers a quiet serenity that will bore those who don't appreciate it, but is the very essence of the good life to those who do. The president of the student council, who left his native Germany to attend Victoria, says: "Victoria is the kind of place you fall in love with at the snap of your fingers. That goes for both the city and university. Once you're here, you'll never want to leave."

THE FACTS

Founded:	1903 Victoria College 1963 Victoria University
Address:	PO Box 1700 Victoria, BC V8W 2Y2
Tuition:	$1,620
Cut-off grade for general admission (per cent):	67
Enrolment:	10,646
Undergraduate full-time enrolment:	6,449
Percentage of foreign students:	2
Percentage of students from outside the province:	3
Residence fees:	$2,654–3,459
Percentage of students in residence:	10
Male-female ratio:	47:53
Athletic facilities:	Very good.
Team name:	(M) Vikings (F) Vikettes
Colours:	Blue and gold
Fraternities/sororities:	Soon. Students are working on founding the first frat.
Typical garb:	Shorts and tee-shirts.
Campus political attitude:	"UBC is conservative. Simon Fraser is Marxist. We're in between." —Student
Best-known fact:	U Vic is located in the warmest university town in Canada.
Least-known fact:	U Vic was founded by McGill University.

| If you had to put it in one sentence: | "This is the most exclusive dating service in the province."— *Student* |

DO'S AND DON'TS

DO consider Victoria if you are an expert basketball player. The Victoria Vikings have won the national men's championships in this sport for six years straight. The record of the women's team is almost as good.

DON'T consider U Vic if you smoke. Even the non-basketball players here are obsessed with fitness and good health. Smokers aren't popular.

DO bring your Frisbee, magnetic chess sets, and Sony Walkman. Lounging around outside is the great joy of attending U Vic.

DON'T live with your parents if you hope to get student aid. The two don't go together.

DO bring your convertible to school. This is the ideal Canadian city for cars without roofs. There are also more Volkswagen "Bugs" in this city than in all other Canadian cities put together.

WATERLOO

Remember the guy in your high-school calculus class who wore thick glasses, flood pants, and carried 16 sharpened pencils in his breast pocket — and would never lend you one because you should have brought your own? The one who didn't go to the prom because not even fat Mabel would go with him? Well, now he's the most popular guy in his class at Waterloo University. And not only that, he's going to get a much better job than you are.

"It's been well documented that Waterloo students are the worst-dressed people in Canada," jokes the arts editor of the student newspaper. But if Waterloo students are square and a little nerdy, they are at least tolerant.

Two years ago, Waterloo got its first punk engineer. One night while he was in the washroom of the pub, a Wilfrid Laurier student named Larry, and his pals, attacked him. The gang grabbed him, beat him up and tried to soap down his Mohawk. But the punk turned out to be tougher than he looked. He broke Larry's nose and nearly broke the ribs of several other gang members. One of them had to be hospitalized.

The university first heard the story when Larry's girlfriend wrote an indignant letter to the editor of the Waterloo paper, warning the punk never to show his face at the pub again — next time, Larry would have a really *big* gang. The Waterloo campus, surprisingly, rallied to the punk's defense. Larry's name became mud. There were anti-Larry dances, anti-Larry buttons (Larry's name with a red bar through it), and an avalanche of anti-Larry letters in the school's paper. Waterloo students work on the assumption that anybody who doesn't like punks probably doesn't like geeks either.

Once you're out of high school, being a geek isn't such a bad thing. Not only do Waterloo students — at least those in computer science and mathematics, science, and engineering — enjoy the ego-thrills of enrolment in one of the most exclusive programs in the country, but they also don't know the meaning of the word "unemployment." "People at Waterloo aren't hung up on jobs," says the president of the student council. "They've *got* jobs."

One reason Waterloo grads are so employable is the Waterloo Co-op program, the second biggest in the world after Northeastern University's. The co-op program combines university-organized work terms with school terms. Students alternate between school and work, earning money, experience, and a degree all at the same time. Waterloo even offers work/study programs in English.

Waterloo students don't compare themselves to students at other universities: they simply pity them. There is, however, fierce intramural rivalry. Who's really on top? The employable engineers? The brainy science and math students? Or maybe — could it be? — the aloof and resentful artsies? The rivalry between math students and engineers is so acute that they refuse to wear the same leather jackets. Math students wear mustard jackets, while engineers wear black ones. (There is unanimity on something — all carry black vinyl briefcases.)

Last spring, artsy spleen bubbled over in an editorial in *Imprint*, the campus paper, entitled "Are engineers stupid?" The sullen conclusion was that engineers might not be stupid, but they have no souls. "While they may be experts at building bridges, they are no better off than high school drop-outs when it comes to ethics, politics or morality. While it is undoubtedly a good thing to train people in engineering, it is also undoubtedly a bad thing to fail to help students place their training and their expertise in the social, political, and human context within which they and their expertise must live."

It isn't just the artsies and the engineers who hate each other. "The campus as a whole does not have a lot of common spirit. People here don't so much identify with Waterloo University as they do with their faculty or college. Someone will say 'I'm a engineer' or 'I'm in St. Jerome's College' before they'll say 'I'm from Waterloo.'"

St. Jerome's is one of four denominational colleges on campus. It's Catholic. Conrad Grebel College is Mennonite, Renison is Anglican, and St. Paul's is United Church. The church colleges contribute both spirituality and academic well-roundedness to Waterloo. Most students in the colleges are students who do not participate in the co-op program. They claim that the colleges give them a sense of community and continuity that they would otherwise miss.

Waterloo sure could use more community and continuity. Fifty per cent of Waterloo students are enrolled in the co-op programs, which means that they are generally on campus no longer than four months at a stretch. Friendships are stunted and love affairs atrophy or never begin. "This campus is never the same from semester to semester," complains a student. "You have to start all over again every four months, making new friends, finding new room-mates. And always in the back of your head when you meet someone new is the knowledge that they will be gone soon." The atmosphere at a school where one-quarter of the student population is away at any given time and the coolest guys on campus are computer whizzes inclines to the chilly.

The co-op program's toll is exacted not just when you leave Waterloo, but when you arrive at work. It's tough to move to a new city, where you probably know nobody, for four months. Waterloo students have sensibly created a network of "WATpubs," so that once a week, at least, Waterloo students in any major city can look forward to a party with people from their school.

Not all the blame for the dismal social life at Waterloo belongs to the co-op program. There's a price to being an engineering, math, and science powerhouse: no women. "There sure are great pickings for the women here," says one young man. Once Waterloo men meet a woman, they don't let go. They never know when they're going to see another.

The place to meet the Waterloo men of your dreams is Federation Hall. Fed Hall is the newest and largest student pub in Canada: it's so spiffy it outclasses all other bars in town. It's so big that a couple can find a corner and be left absolutely alone; it's so crowded that you can always find someone you know — or someone new.

Kitchener-Waterloo is a tough housing market, and the co-op program makes finding a bearable apartment even tougher. Students often return to school just days before the start of a new term, and don't have time to be choosy. Many have to settle for expensive housing miles away.

The denominational colleges have dormitories attached, and the university maintains two large residence complexes, Villages One and Two. (There's room for 2,000 on campus, but the university has another 2,500 spaces off campus.) First-year students have taken over Village Two, and it's the wilder. "Guys drink a lot more than they would if there were girls around," explains a male computer-science student. "You sometimes have to step over the collapsed bodies at res parties, or else sometimes fights will break out. It's just all that pent-up male energy, I guess."

Not all that energy is channelled into aggression. Waterloo has made major advances in computer technology, and as a research institution it has brought great honour to Canada. Not only has Waterloo produced over one-quarter of Canada's computer scientists, but it has also invented three new computer languages that together earn the university $2 million in royalties each year. Waterloo will soon be opening a brand-new computer facility which will — it's claimed — "have more computer scientists under one roof than any place in the world." Waterloo already has the largest university math department in the free world. Waterloo computer scientists are computerizing the Oxford English Dictionary. Let's hope "computerizing" makes it in.

The ideal Waterloo student did brilliantly in math in high school. He (or she) either wants to, or needs to, work to put himself through college. He's highly career-oriented. He likes packing. And he thinks the pocket calculator is the ultimate fashion accessory.

THE FACTS

Founded:	1957
Address:	Waterloo, Ontario N2L 3G1
Tuition:	$1,654
Cut-off grade for general arts admission (per cent):	mid-60s
Average grade 13 mark of entering class (per cent):	77.3
Enrolment:	25,000
Undergraduate full-time enrolment:	14,540

Percentage of foreign students:	3
Percentage of students from outside the province:	7.5
Residence fees:	$3,430
Percentage of students in residence:	13
Male-female ratio:	70:30
Athletic facilities:	Good.
Most impressive major:	Computer science
Least impressive major:	General arts
Fraternities/sororities:	The two frats and one sorority are located off campus, and are not recognized by the university. There are approximately 130 members.
Typical garb:	Flood pants, polyester shirts, sweats.
Favourite movie:	*Revenge of the Nerds*
Campus political attitude:	According to the *Imprint*: "Issues that are trendy to be concerned about: apartheid, Nicaragua, cults, gay rights, nuclear power, the type of music at Fed Hall, the volume of the music at Fed Hall, the kind of lighting at Fed Hall."
Best-known fact:	Waterloo is Canada's top computer-science school.
Least-known fact:	The university uses 470,590 gallons of water per day, 2,700 gallons of paint each year, and produces 54,000 cubic yards of garbage annually.
If you had to put it in one sentence:	"When people think of Waterloo, they think computers and that's what this university is all about." —*Arts student*

DO'S AND DON'TS

DO bring a durable suitcase with you to school. Students at Waterloo move, on average, four times a year for four years.

DON'T be too hasty about breaking up with your high-school girl-friend, since "ten times more guys show up at Waterloo parties than girls." You might miss her more than you suspect.

DO start saving up your money for your own computer, as Waterloo is soon going to demand that students buy their own machines.

DON'T look for the engineers' newspaper, *Enginews*. It was closed down after campus feminists protested its crude humour.

DO look for these weekly columns in the *Imprint*: "A Different Light" (about homosexuals) and "Vegetarian World" (about fruits and nuts).

UNIVERSITY OF WESTERN ONTARIO

If you want to see the Western student council president, you have to call his secretary for an appointment. "The nice thing about this job," he says, "is that it's good training for life." Student leaders at Western carry engraved business cards. They say goodbye with an enthusiastic "we must do lunch sometime." They manage multi-million-dollar budgets. They have buffed fingernails and precision haircuts. The real big shots get modern corner offices brightened by huge picture windows. This is also good training for life. Good training for the Good Life.

The University of Western Ontario is the most popular university in Ontario. It receives more applications than any other university in the province. And with good reason. Western is a large, diverse university of 23,000 students that has the feel of a tight-knit community. It is blessed with a century of history (and therefore some good architecture) as well as a modern, well-equipped, amply-endowed campus. It's located in a charming university town, far enough away from Toronto to feel distant, close enough for spontaneous visits. Best of all, it commands a great deal of snob appeal without exacting harsh entrance requirements.

The snob appeal is the natural consequence of Western's wealth. Western is better endowed than almost any other school in Canada.

Western alumni are among the most generous in the country. Seventy per cent of Canada's private-school graduates apply to Western each year. Fifty per cent of the school's population comes from posh Toronto, and another 25 per cent comes from London, Ontario, one of Canada's wealthiest communities. About 30 per cent of students are children of Western alumni. The student council president says, from his comfortable chair in the nicest student council president's office in the country: "Not many people here make use of OSAP."

Western students think ahead. "Everyone you meet in first year is either pre-med, pre-law, or pre-business," explains one senior. "But a lot of them change their minds later." (When socializing, be prepared for two familiar Western opening lines: "Where did you go to high school?" and, "What does your father do?")

Almost as important as money — maybe just as important — are looks. The Western application form does not ask students if they are thin, blonde, and beautiful, but it's clear that someone in the admissions office is keeping track of this information. I cannot, with a good conscience, recommend Western to fat or ugly people. Unless you are *very* rich.

You'd be crazy to show up at the main student hangout, the University Community Centre (UCC for short — sound familiar?), without having spent a good portion of your morning grooming and primping, preparing yourself for a scrutiny that even Miss America contestants seldom face. Big, open lunch areas allow beautiful people to nibble at celery sticks while making flirtatious eye contact with other beautiful people, and chortling at those who don't make the grade. "It's true people go to the UCC to stare. If you're a girl who can't stand being looked at that way, it may not be a very nice place," says a former private-school boy. "But fortunately the girls who go there do like being stared at."

Western hasn't gotten the news that vanity is one of the seven deadly sins. Western is the only school in Canada that could support an exposed, glassed-in gymnasium and a swimming pool in the middle of its student centre. Throughout the day, co-ed aerobics and swim classes are held in full view for all to enjoy. Judging by the overflowing attendance, it's clear that few Western students are put off by a public display of their scantily clad bodies. They thrive on it.

The 4 o'clock aerobics class is the worst, or best, depending on your point of view. Hundreds of beautifully toned bodies pack the large gym. One student was heard to remark: "I've never seen so many bodies doing anything together, ever." Learning how to work out in Yves St. Laurent exercise outfits, without sweating, is also good training for life.

Success at Western depends, not so much on academic achievement as on social ability. How you perform at the year's various formal balls is

202 LINDA FRUM'S GUIDE

very key. The frats, sororities, residences, clubs, student council, even the orientation committee, all stage their own balls. Vast expenditures of time and money are lavished on all the balls, but the ball of balls, the very tippy-top social event of the year, is the great Western Charity Ball. For this important night, the young men and women of Western spend hundreds and hundreds of dollars on gowns, tux rentals, champagne, manicures, hair-dos, limos, and shoes. Tickets cost $16, and the profits go to local charities. Who says Western lacks a social conscience?

Not everyone at Western is into black tie, however. The students on the Committee against War Criminals, for example, probably haven't been to a formal dance in a while. The committee was formed in 1986, when Western's student council announced that it had engaged Henry Kissinger as a guest speaker. The committee doesn't like Henry Kissinger, and didn't want him to come. Although they failed in their attempt to have the invitation revoked, they did manage to provoke some thought on the Western campus. As one observer points out: "Even if their opinion is a little warped, at least the people on the committee know who Henry Kissinger is, which is more than most people here can say."

It's not that people at Western are stupid, it's just that they find the rest of the world so much less interesting than their own fascinating little corner of the globe. The student president says of the Kissinger visit: "It was gratifying to do something that raised interest on campus beyond the normal concerns of who was at Ceeps last night, and did you see what so-and-so wore to the formal?"

The PR department has ambiguous feelings about Western's image as a playground for the glossy. A school liaison officer frets: "It's thought that Western students are preppy. And if that means they dress well and are good kids, well, then we don't want to discourage that image. Just like Harvard wouldn't want to discourage preppy students from going there either. But if that image of our school discourages intellectuals from coming here, then it's not good."

If only to keep up appearances, Western does have a faculty. The only department at Western that has an outstanding reputation is business. It's usually held to be the best in Canada. Students are only admitted after two years of general study, and successful entrants to the program must have exceptional records. Many of Canada's most important CEOs are Western graduates, among them Galen Weston. The rest of Western's undergraduate programs are fine, and certainly an undergraduate degree from Western carries clout with graduate schools. Western doesn't have a superfluity of big-name professors, but the quality of teaching is probably better than most. Still, business so overshadows all other departments that one Western liberal-arts student complains: "When I tell people I go to Western they say, 'Oh, so you're in business!' Everyone assumes it's the only thing taught here."

One thing that's definitely learned here is school pride — only Queen's equals it. London's hotels and motels are booked months in advance for the fall homecoming weekend. Over 30,000 graduates return each year to remember their happy college days, to watch the Mustangs play football, and to shed a proud tear for their alma mater. The Mustangs came within an inch of winning the Vanier Cup in 1986.

Students are also very proud of their madcap residences, especially Saugeen-Maitland Hall, which is known across the country as "the Zoo." Saugeen houses 1,200 students, making it the largest co-ed residence in North America. "If you're not used to being around a lot of loud and obnoxious people," cautions one resident, "then you won't like it here. Especially on Thursdays, Fridays, and Saturdays." Saugeen is too big for everyone to know everybody else, but regular floor parties ensure a great deal of socializing.

Other Western residences are more sedate, although none is dull. The new Alumni House provides apartment-style living; Delaware is co-ed and has some of the biggest rooms; Medway is all male, and Sydenham is all female.

Housing for students who live off campus is relatively easy to find, but it's usually far from campus. There's no student ghetto. Western students look to the campus for their fun. When students do go into town, Ceeps in the old CP Hotel is the favourite hangout.

To have a great time at Western, be beautiful, rich, private-school educated, athletic, extroverted, and not too serious about your studies. If you can't be all these things, you should at least be some. Western is certainly one of Canada's best universities — few others offer the extensive resources, prestigious reputation, and the happy-go-lucky tone of Western. All it asks in return is that you buy five ball-gowns a term.

"If you want to see the Western student council president, you have to call his secretary for an appointment."

THE FACTS

Founded:	1878
Address:	London, Ontario N6A 3K7
Tuition:	$1,264
Cut-off grade for general admission (per cent):	71
Average grade of entering class (per cent):	76.1
Enrolment:	23,606
Undergraduate full-time enrolment:	15,261
Percentage of foreign students:	4
Percentage of students from outside the province:	15
Residence fees:	$2,848–3,274
Percentage of students in residence:	16
Male-female ratio:	50:50
Athletic facilities:	Excellent. Three gyms. Stadium (seats 10,000), arena (5,000).
Team name:	Mustangs
Colours:	Purple and white
Coolest major:	Business
Fraternities/sororities:	Definitely.
Typical garb:	Preppy — button-down, penny-loafer style. Important to have at least $300 to $400 worth of clothing on your body at all times.
Campus political attitude:	Big fans of the status quo.
Best-known fact:	Western has the most prestigious biz school in the country.
Least-known fact:	Western students are required to go to classes between balls.
If you had to put it in one sentence:	Western is good training for life.

Alumni: Alice Munro, Premier David
                           Peterson, Don R. Getty, Senator
                           Jerry Grafstein, Robert Elgie, Perrin
                           Beatty, Sinclair Stevens, Richard
                           Lawrence (CEO of Burns Fry).

HURON COLLEGE

There are some students who feel that Western would be okay if it could just be a little snobbier. For these students, there is Huron College. Located on the other side of Western Road, Huron students refer to the main campus as the place "across the road." "Huron is a very distinct place from across the road," says one student. "We're rather insulated here and that's how people want it. Most people don't start taking classes across the road until third year. It's too big and intimidating over there."

Huron was the founding college of Western, and is now an affiliated body. The college runs its own admissions and has a strict entrance requirement of 75 per cent. The college holds only 620 students. "Huron wants to stay exclusive," says one student. "Our standards will always be slightly higher than Western's. Not a lot, but just enough to say we're better."

Huron students have their own residences, their own refectory, and their own tea parties twice a week. They are also their own clique. "Huron College students are different from Western students and they are aware of that difference. We dress differently. We vote as a bloc."

Since Huron resembles nothing so much as an enlarged version of Bishop Strachan School in Toronto, it is not surprising that over 50 per cent of the students Huron attracts come from private schools. Most of the students from the private-school axis know each other already. They don't make the effort to meet anyone new. For the rest of Huron's students this can be annoying. "There are certain people here who will never talk to you. You know, you don't belong to the Toronto Cotillion, so you're nothing. Those people are not a majority, but they are very well known. They assume that if you didn't go to private school, you have zero cash."

The best part about going to Huron is that the college's registrar, Miss Ridley, will watch over you. Miss Ridley has been with the college 25 years, and some say she *is* the college. Student attitudes about her range from deep affection to deep fear. Yet all agree that her personal care with each student's academic orientation, registration, and course selection is a symbol of the warm and caring atmosphere of Huron. Miss Ridley calls this "the joy of working with real people, helping them prepare for their future. Here we deal with people, not with paper and numbers."

Although students may take a majority of their courses at Huron, it's not possible to take all of them there. By third year, most Huron students are itching to get to the big campus anyway. Huron students disagree on whether it is easier to get an "A" on the big campus, where the kids are dumber, or at Huron, where the profs know you and are inclined to be generous. Huron students are entitled to use all of Western's facilities except the residences. Several Huron students over the years have been president of the Western student council.

A case could be made that, if you're already into doing the "Western Experience," you might as well go all the way and apply to Huron. However, a case could also be made that, once you've graduated from high school, there's no reason to go back.

THE FACTS

Founded:	1863
Address:	London, Ontario N6G 1H3
Tuition:	$1,432
Cut-off grade for general admission (per cent):	75
Enrolment:	724
Undergraduate full-time enrolment:	661
Residence fees:	$3,255
Percentage of students in residence:	50
Male-female ratio:	52:48

WESTERN DO'S AND DON'TS

DO be sure to attend the traditional "O" Ball. This ball is held in the first week of classes to get you used to the social thrust of the next four years of your life.

DON'T waste your money on a stadium ticket when you can watch games from the hill that overlooks it.

DO get a hold of the "Western Gold Card," which entitles you to discounts in town. Having a Gold Card is good training for life. So is joining the squash club.

DON'T limit your courses to those offered at Western. Charlie Brown University, operated by the UWO student council, offers courses in mixology, yoga, knitting, sign language, and, of course, investing your money.

I REMEMBER...

"My memories of university are very happy. As for impact on my life, I guess it must be having been coached by the late John Metras. I wish my four sons could have been coached by someone like him. I will always be grateful to him and Western for helping me make the transition from a youth to a man." — *Don R. Getty*

WILFRID LAURIER

There are two kinds of students at Wilfrid Laurier University — the biz-nobs (business students), and everyone else. "There is mutual avoidance between the two groups," explains one biz-nob. "It's a considerable gap," says another. "*Are* there other departments here?" a third inquires snootily. Biz-nobs have high-school averages about 10 per cent higher, wardrobes 20 per cent fancier, homework 30 per cent harder, egos 40 per cent bigger, and a new building 100 per cent nicer than anything else on campus.

Waterloo Lutheran University went public in 1973. It abandoned its denominational past, and became secular Wilfrid Laurier University. To survive the competitive Ontario university market, Laurier needed to find some device — any device — to win itself some glory. "The new mind frame of universities is to develop some specialties and then do those things very well," says one of the university's vice-presidents. "Here, specialization is most observable in music, social work, and, of course, business economics." Biz-nobs are the result.

The Peters Building, in which biz-nobs learn to crunch numbers, is clearly meant to prepare them for a lifetime of Ramada Inns. It's luxurious in an utterly impersonal way; still, the potted plants, bright murals, modern classrooms, and carpeted study lounges make the red-brick instant-buildings of the rest of the campus seem distinctly proletarian.

The biggest appeal of the Laurier business program is that students can enter it in first year, and so minimize the time wasted on non-utilitarian subjects. Western's business department, in contrast, requires students to study general arts for two years, and then a great number of applicants are denied admission. "I really wanted to take business," explains one student who decided against Western. "I like the way you can start right away here. Western may be more fun, but it's more risky, too. I wouldn't want to spend two years in general arts only to find out I wasn't accepted into the program." Another attraction of Laurier's business program is that it has a co-op option.

Now that Laurier is stealing business students from Western, it hopes to start stealing music students from U of T. Perhaps the nearly completed Aird Centre for the Arts will help. And if that's not enough, the recent appointment of Maureen Forrester as chancellor of the university means that music students will receive their degrees with a pat on the head from Canada's most famous diva.

Just down the street from WLU, the University of Waterloo is making itself a national reputation. But this is just one of the ways the two neighbouring universities differ: most of Waterloo's students are scientists; most of WLU's are artsies. Waterloo is big and rich, WLU is tiny and hungry. Waterloo has an established reputation. WLU is still working on it.

When asked what they like best about their university, WLU students consistently answer: "I like its small size." When asked how it could be improved they consistently answer: "I wish it was bigger." One university vice-president who agrees with both responses admits: "It's a bit of a conundrum."

The Wilfrid Laurier campus occupies all of one city block. Its location, in a heavily developed residential neighbourhood, probably precludes expansion. The Aird building will likely be the last addition the school will ever see. WLU's vice-president says: "Our location guarantees that we will always maintain our philosophy of being a small, personalized institution." It also guarantees that the hopes of many WLU students for improvement will be thwarted.

Nevertheless, WLU students feel increasingly proud of what they have now. "You can tell the difference just by looking at how much more memorabilia there is in the bookstore," a senior notes. Wilfrid Laurier students are big supporters of their varsity teams. "When you go to a game, and kids have their faces stained purple and the letters WLU painted across their foreheads, you can see that they are really into it," says one WLU enthusiast. "When the teams do well, the place is insane," claims the editor of the student newspaper. "And when they don't do well, the place is insane! Last week they had to turn away 200 fans from the hockey arena." Football and hockey are Wilfrid Laurier favourites, but, in a pinch, basketball will do.

What students like best about basketball is not so much the game but the coach, Dean of Students Fred Nichols. In fact, the students like him so much that last year they decided to rename the student union building after him. The administration, which also likes Dean Nichols, but not *that* much, forbade the renaming. The students took the administration to court to find out who really controlled the student union building. The answer? The administration. There's a lesson for everybody here.

The no-name student union building is the home of Wilfrid Laurier's pub, the Turret, an extremely popular establishment. One student boasts that the round tables in Wilfrid Laurier's bars encourage circulation and mingling. Waterloo may have a sybaritic new pub, but WLU students congratulate themselves on their superior friendliness. "Waterloo students go to Fed Hall with one group of friends and stay with the same group the whole night. At Laurier, you go to the Turret and talk to lots of people. You'll always meet someone new. That's the kind of place it is." Laurier students flock to the "Loo" at the Waterloo Hotel, too.

Although Laurier is a friendly campus, the friendliness is — complain the young men — strictly platonic. "This is not a promiscuous place. If people 'do it,' they only do it with their boyfriends or girlfriends." One young man in residence complains that WLU girls aren't interested in men: "I can't even think of a girl who's got a reputation. But the girls here aren't much, anyhow. It doesn't take a lot to be considered hot stuff. The best girls here wouldn't get a second glance where I'm from [Sudbury]." When this young man and his friends get desperate, they take field trips to Western, where, they say, "you really have to look hard to find an ugly girl."

The women in the new Bouckaert residence — "the prissiest women in Canada" — are the most derided by WLU's men. WLU women do notice that they don't get asked out much; they have no theories as to why. Since all Laurier residences are sex-segregated, men and women keep to themselves. Single-sex dorms enforce studiousness rather than chastity: women are forbidden to have men in their rooms after midnight, Sunday through Wednesday; but they can entertain bikers until dawn Thursday, Friday, and Saturday. There are no effective restrictions in the men's residences.

Off-campus housing in Waterloo can be tough to find. Many students end up in Kitchener, which deters them from joining in an otherwise lively extracurricular life. "It's just too much of a drag to take the bus more than twice a day. That's why I don't participate in any after-school activities. I don't want to have to come back to the campus at night," a Kitchener resident explains. To find housing in Waterloo, start early.

WLU will probably never catch up with Waterloo in popularity or prestige. Still, it's attracting more students all the time. In the last 10 years, the first-choice applications have more than doubled. "Our first-choice applications are up 12 per cent from just last year," boasts a vice-president. "There's a terrific demand. It's just like the way everybody suddenly needs to have Beaver Canoe shirts when the identical no-name shirt goes for a quarter of the price. Demand fosters demand."

THE FACTS

Founded:	1911 Waterloo Lutheran 1973 Wilfrid Laurier
Address:	Waterloo, Ontario N9B 3P4
Tuition:	$1,264
Cut-off grade for general admission (per cent):	65
Enrolment:	6,964
Undergraduate full-time enrolment:	4,308
Percentage of foreign students:	2
Percentage of students from outside the province:	2
Residence fees:	$3,050–3,205
Percentage of students in residence:	14
Male-female ratio:	52:48
Athletic facilities:	Excellent. Athletic Complex, Stadium (seats 6,500).
Team name:	Golden Hawks
Colours:	Purple and gold

Coolest major:	Business
Fraternities/sororities:	None.
Typical garb:	Yuppy-garb for biz-nobs (navy suits, floppy bows, sensible navy pumps, ties). Purple and white WLU clothes for everybody else.
Campus political attitude:	Student concern with drinking and driving is the biggest issue on campus.
Best-known fact:	Wilfrid Laurier has had two names but always the same initials: WLU.
Least-known fact:	Wilfrid Laurier University is just steps from Waterloo University and so enjoys the benefits of extra university facilities and a built-in rival.
If you had to put it in one sentence:	"School spirit here improves daily." — *Student*
Alumni:	Alan Pope.

DO'S AND DON'TS

DO consider attending Wilfrid Laurier if only for the opportunity to participate in Kitchener-Waterloo's famous Oktoberfest celebrations. You will be treated to a week full of accordionists and polka parties.

DON'T make any investment decisions without checking first with your friends in the WLU Stock Market Club. Stocks, bonds, and investment competitions are major passions with WLU students.

DO go to the University of Waterloo library if you can't find what you need at Laurier. Your card is good at both places.

DON'T fail to visit the Kitchener farmer's market on Saturday mornings for breakfast. You can take home some fresh eggs or gorge on the spot with some homemade baked goods.

DO watch a lot of *The Flintstones* reruns before you come to school. Fred and Barney trivia is very important here — especially to the members of the campus' biggest club: the Water Buffaloes.

DO buy your morning cup of coffee from Eileen Stumpf, Wilfrid Laurier's beloved coffee trolley lady. The cheerful Mrs. Stumpf not only dishes out cakes and cookies, but is a friend to all, and a repository of WLU sports trivia.

UNIVERSITY OF WINDSOR

Unlike many universities in Canada, the University of Windsor is not overcrowded. It's not for lack of trying. It's just that nobody wants to come. Windsor's a city you leave. "It's hard to get people to realize that there is another Ontario university west of London," laments a member of Windsor's student council. "I think this school needs better marketing."

Marketing Windsor better would not be easy. Windsor did briefly advertise itself as Canada's southernmost university. The posters said: "Come South," and bragged that it was located in Canada's banana belt. It fooled nobody. A successful marketing campaign would have to gloss over a lot. It would have to gloss over how much Windsor students dislike their school. "I think most people here would go somewhere else if they had the chance," says one of the editors of *The Lance*, the student newspaper. "I know I would." "I'm blown away whenever I meet someone here from Toronto," says another *Lance* staffer. "I mean, why would someone come to Windsor if they didn't have to?"

The campaign would also have to gloss over low — maybe mythical — admissions standards. A third-year student from Toronto complains that "there are a lot of students here who really have no business being anywhere near a university. There are a lot of dumbos who can't read or write, and they don't improve even after three years." Only 2.2 per cent of Ontario Scholars attended the university in 1984–85.

Finally, the campaign would have to gloss over Windsor's faculty. "You have a lot of profs here giving multiple-choice exams for third-year courses. They're too lazy to do anything else, and they probably haven't updated their courses in 20 years."

A sufficiently determined marketer could find a few items to brag about. The fine-arts program is well respected, generally considered second only to York's within Ontario. The university has also attracted some prominent writers. Joyce Carol Oates was writer-in-residence for a year, and W.O. Mitchell served on the faculty for eight years before retiring in 1986.

Before she left, Oates plugged Windsor in an interview in the *Paris Review*: "Windsor is really an international, cosmopolitan community, and our Canadian colleagues are not intensely and narrowly nationalistic. There is, generally, a closeness between students and faculty at Windsor that is very rewarding." Mr. Mitchell said of the program, "In no other university have I found as fine a creative-writing program." The appointment of Richard Rohmer as chancellor demonstrates further Windsor's commitment to literature.

Windsor also has a well-known law school; unfortunately, it is well known for being the Last Chance U of law schools, though our marketing campaign doesn't need to mention that. It would mention, proudly, that Mark MacGuigan taught here, and returned as dean after serving as Attorney-General of Canada. The business school is also not too bad. Two University of Windsor institutes have won some renown and a lot of grant money: the Centre for Canadian-American Studies, and the Great Lakes Institute.

The Windsor campus is remarkably attractive. The usual high-rise blahs don't wreck the central campus with its old ivy-covered stone buildings, inherited from Windsor's precursor — Catholic Assumption College. The imposing Ambassador bridge overwhelms even the most appalling of the 1950s residences. Best of all, the campus is green, treed — no bananas, though — and built to human scale.

Windsor has about the least pretentious and most easygoing atmosphere you could want. There's something about heavy industry that makes people realistic, unassuming, open. "I love it here," says one young woman in residence. "I wanted to come here because it's small, the profs are good, and the people are nice. I could have gone to Western but I'm glad I didn't. When I meet up with my friends who go there, or to places like it, I don't envy them. I can tell that I'm having a better time."

Our marketing man will have to consider carefully whether to mention Windsor's proximity to Detroit. Detroit does offer students the benefits of a truly urban environment: shopping, theatre, big-league sports, concerts, fancy bars, restaurants, and the excitement of being in a border town. It's also Murder City. Detroit leads American cities in murders per capita.

Windsor students glumly compare themselves not only to Western, but also to the school-spirit capital of the world, the University of Michigan. "You think about those guys getting 100,000 people out to their football games ... if we get 300, we're laughing. I suppose the great advantage of the U of M is that it is in Ann Arbor, a town that exists exclusively for the university. Windsor is not a university town, it's an automotive town."

Being a woman at a university in an automotive town can be hard. Everybody assumes that your only goal is to meet somebody who'll take you away with him. More than one one young man believes that "you just can't help thinking that these girls are here to land a husband. You can't blame them. What else is there for them to do in Windsor?"

Although most students look forward eagerly to the day when they leave Windsor, they seem to have a good time while they're here. "It's the people in residence who have the best time," says one non-resident.

"The guys in Mac Hall are real party animals. They brag that they have the lowest collective GPA (grade point average) in Canada. They think that's something to be proud of." Another young woman claims that life in the dorms is so exciting, "nobody needs the networks. We've got the best soaps going on right here." The 35 per cent of students from the Windsor area — and who therefore live off campus — don't usually share her enthusiasm. "Windsor is a very boring city," says one. "The place is dead by two o'clock in the afternoon," says another.

Finding housing both on and off campus is, for once, easy. Windsor guarantees a berth in residence to all first-year students, and students who want to return to residence in the upper three years usually can. Off campus, a two-bedroom apartment goes for about $350. Naturally, the best places are snatched up quickly, so the sooner you look for a place the better. The university is located in a residential area, easing apartment-hunting.

Bullet-shy students prefer Windsor bars to the more glamorous bars in Detroit. So do ID-shy students: the drinking age in Michigan is 21. Tune Up's, Bentley's, Faces, Peachies, and California's are important student hangouts, as is Subway's, the campus pub.

The real marketing campaign for the University of Windsor is run by every University of Windsor graduate. "If I get a job, especially in a place like Toronto, it won't be because some employer was impressed that I went to the University of Windsor," says one senior. The education you receive at Windsor is no worse than that of many other schools, but you'd better get used to the idea that people will always ask you, "Windsor? Why would you want to go there?"

THE FACTS

Founded:	1857 Assumption College 1963 University of Windsor
Address:	Windsor, Ontario N9B 3P4
Tuition:	$1,262
Cut-off grade for general admission (per cent):	63
Average grade 13 mark of entering class (per cent):	70.5
Enrolment:	12,744
Undergraduate full-time enrolment:	7,533

Percentage of foreign students:	10
Percentage of students from outside the province:	Not available
Residence fees:	$2,133–3,730
Percentage of students in residence:	25
Male-female ratio:	53:47
Athletic facilities:	Medium.
Team name:	(M) Lancers (F) Lancerettes
Colours:	Blue and gold
Coolest major:	Business Administration
Uncoolest major:	Fine arts: "those people are freaks."
Fraternities/sororities:	Yes. But only about 100 students involved. Very low profile.
Typical garb:	"The feather haircut is still in style here." Fine-arts people wear black, others wear highly casual clothing.
Campus political attitude:	Obsessed with politics of the US.
Best-known fact:	Proximity to Detroit allows Windsor students to enjoy cultural, social, and sporting opportunities in two cities.
Least-known fact:	In 1986, a Windsor student was abducted in Detroit. She was released three days later in Las Vegas.
If you had to put it in one sentence:	"What people at this school want is a guarantee of a job ... in Toronto." —*Student*
Alumni:	Richard Rohmer, Ed Lumley, Mark MacGuigan, Al Strachan (*The Globe and Mail*), Larry Stout, Vicki Russell (CBC news), Richard Peddie (president of Hostess Foods).

DO'S AND DON'TS

DO take advantage of the free library privileges for Windsor students at Wayne State University in Detroit. Windsor and Wayne State have the closest international relationship of any two universities in the world. They are only ten minutes apart from each other.

DON'T wear your Walkman in the library. A plain-clothes student guard will boot you out, since Walkmans are forbidden according to the library's anti-noise rules. Feet on desks are also a no-no.

DO bring some light clothing with you. Windsor likes to brag that it is located in Canada's banana belt and has posters that encourage potential students to "Come South." Windsor gets very little snow.

DON'T come to Windsor if you are gay. "This would be a scary place to be like that," advises one student.

UNIVERSITY OF WINNIPEG

Winnipeg is a city of two universities. The general perception in Winnipeg is that U of W is the city's *other* university. The one people go to if they're not very smart or if they didn't get into U of M. This unflattering reputation has some truth to it, because of the university's mandate: to offer all Winnipegers a chance to go to university, no matter what their academic past has been like. Half the population of U of W are "mature" students — defined as anyone who begins university at 21 or over. They may enrol in any program with virtually no questions asked. But U of W is not just a school for those with bad high-school transcripts. It is the school of the eccentric, the shy, the immigrant, the poor, the off-beat. It is also the school chosen by those who can't face the long commute to the edge of town where the University of Manitoba is located.

For U of W students, attending Manitoba's less-prestigious school can be humiliating. "A lot of first-year U of W students think to themselves, 'What am I doing here?' But they like it after a while," explains one student. Says another: "The hardest part is when you're still in high school and you tell your friends you're coming here. There is some stigma."

For ambitious students coming out of high school, the open-door policy and community orientation of their university may destroy the sense of intellectual rigour they expect university to represent. However, while the U of W may not be exclusive, it is one of the most cosmopolitan, diverse, and sophisticated universities in the country. "It's incredible, all the different kinds of people you meet," says one student. "And, of course, that's all part of a good education."

Another part of a good education is the feeling that you belong to a community that cares about you. U of W students insist that the relative smallness of U of W is its best attribute. "The old joke in the 1970s was that we called the University of Manitoba 'the farm,' and they called us 'the factory.' People at U of M were treated like cattle and we were treated like items on an assembly line. The difference is, it's true about them but not true about us. This is actually a very personal, very warm place."

"Yeah! Not like it is over there at the jungle [U of M]," adds another student for emphasis. Compared to U of M, which has 25,000 students, U of W with 7,000 feels intimate.

The University of Winnipeg specializes in the liberal arts, small classes, and urban chic. It is downtown, surrounded by plentiful cheap housing, and all the best night-clubs. A U of W student journalist, writing in the school's newspaper, summed up the differences between the two universities this way:

"The University of Winnipeg has never been a school known for its career-oriented focus. People come here to study Psychology, English, Political Science. None of these fields of study is a particularly outstanding path to a career in the outside world. No way. You want a career? Go to the U of M and study Computer Programming, Business Administration, Law or Engineering. Being hip is the essence of attending the University of Winnipeg."

There is definitely something cool about the students at U of W. They wear black. They dye their hair purple. They wear big earrings through their noses. They shave the back of their heads. The editorialist quoted above suggests, wishfully, that they are "dropping gossip gleaned from back issues of the *Village Voice*." But even if they're not, they do look as if they could be.

U of W students are more politically active than most Canadian students. When Riddell Hall isn't filled with funky musicians putting on a concert, it is often filled with booths protesting this cause or that. "We have near-riots here sometimes. There are a lot of different people with a lot of different beliefs here. And people are very vocal."

Being downtown is U of W's great advantage over U of M. For one thing, the location is a great ally in the student leaders' battle against apathy. "Put up 25 flyers around campus and you can be sure almost every U of W student will see one," says a student journalist.

U of W's detractors say it looks just like a high school: a big building with lockers in it. In fact, the architects — Jim Christie and Michael Rattray — have put up a terrific piece of modern design, combining one old building (built in 1896 from the days when the U of W was Wesley College) and 10 newer buildings into one big, bright, airy complex connected by tunnels and overpasses.

The interior of the university is painted in cheerful (okay — garish) reds and yellows and purples and greens. And there are truly neato bits like the huge yellow spiral staircase enclosed in a glass cylinder in Riddell Hall, and the black and orange library in Centennial Hall. But the best part is that you never have to go outside, which for Manitobans is bliss.

But Buck Rogers architecture cannot compensate for shaky academic standards. Fortunately, not everything is shaky. "We're strong in the areas where the only equipment you need is someone who will sit down and think things out with you" — the liberal arts. However, other students argue that the sciences are also worth taking at U of W. A graduate of St. Mary's Academy, a very fancy private girls' school, notes: "After our science teacher told our class that we'd be better off studying science at U of W because classes at U of M were just too big, over half my graduating class decided to go to U of W."

That may represent a real change in thinking at St. Mary's, whose students — at least, those who passed — would never have considered U of W 10 years ago. But the expensive private schools are not yet breaking down the doors at U of W: the main feeder schools remain Kelvin, St. Paul's, and U of W collegiate.

It's not just lack of prestige that keeps bright undergraduates away from U of W, but also the restricted choice of courses. A University of Manitoba student points out that "sure, they have computer science at U of W, but with only one speciality — business computing. Our computer-science program has six choices of specialities. So where are you going to go if you're serious?" The serious are also bothered by the lack of graduate programs — French is just about the only one. And Winnipeg students fear that U of M discriminates against them when they apply to its graduate programs. "If you want to do grad work, U of M is your only choice," says one U of W student. "Otherwise, you're at a real disadvantage when it comes time to apply to grad school. If you aren't yet acquainted with someone you want to study under, or if you don't know anyone who can pull a string to get you in, it may be hard to get accepted."

A U of W guidance counsellor disagrees, however: "Statistics show that a larger proportion of U of W students get into medical school than do U of M students, probably because our classes are smaller and so students learn better here." "And because they mark easier at U of W," says an unimpressed U of M student.

To maintain its reputation for intimacy and smallness, U of W enforces a limit on the number of students any one professor may teach, something inconceivable at U of M. Average class size is between 20 and 30 students, and the biggest single class in the whole university numbers only 227.

There's no student union building or campus pub at U of W, so the student buffeterias (Manitoban for "cafeteria") are used as hangouts instead. "The building closes at eleven, and the security guards always have to chase people away. This is not the kind of school where people come just for classes. People linger around campus just for fun." Different buffeterias appeal to different students. Punk rockers eat Mars bars at Lockhart, preppies sip Diet Coke at Riddell, and a motley assortment crowds the main dining hall. Off campus, U of W students frequent either fancy places like Night Moves (Winnipeg's version of Edmonton's Goose Looney's) and the Times, or they go to the cheap and rowdy Union Centre, which is a clubhouse for Winnipeg's union workers. Beer at the Union Centre is only $1.80, and between beers you can amuse yourself with pool-tables and juke-boxes. It's not the crowd you'll meet in yuppy bars — nobody's networking here.

U of W is closing down its residences. "When you're downtown, and you need to expand, you don't have any choice but to refocus your existing space," says a housing officer. In any case, there were only 125 spaces in residence, and those spaces were seldom filled, because good cheap housing in the area is easy to find. Of course, many students live with their parents. Students either walk or take the bus to school, because parking in downtown Winnipeg is a nightmare.

If you live in Winnipeg, and impressing others — especially potential employers — matters to you, then you really must go to the University of Manitoba. But if you'd like to do something a little different, a little risky, that exposes you to wider experience and a fuller sampling of humanity, then you might just buck the trend and opt for the undervalued University of Winnipeg.

THE FACTS

Founded:	1967 as the University of Winnipeg. History of institution dates back to 1871.

Address:	515 Portage Avenue Winnipeg, Manitoba R3B 2E9
Tuition:	$981
Cut-off grade for general admission (per cent):	60
Average grade 12 grade of entering class (per cent):	65
Enrolment:	7,774
Undergraduate full-time enrolment:	3,422
Percentage of foreign students:	5
Male-female ratio:	41:59
Athletic facilities:	Good. Also YWCA across the street.
Team name:	(M) Wesmen (F) Lady Wesmen
Colours:	Red, white, and black
Fraternities/sororities:	None.
Typical garb:	Urban chic.
Campus political attitude:	"Very left-wing. After all, there are no engineers here." — *Student*
Best-known fact:	It produced a lot of stars in its golden-olden days.
Least-known fact:	The University of Winnipeg is home to some extremely hip dudes and chicks.
If you had to put it in one sentence:	"U of W is for alternative type of people, you know?" — *Student*
Alumni:	Lloyd Axworthy, Allan Gotlieb (Canadian ambassador to USA), Sterling Lyon, Howard Pawley (premiers of Manitoba), Heidi Quiring (Miss Canada 1978), Ramsay Cook (historian), Stanley Knowles, Peter Herrndorf (publisher, *Toronto Life* magazine), Margaret Laurence.

DO'S AND DON'TS

DO attend the concert series held in Riddell Hall: Jazz Riddell, Blues Riddell, Reggae Riddell, Rock Riddell, and Classics Riddell. The whole city shows up.

DON'T try to do serious studying in the U of W library. It's not that great for research, and besides: "You need to put a bag over your head if you don't want to be bothered by your friends." You're better off at the public library, which is only four blocks away.

DO read the *Unitergram*, the administration's daily on-campus news-letter, whose distribution makes up for the fact that the school newspaper, the *Uniter*, is only published once a week.

YORK

Is York really as terrible as everyone says? Yes. It's ugly, isolated, impersonal, impoverished, bleak, and depressing. Attacking York is no fun, because it's not sporting. York is a sitting duck.

York University is situated on the industrial prairie of Downsview, Ontario. The campus is remote from the centre of town, and virtually inaccessible by public transit. The 85 per cent of York students who commute must choose between the expense of a car and one of Toronto's longest bus rides. It takes 45 minutes to get from Wilson subway station to the York campus. When you get off the bus, you face the ramp of the immense Ross Building, which looks and feels remarkably like one of those pyramids the Aztecs used for human sacrifices.

Although it was originally founded to promote the educational ideals of the 1960s (open admissions, small classes, even smaller academic demands), York's real purpose in life is to serve as the spill-over school for U of T. (U of T has always enthusiastically supported York as a perfect solution to its own overcrowding problems.) York's Downsview campus was designed in 1965 to accommodate 20,000 students. In 1972, when the project was only half-finished, the Ontario government imposed a moratorium on university capital spending. York refuses to relinquish hope that the money for the rest of the campus will materialize any day now. Forty thousand students attend York —twice as many as planned for in half the space.

To humanize what is now the fourth-largest university in Canada, York created Oxford-inspired colleges. Sadly, the college system has not been a great success. Few students are even aware of which college they belong to. "It's just a name written on your student card," says the editor of the student newspaper. The university claims that each of the seven colleges has a distinct personality, but these personalities prove hard to define. The most elusive is that of Calumet College, which doesn't, in fact, exist. Calumet College is the name on the door of the common-room in the part-time student building. Just one college does stand out a bit, Norman Bethune College, named after Canada's most admired Stalinist. The Bethune student council is alleged to be a little more radical than the others.

York students are painfully aware of their university's unfavourable reputation. "We all know the jokes about how all you need is a pulse and a cheque-book to get into York," says the student president wearily. "When I was in high school, and people asked me where I was going to go to college, I told them I didn't know, even though I knew I was going to go to York. There is a stigma." A member of York's administration complains: "It's astonishing to contemplate in what low esteem people within a one-hundred-mile radius view us. People love to dismiss us. We've changed a lot. We keep getting better. But it's hard to get the outside world to believe that."

There are, however, enough people in the outside world who believe in York to allow the university a rejection rate of three out of four applicants. Because of its location, York attracts many suburbanites who are glad to be spared a long daily journey downtown to do their studies. Other students choose York because U of T seems either too intimidating or too snooty. York welcomes Jewish, Italian, and West Indian students who might only receive a condescending smile from the sherry-sipping guardians of the Trinity College junior common-room. And York enthusiastically believes in part-time education, making higher education and university degrees available to working people, mature students, and others who weren't ready for university when the universities were ready for them.

Outsiders see York as a very social, non-academic place. This mystifies York students. "I think that if you compared us to Queen's, Western, or Waterloo, you wouldn't think we were especially social," says the student president. The editor of the paper theorizes that "maybe that image can be explained by the fact that we don't have much student space at York. People are constantly thrown up against each other. That makes for a more social environment, I guess. Most of our classes are held in the Ross Building, and, between classes, Central Square resembles Sam the Record Man on Boxing Day."

York has no student union building, although a plan for one is in the works. For now, Central Square, underneath the Ross Building, is the closest thing there is. York students call it a mall; Albertans would sneer. It's just an underground collection of shops. Between classes, students squat along the walls, assorted by ethnic group. "It's dingy and depressing," complains one student. Still, it's warm. Students dread leaving the Ross Building between November and April. "During the winter, this place, because of its vast open spaces, turns into a wicked wind tunnel. It may only be a five-minute walk between your car and your class-room, but those are five minutes spent in HELL," says the editor of the newspaper.

York's problems are more spiritual than academic. "I think the biggest misunderstanding people have about York is that the academics here are not good," says the student president. Indeed, York's business school, law school (known at York as Club Oz), fine-arts department, history, and political-science departments easily rank among the "top three" in Canada. And even though the sciences are desperately short of money, York has an excellent faculty of arts. Canadian Studies is particularly well thought of: Ramsay Cook, Donald Smiley, Jack Granatstein all teach here. And, for a new university, York's library is unusually good.

It's the students, not the faculty, who depress York's academic reputation. With a current cut-off grade of 68 per cent for most programs (it's going up to 70 per cent for 1988), some York students find their class-mates to be "mediocre and unmotivated." "You get some real goofs in your classes."

Since most students board the buses for the long journey home immediately after class, extracurricular activities at York are limited. A few energetic students do play on the generally respectable varsity teams, and ethnic clubs are visible and robust.

What extracurricular life there is depends on the residential students. "Living in residence is a lot of fun," says one student. "Most people get very involved in something." Residences are also where the majority of campus parties take place. "The best residence parties are in the dead of winter, when, after being locked up in the middle of nowhere for months and months, people go really crazy," says one resident.

Students who don't live with their parents, but want to escape the grim campus residences, would be well advised to find an "inconvenient" apartment somewhere in central Toronto rather than a "conveniently located" basement apartment at, say, Jane and Steeles. A recent graduate believes that "it's better to take the hour to drive to school than to shunt yourself off in some depressing hole far from civilization. I tried it, and it sapped all my energy. I felt like I had been sucked into a black hole."

Students eat and drink on campus during school hours, because "off-campus places are too far away." (The nearest Harvey's is five minutes away by car.) After class, students flee, and so the campus pubs are not much in demand. Each college building has its own pub, and there are several cafeterias and one deli on campus. The faculty lounge boasts a Bersani and Carlevale's franchise. Theoretically, students aren't allowed in, but during off-peak hours the restaurant's staff are unlikely to challenge interlopers.

The best thing that has happened to York in a long time was the appointment of Harry Arthurs, the dean of Osgoode Hall, as president. Arthurs admits willingly that, in its current state, York's environment is far from exciting. To solve the problem, he has created the York Development Corporation. He plans to sell some of York's excess property, and use the profits to fund expansion. He expects that in the future York will have "extensive residential accommodation, nearby cinemas, dry-cleaners, and other services and cultural amenities." Arthurs points out that Downsview is the fastest-growing urban community in North America and that it will only be a short time before York becomes "a first-class, synergistic, high-quality community." Furthermore, Arthurs is currently negotiating with the Toronto Transit Commission for a York subway stop. This in itself would be a massive improvement. However, as laudable as Arthurs' initiatives are, they won't happen in time for you.

If you have an average of 70 per cent, should you go to York? You have a tough choice. Of schools with equal admissions standards, York, with the possible exception of Dalhousie, has the best academic program available to you. But York is not generally a happy place, or a fun place, or a pretty place. It is a serious place with a fine faculty and a pretty good library. For Torontonians, it's also a cheap place. Much depends on whether you are going to university to work or to play. If you want to work, go to York. But if you want to live a little, and you can afford it, you'd be smart to take your 70 to Acadia, St. FX, Dalhousie, Memorial, UNB, or Trent.

THE FACTS

Founded:	1959 Glendon Campus. Moved to Downsview 1964.

Address:	4700 Keele Street North York, Ontario M3J 1P3
Tuition:	$1,479
Cut-off grade for general admission (per cent):	70
Enrolment:	33,632
Undergraduate full-time enrolment:	18,188
Percentage of foreign students:	4.4
Percentage of students from outside the province:	7.4
Residence fees:	$2,681–2,964
Percentage of students in residence:	8.5
Male-female ratio:	43:57
Athletic facilities:	Shared with city of North York, limited hours, but good. Gym, ice palace, tennis centre.
Team name:	(M) Yeomen (F) Yeowomen
Colours:	Red and white
Coolest major:	Fine Arts
Fraternities/sororities:	None.
Typical garb:	Vuarnet sun-glasses in summer and winter, fancy Italian leather jackets, shiny leather loafers.
Campus political attitude:	York students support whichever political party is for malls and Trans Ams.
Best-known fact:	The campus is ugly.
Least-known fact:	85 per cent of York students are first-generation university-attenders.
If you had to put it in one sentence:	"No matter what else you say about York, the academic quality is sky-high. We've advanced faster than any other university in the nation." —Student president

GLENDON

Whether Glendon students like it or not, they are York students. But they can be forgiven the flattering delusion that they are something else, since Glendon, in both location and attitude, is miles away from the Downsview campus of York. In fact, Glendon students can sometimes be the harshest critics of what they call York Other. "We're only loosely affiliated, in my mind," says the editor of the student paper. "The two places are very different. We're a green campus; they're grey. York Main is a concrete jungle located in Downsvoid, or is it Dullsview? We have this!"

"This" is beautiful, lush parkland in North Toronto, graced by a spectacular old mansion that once belonged to the man who created Dominion Securities, and disgraced with red-brick boxes. But if you look at the trees, the hills, the grass, and the birds, Glendon is a lovely, peaceful campus.

The most important distinction between York and Glendon (actually, Glendon *was* York before York moved to Downsvoid) is that Glendon is bilingual and getting more so every day. In the old days, bilingualism at Glendon was strictly enforced. When enrolment fell below "viable levels" in the mid-1970s, standards were relaxed, so that bilingualism meant only coexistence and cohabitation. These modifications caused enrolment to climb again.

This year Glendon will resume shoving French (or English, as the case may be) down students' throats. You'll have to demonstrate an ability to speak French or English at a level appropriate for second-year university students. "We're going back to the original concept of Glendon," explains a liaison officer.

Many current Glendon students, especially the English ones, have been disappointed to find how little their French has improved during their time at Glendon. "I came here bilingual and lost it," says the editor of the student newspaper. "I'm still comfortable with syntax and grammar, but I don't flex my vocabulary." If nothing else, some anglophone students acquire an eerie Québécois accent.

For French students, the college seems to be more effective, although it may be the Toronto transit system and the Eaton Centre that deserve credit for their linguistic immersion. Says one student from Quebec, "The co-operation between French and English students is very good. When I came here I could barely speak English. But people here help you. They will talk with you if they see you are making the effort to learn the language. And once you are out on the street, you must speak English." One student from Trois-Rivières explains that "at home, Glendon is prestigious. That's because it's in Toronto. Toronto is big and they know it is difficult to come here. People are impressed. And it's also good to know two languages."

Glendon students are a chummy bunch. Residence life is very convivial. Since the college has only 3,000 students, everyone knows everyone else. And everyone knows everything about everyone else. Not that there's much to know, since Glendon has a serious man shortage. There are 255 women in residence, and 100 men. Says one male resident: "You can live and breathe Glendon if you want. You always know there are people here waiting for you. You just have to watch out for the Glendon grape-vine. After hearing gossip about all the different women who have spent the night in my room — I wish I had been there!"

Of the two residences, Wood is rowdier and "more" co-ed. Hillier is mostly girls and accordingly nicknamed "the convent." "The dances here are great for guys," says a guy. "But the whole community is really close-knit." When Glendon women need to remind themselves that there are men in Toronto, they head out to the Yonge-Eglinton strip. Toronto legend has it that a woman did once meet a man in a Yonge-Eglinton bar, but there is no independent corroboration.

Glendon students are entitled to use all York facilities, although few take advantage of the privilege. The Glendon library is acceptable, and there are excellent sports facilities. Only those students interested in varsity sports make the regular trek to Downsview. All other Glendon students are loath to remind themselves of the connection.

THE FACTS

Founded:	1959
Location:	2275 Bayview Avenue Toronto, Ontario M4N 3M6
Tuition:	$1,479
Cut-off grade for general admission (per cent):	70
Enrolment:	1,900
Undergraduate full-time enrolment:	1,900
Percentage of foreign students:	.7
Percentage of students from outside the province:	7.5

Residence fees:	$2,771–2,994
Percentage of students in residence:	21
Male-female ratio:	26:74

YORK DO'S AND DON'TS

DO wear protective gear when you remind Osgoode law students that they're students at "YORK!" They hate that.

DON'T forget to bring your complete shopping list with you when you go downtown. It takes an hour and a half to get to the Eaton Centre, and you don't want to forget anything.

DO try to pay for your cafeteria meals with "scrip" bought off res students. Scrip is the Monopoly money res students must buy to pay for their meals. They're usually willing to sell some at a 20 to 50 per cent discount, depending on the time of year.

UNIVERSITIES NOT INCLUDED IN THIS BOOK

Athabasca University, Box 10,000, Athabasca, Alberta, T0G 2R0, (Correspondence university)

Université Laval, Cité Universitaire, Quebec, G1K 7P4

Université de Moncton, Moncton, New Brunswick, E1A 3E9

Université de Montreal, Cas postale 6128, Succursale A, Montreal, Quebec, H3C 3J7

Université du Québec, 2875 boulevard Laurier, Sainte-Foy, Quebec, G1V 2M3

Université Sainte-Anne, Pointe-de-l'Église, Nova Scotia, B0W 1M0

Saint Paul University, 223 Main Street, Ottawa, Ontario, K1S 1C4 (Divinity University)

Université de Sherbrooke, Cité Universitaire, boulevard de l'Université, Sherbrooke, Quebec, J1K 2R1

Technical University of Nova Scotia, P.O. Box 1000, Halifax, Nova Scotia, B3J 2X4

CAMPUS POLITICS

Few Canadian campuses are very political. When you ask about it, most students look at you suspiciously and reply: "You mean South Africa 'n' stuff?" To most students, the word "politics" means being hectored by some unfragrant Sandinistan bore. Naturally, they try to avoid the subject.

There is one issue on which large numbers of students can be relied upon to show some passion: underfunding. Understandably, students want to pay for as little of their own education as possible, and shift as much of the cost as they can onto the taxpayer. On virtually every other issue, students are doggedly conservative. The most popular under-graduate major in Canada today is business.

Junior branches of the political parties flourish on most campuses. Aspiring politicos mimic the example of Brian Mulroney, Jim Coutts, Joe Clark, and Keith Davey, and start early. The Young Tories have dominated campuses during the mid-1980s, but since campus political trends track those in the country at large, expect a Liberal resurgence. On no campus, not even in Manitoba (where there is an NDP government) can the Young NDP fill a telephone booth.

At every urban university there is a tiny, highly visible clique that cares passionately, but fleetingly, about El Salvador, Nicaragua, East Timor, South Africa, or whatever issue the Soviet Union is pushing at the moment.

Campus newspapers usually have leftist politics of varying degrees of intelligence. The most doctrinaire are the *McGill Daily* and the UBC *Ubyssey*. When campus writers fail to produce enough material, the newspapers rely on CUP — the Canadian University Press — to fill their pages with a steady stream of post-modernist feminism. Fortunately, nobody reads anything in the campus papers except the sports page and the personals.

THE FRESHMAN FIFTEEN

It's difficult to explain to your parents, after you've complained all semester about the food in the cafeteria, how you've managed to gain 15 pounds. Woody Allen, talking about a hotel in the Catskills, once quipped that the food there was really terrible, but at least the portions were big. He could have been talking about any university in Canada except Brock.

I know what you're thinking: you won't eat dessert, you won't take second helpings, and you'll never touch snacks. It won't happen to you.

Oh yes it will. Here's why. One helping of every dining-hall director's favourite, Chicken à la King, has 702 calories. One triple-decker club sandwich has 709 calories—before the French fries. Macaroni and cheese is a comparatively slimming 450, but with ketchup on top (never do this!) you're up to 550. Peanut butter and jelly sandwiches, which many deluded weight-watchers opt for when the chef serves liver, can be—depending on how thickly the extra-chunky is spread—as much as 500. Modern science cannot register the calories in a peanut butter and fluffer nutter sandwich. These statistics go far to explain the popularity of track pants as college fashion.

DRUGS AND ALCOHOL

Tell Mom not to worry. Drugs are out of favour on Canada's campuses. Recently the Nova Scotia police raided residences at Acadia and St. Mary's, where many students had been growing their own little marijuana plants in closets, but beer is everywhere regarded as cheaper, safer, tastier, and more respectable. A recent study at Simon Fraser, not an especially abstemious place, found that the typical student smoked marijuana only twice a month but drank alcohol ten times a month. Modern students smoke tobacco far more than hashish.

Waterloo and Memorial both boast that their campus pubs are the most profitable in Canada. Whoever's right, the race is close. UNB and Western seem to have the most-soused dorms. Alcohol-awareness campaigns are proliferating, but students on even the booziest campuses deny that alcoholism is much of a problem.

In general, the west coast seems to be the most wholesome. Parties, when they are thrown at all, are impressively sober. It's hard to wake up for your six o'clock run if you're hung-over. A depressing environment may explain the heavy drinking in Manitoba and at the northern Ontario universities. The farther east you go, the more alcohol is consumed; Maritimers lead the rest of the country; Newfoundlanders win the trophy.

SEX AND LOVE

In later life, when people say they were happy in college, they're not talking about the classes they took or the essays they wrote. They're thinking about the love affairs that made the concrete seem a little less grey, and the pre-law curriculum a little less unbearable. Leonard Cohen says: "Of course I remember my love affairs at McGill. They're the only ones I remember. You never forget the first ones."

Canadians have traditionally married old. For 50 years, the average age at marriage for women has been about 25, and for men about 27. For 19-year-old freshmen, licit sex is a long way off. Almost all Canadian students are prepared to settle for the illicit stuff. Actually, they sort of prefer it.

There are some campuses where serious, long-term, romantic relationships either predominate or at least set the tone for social life. These are usually schools where there are more men than women — Waterloo and UNB, for example. But since 52 per cent of Canadian undergraduates are women, most schools conform to other patterns.

Those other patterns fall roughly into three groups. The most worrisome to parents is the carefree promiscuity reputedly associated with Memorial and UPEI. The most worrisome to students are the alienating wastelands of places like Manitoba and UBC, where finding a friend is almost impossible, never mind a lover. Between these extremes falls a social life very much like that which you remember from high school — dating. At Western, Queen's, Acadia, Mount Allison, and other schools with many formal social events, a girl or boy without a date is cut off from the main current of life.

The universities themselves have long since despaired of protecting their students' morality. Most residences regulate stereo-playing and leave it at that. Formerly Catholic schools have never repealed their strict dormitory rules, but they go unenforced. St. FX alone forbids something: one dormitory, for first-year female students, is zealously policed by nuns. (After first year, of course, women can move into co-ed dorms, and from there go straight to Hell.) More typical are the rules at the women's dorm at Catholic St. Thomas University: a woman caught with a man in her room after hours is fined $25.

Generalizing about the sexual practices of 470,000 undergraduates is impossible. You find the same mix of the chaste and the loose, the frustrated and the fulfilled, the deviant and the normal as in the population as a whole. With that caveat, the following tips may help you match yourself to the most appropriate school.

If you want to be married by commencement, Newfoundland has the lowest average marriage age in the country: 23 for women, 25 for men. Memorial therefore looks promising. St. FX, Acadia, and Mt. Allison graduates show a remarkable propensity towards marrying other St. FX, Acadia, and Mt. Allison graduates. At woodsy, athletic, and placid U Vic, one recently-wed undergraduate mused: "I sometimes think Victoria is nothing more than a high-priced dating service." The women at Queen's and Western are maligned as single-minded pursuers of rich husbands. In fact, the women at Queen's and Western are probably more ambitious than the men; they may be blonde, but they're not bimbos.

If you're gay you'll find Ottawa, Trent, McGill, Toronto, and UBC the most tolerant. Concordia homosexuals may want to join the Coalition against Skinheads, which patrols the streets of downtown Montreal to protect gays against the local hoodlums. Montreal, for some reason, abounds in lesbian bars. Homosexuals and lesbians will want to avoid Catholic universities and those located in blue-collar communities, notably Windsor, McMaster, Lakehead, and Laurentian.

What to do about your home-town honey: A prudent but ruthless approach is to dump him or her in September, see how first term goes, then reassess at Christmas. An even more ruthless approach is to do exactly the same thing but not say anything in September. Be prepared for the possibility that your high-school sweetheart may have the same plan in mind for you.

If your parents are protective or nosy, be sure to live with a room-mate. He or she can tell them, when they call at 8 a.m. and you're not there, that you've just set out on your morning eight-mile run, or you're already in the lab. Your parents won't believe this, of course, but they'll be glad you made the effort.

If you're a woman determined to hold onto your innocence, go to a school ridiculously overpopulated with women: Mount St. Vincent, St. Thomas, or Glendon College. If this seems extreme, go to a big-city school where you won't meet anybody anyway. And be sure to live in an all-women's residence.

If you like sex but want to preserve your reputation, resolutely avoid small schools. At Acadia or Brock you may think nobody knows what you're up to, but everybody does. And, whatever school you're at, stay out of the dorms.

SPORTS

If you care deeply about college sports, buy a TV so you can watch the Orange Bowl. College sports in Canada are a major non-event. Since sports scholarships are forbidden to first-year students by the Canadian Inter-University Athletic Union, Canadian universities cannot offer student athletes material inducements to select a school, nor may they bribe or coddle them in any way once they're on campus. Some universities — Brandon and St. Mary's, for example — have broken these rules in the past, but most seem to obey them. Still, some universities do develop good teams — even dynasties. The University of Victoria holds the record for men's and women's basketball championships; Calgary has the lead in football; and Concordia is the nation's wrestling king. Dynasties emerge by accident. If you win the basketball championship once or twice, students interested in basketball begin to prefer your school, which helps you win again, which attracts more basketball players.

At only a few Canadian schools do campus jocks bask in the hysterical adoration that American colleges lavish on theirs. If you're a potentially talented athlete who wants girls to stare at you when you flex your muscles in the cafeteria, send your application to St. Mary's, Acadia, Mount Allison, St. FX, or Queen's. If you're a woman athlete at a Canadian university, try to remember as you play to the empty stands that your mother loves you.

WHAT'S WINTER LIKE?

Mean daily temperature in January, and lowest recorded temperature in Canada's college towns (Celsius degrees).
(Source: Statistics Canada)

	MEAN TEMP.	LOWEST TEMP.
NEWFOUNDLAND		
St. John's	- 3.5	-23.3
PRINCE EDWARD ISLAND		
Charlottetown	- 7.1	-30.6
NEW BRUNSWICK		
Fredericton	- 9.2	-38.9
Sackville	- 6.8	-31.7
St. John	- 7.8	-30.0
NOVA SCOTIA		
Antigonish	- 6.1	-24.4
Halifax	- 3.1	-25.0
Sydney	- 4.7	-23.3
Wolfville	- 6.8	-27.8
QUEBEC		
Lennoxville	-10.7	-44.4
Montreal	- 8.7	-32.8
ONTARIO		
Guelph	- 7.2	-37.2
Hamilton	- 6.4	-27.8

Kingston	- 7.7	-32.2
Kitchener	- 6.9	-28.9
London	- 6.6	-31.7
Ottawa	-10.6	-37.8
Peterborough	- 8.6	-33.4
St. Catharines	- 4.5	-22.8
Sudbury	-12.3	-42.8
Thunder Bay	-14.8	-41.1
Waterloo	- 7.2	-31.1
Windsor	- 4.2	-23.9
Toronto	- 4.6	-32.8
Downsview	- 6.5	-28.4
Etobicoke	- 5.0	-27.8
Scarborough	- 5.0	-27.8
MANITOBA		
Brandon	**-19.7**	**-46.1**
Winnipeg	-19.0	-41.7
SASKATCHEWAN		
Regina	-17.9	-47.2
Saskatoon	-18.8	-46.1
ALBERTA		
Calgary	-11.1	-39.4
Edmonton	-15.0	-42.2
Lethbridge	-10.3	-42.8
BRITISH COLUMBIA		
Burnaby	1.6	-13.9
Langley	2.0	-13.9
Vancouver	2.9	-13.9
Victoria	**3.8**	**-12.2**

THE BEST

Most attractive campus: Acadia; runners-up, St. FX, UNB
Best-looking men: Western
Best-looking women: Western
Friendliest campus: St. FX
Best school spirit: Queen's
Best dining hall: Trinity College, U of T
Best athletic facilities: University of Calgary
Best campus newspaper: Memorial (*The Muse*)
Best campus pub: Waterloo, Federation Hall
Best off-campus student ghetto: Queen's
Best residence life: Acadia

Best bookstore: U of T; runner-up, UBC
Most elegant faculty club: McGill; runner-up, Dalhousie
Best international reputation: University of Toronto. Thanks, Dr. Polanyi
Best promotional material: Brock
Best university town: Kingston
Best university city: Montreal
Best library: U of T
Best orientation: University of New Brunswick
Most expensive tuition: Trinity Western University; runner-up, UBC
Best alumni magazine: Dalhousie
Best scandal: Brandon University re: President Harold Perkins

THE WORST

Ugliest campus: University of Calgary; runner-up, York
Least-friendly campus: U of T; runner-up, University of Alberta
Worst school spirit: University of Regina
Worst sports facilities: Memorial; runner-up, UPEI
Worst campus newspaper: Acadia and Lakehead (both were closed down by their student councils)
Worst campus pub: Lakehead (customers have been known to beat up staff)
Worst off-campus housing: Dalhousie; King's; St. Mary's; Mount Saint Vincent; Carleton; U of O.
Worst residence life: York
Worst bookstore: Trinity Western University
Worst university town: Brandon
Worst university city: Saskatoon
Worst library: Trinity Western

ACKNOWLEDGEMENTS

This book was written with the help of thousands of people. (NB: this approach works for books, but don't try it on term papers.) I must express my deep appreciation to all the young Canadians and administrators who agreed to be interviewed for this book. It was inspiring to discover that most Canadians, when approached by a total stranger asking questions, are kind, forthcoming, and often extremely charming. It is to these wonderful people who gave so freely of themselves, that I am most truly grateful.

On the home front, I must thank my cherished friend Edward Hore who kept me company, returned a lot of long distance phone calls, and made a lot of helpful suggestions. I am also extremely grateful to my wonderful parents and my grandmother Florence for their endless, loving encouragement, and for their own helpful suggestions. Still more helpful suggestions came from my brother David. I owe thanks to David Matthews of the Upper Canada College Guidance Office, Heather McArdle of *Campus Canada* magazine, and my friend Alister Campbell. To the lovely people at Key Porter Books I give a hearty thank you.

ATTENTION STUDENTS!

I'd love to know what you think of this book. An update is planned and I would like to have your input. If you agree or disagree with what you have read here, or think I have left something out, write and tell me c/o Key Porter Books Limited, 70 The Esplanade, Toronto, Ontario M5E 1R2.